Kenya at a Crossroads

Kenya at a Crossroads

Administration and Economy Under Sir Percy Girouard, 1909–1912

Abdullahi Sara

LEXINGTON BOOKS
Lanham • Boulder • New York • London

Published by Lexington Books
An imprint of The Rowman & Littlefield Publishing Group, Inc.
4501 Forbes Boulevard, Suite 200, Lanham, Maryland 20706
www.rowman.com

Unit A, Whitacre Mews, 26–34 Stannary Street, London SE11 4AB

British Library Cataloguing in Publication Information Available

Library of Congress Control Number: 2015949342
ISBN: 978-1-4985-1065-3 (cloth : alk. paper)
eISBN: 978-1-4985-1066-0

∞™ The paper used in this publication meets the minimum requirements of American National Standard for Information Sciences—Permanence of Paper for Printed Library Materials, ANSI/NISO Z39.48-1992.

Printed in the United States of America

This book is dedicated to the memory of Adama, Walid, and Fatimah

Contents

Preface

The study is significant because it is a contribution to the debate on the best practice of a colonial service. The career of Sir Percy as a British proconsul and colonial official will be examined with particular attention to the period when was in charge of the EAP. The circumstance that resulted in his untimely resignation will be spotlighted as a nonconventional norm and practice in the colonial service. His failure to measure up to the expectations of London will be gauged based upon conventional wisdom as the best administrative practice of the colonial service. For example, Sir Percy erred in failing to comply with the directives from London to deport Mr. Cole. He failed to inform London on the relocation of the Maasai from Laikipia to Ngong. Sir Percy's partiality toward the European community and disregard toward the rights of both the African and the Indian communities, among others, combined to discredit him before the Colonial Office (CO).

Double-dealings in the colonial service or reluctance in the implementation of directives, the failure to make timely communications and a lack of clarity of dispatch, among other things, are not normally considered as the best practices within the colonial service. However, Sir Percy fell short in this regard, and had to resign. His untimely resignation following his double-dealings could in no way be considered to be in the best interest of the colonial service. Thus, Sir Percy should not be considered one of the best administrators, but he may be considered a hardworking officer. Sir Percy failed to measure up to the expectations of London, and that led to his untimely resignation. This study will lay to rest the argument as to whether or not Sir Percy could have been considered an outstanding and successful colonial administrator, drawing from his action in the field of administration vis-à-vis the expectations of the colonial service.

Acknowledgments

This book owes its origin from my Ph.D. dissertation titled "Rush to Failure: The Kenya Governorship of Sir Percy Girouard, 1909–1912." This book and the original dissertation from which it owes its origin would not have been in its presence without the assistance of many individuals and organizations. My thanks go to West Virginia University Chancellors Award who financed my research project, History Department of the West Virginia University, and to the University of Maiduguri, which granted me leave of absence to embark upon this research. Thanks are also due to the archivists and librarians of the Wise Library in West Virginia University and the Library in Syracuse University who readily combed through their archival records and made relevant documents available for my inspection.

Also I wish to acknowledge the debt I incurred in the course of all those running between West Virginia University and the Syracuse University, who are too many to be mention in here, but whose help during the course of my research would never be forgotten. I am also grateful to Professor Robert Maxon who provided useful supervision of the original dissertation and counseled me on the direction of this book. Thanks are due, also, to Professor Elizabeth Fones-Wolf, Chair, History department in the West Virginia University, who approved for my graduate student research travel fund for my travels to Syracuse University, and to the Director, Center for Trans Saharan Studies in the University of Maiduguri, Professor Muhammad Nur Alkali who supported my leave of absence and travel to the United States to undertake this research study. I am also using this medium to acknowledge the help and assistance given me by Professor James Siekmeier of the History department at West Virginia University, Professor J. D. Amin of the Faculty of Veterinary Medicine at the University of Maiduguri, and Dr. A. A. Fari of the History department at the University of Maiduguri.

Finally, my thanks go to my family members, friends, and to my colleagues at the Center for Trans Saharan Studies in the University of Maiduguri who supported me in various ways in the course of this research study.

List of Abbreviations

CO	Colonial Office
EAP	East Africa Protectorate
FO	Foreign Office
IBEA	Imperial British East Africa Company
S of S	Secretary of State

Chapter 1

Introduction

Sir Percy Girouard's career prior to the assumption of governorship of the East Africa Protectorate (hereafter, EAP) had taken him from Canada to Great Britain, the Sudan, the Transvaal and Orange River colonies, the Northern Nigeria, and the EAP. His achievements in Africa included distinguished service as railway engineer, an administrator of railways, and a colonial governor. Sir Percy's success as a railway builder impressed his superiors and was a key factor in his winning distinction and honors. This experience also led to his appointment to important railway administrative positions in Egypt and in the Transvaal.

While his work in South Africa ended in some disagreement over railway policy, Sir Percy met his wife while there (Transvaal). He also had drawn favorable attention from the Colonial Office (hereafter, CO) and this led to his appointment to head the colonial administration of Northern Nigeria. Sir Percy's governorship of Northern Nigeria was characterized by success in railway building and in general administration. He supervised the construction of Baro to Kano railway that linked Baro to Southern Nigeria and Lagos, as gateway to the coast. In Northern Nigeria, Sir Percy was credited for the implementation of policies with regard to land, taxation, education, and general economic development that advanced Northern Nigeria's economic, social and political condition. By 1909 this, together with his earlier work in North and South Africa, had won Sir Percy the admiration of many within the CO as a strong and effective administrator. Viewed from that perspective, it is not surprising that Sir Percy would be chosen to head the administration of the EAP.

His prior achievements were important in his success, as it had informed his successive appointments to important colonial administration positions. The latter was out of the CO's consideration that Sir Percy was one of the best

Canadian administrator in the British colonial service.[1] The CO pointed out that Sir Percy had carried through remarkable development projects aimed at modernizing the territories assigned under his administration; especially in Northern Nigeria. The latter notwithstanding, Sir Percy's tour of duty in the EAP in 1909–12 was beclouded with altercations between him and his home government, over the removal of the Maasai among others matters, and this led to his untimely resignation.[2] The quarrel with his home government ended his official career. In spite of all the development projects he had carried through (railroad building and agricultural development among other things), his career ended in a regrettable incident relating to the Maasai move in the EAP.[3]

In determining as to whether or not Sir Percy was an outstanding administrator, this work examines his governorship of the EAP. The assessment included the development projects that Sir Percy implemented or sought to implement and circumstances that caused his untimely resignation from his unenviable post of governor of the EAP. Admittedly, he carried through remarkable development projects aimed at modernizing the protectorate, but his relations with the CO and the local people he governed left a lot to be desired.

This study contends that his tragic failure in the field of colonial administration proper suggests that Sir Percy was not an outstanding administrator because he failed to adhere to regulations governing his official duties. This could be seen from his attitude toward the deportation of Galbraith Cole and the removal of the Maasai, all between 1910 and 1912, among other things.[4] Current and past scholarship suggests a mixed evaluation of the career of Canada's proconsul and colonial administrator, Sir Percy. A. H. M. Kirk-Greene suggests that Sir Percy was the most outstanding administrator Canada produced in the British colonial service.[5] Kirk-Greene points to Sir Percy's track record of initiating development projects aimed at modernizing African colonies.[6] While on the other hand, M. P. K. Sorrenson contends that Sir Percy was a hardworking officer, but he opined that Sir Percy failed to fix the colony's problems as expected of him and he was therefore forced to resign.[7] However, this work examines by colonial standards what should be considered to be the best style of administration, reflecting the circumstances that ended the career of Sir Percy. This work argues that a positive assessment falls short of considering measures expected of an outstanding or a successful colonial official. Devising and implementation of development programs alone should not be used as a measure in determining the success or failure of administration or an administrator. Admittedly, Sir Percy was hard working, but that was only part of the expectations of an outstanding administrator, there were other qualities worth consideration in critically addressing that issue. This work argues further that part of qualities expected in outstanding performance for one who could also be credited to an outstanding administrator involved good working relations with his subordinate staffers and with the CO.

An administrator judged to be the best proconsul should be in a position to carry through instructions accurately. He should act within the established rules and regulations governing the colonial service. An outstanding officer should not engage in double-dealing or any act that was capable of embarrassing the metropolitan government. An outstanding officer should subordinate himself to his superior officers and to the rules of the colonial service. A governor like Sir Percy should respect and deal with his subordinate staff according to the rules and regulations of the colonial service. Yet Sir Percy had difficulty dealing with subordinates with whom he would work to move the economy of the Protectorate on.

The question of the economic development of the EAP preoccupied Sir Percy's attention and was a key factor in his proposed economic development policy for the EAP. Sir Percy proposed policy for export economy for eventual solvency of the protectorate's economic difficulty. This export production regime was to integrate Kenya's economy into the global market so that the EAP could earn the needed finance from exports, for both the agricultural sector and the government.[8] These measures were supposed to make the colony self-reliant and to do away with its dependence on grants-in-aid from the British Treasury.[9]

This led Sir Percy to initiate the construction of the railways, reinvigoration of the colonial service, and the introduction of economic initiatives aimed at the development of agriculture, the relocation of the Maasai and the consolidation of European settlement. These initiatives were partly intended to make the colony effective and efficient in terms of the establishment of an efficient colonial system of administration and self-supporting economy through the development of the economy that would generate the needed revenue to support the administration of the colony. Sir Percy considered the establishment of European settlement indispensable to agricultural production for export.

In this, the building and development of railway will serve as one example. Railway transportation would ease the movement of people and goods from one place to another, especially the movement of goods to the major coasts, from where goods would be shipped abroad. Despite his desire for the economic development of the colony, his nonconventional norm and practice in the governance of the EAP that are contrary to the expectations of the CO ended his career.[10] This work covers the stewardship of Sir Percy in the EAP, from 1909 to 1912. It examines and highlights areas where Sir Percy initiated development projects aimed at modernizing EAP, and the areas in which he erred. All aspects that resulted from his service and resignation will be examined and analyzed. To this end, issues relating to the reinvigorating of the EAP administrative system, staff redeployment or retirement, and his relations with the settler community vis-à-vis the African and the Asian are examined. His relations with London, especially his official correspondence on issues relating to Cole's deportation and the Maasai move, and his subsequent altercations with his home government over these issues that led to his resignation formed the scope of this work. Issues that combined to portray a picture of Sir Percy's stewardship in the EAP are examined with a view to capturing a clear and correct picture of his administration. These issues provided justification that could be used to measure what would be the best administration or administrator based on the colonial service subsisting rules, regulations, and expectations.[11]

In carrying through a magisterial account of Sir Percy's stewardship in the EAP, a brief biography of Sir Percy and his prior achievements in the Sudan, Transvaal, and the Northern Nigeria was considered necessary. I also deemed it necessary to sketch a background history of the EAP, on Sir Percy's assumption of government of the protectorate, policy of government administration and Sir Percy's proposed policy reform. In Sir Percy's formulation of government policy of administration, he reviewed the condition of administration of the colony and recommended policy reform to the CO, especially on official circulars, taxation, economy, executive, legislative, judicial departments and officials, structure of administration and staff, as well as provincial administration.

Sir Percy also proposed a policy for the European settlers and Indian residents, his proposed application of settler involvement in county, local government and other government bodies, establishment of a separate settlement in the highlands and their access to land. The effective application or failure to apply these proposed policies suggests his competence or otherwise in the field of policy of administration of the two races (Europeans and Indians). In addition to the latter, was Sir Percy's policy of African administration that he proposed and recommended a separate administration in separate African settlements or reserves for the Africans. The policy was informed by his belief that Africans should not be governed by a European method of administration. He reflected on his experience in administration in Northern Nigeria where his predecessor, Lord Lugard, introduced an effective method of administration of Africans that came to be known as indirect rule.[12] Sir Percy's administration of this policy and his failing as to its application has implications to his outstanding performance or his failure.

On the coast of the EAP, Sir Percy examined and recommended separate coast's lands policy that provided an approach to the resolution of competing title claims between the Sharia and the Mijikenda land tenure systems. His desire to apply a British land ordinance so that land could be granted to European estate developers was complicated by the legal abolition of the status of slavery and the dispersal of the slaves that became a serious challenge to his administration in defining limits of each estate owned by Arab slave masters, for demarcation and distribution to prospective European farmers.

As to economic development of the colony, Sir Percy recommended to the CO his economic development policy for the eventual solvency of the colony's economic predicament. He introduced a policy of reduced railway rates on coastward bound agricultural products so that farmers could be induced to produce more for export. He applied the policy on European settlers only, to the exclusion of other races. But the settlers could not produce enough in view of their insignificant numerical strength and his policy could not have afforded the colony the desired economic relief he sought to introduce. His view on the policy and his process of implementation defines his policy capability or failing as far as economic development of the colony was concerned.

In his economic policy consideration, other than the development of European settler agriculture for export, Sir Percy considered the development of railways so as to ease communication and shipment of goods for the eventual solvency of the colony's economic predicament. Even though the purpose of some of the railways was for communication rather than economy, they had at the same time provided relief in the shipment of goods. The construction of railways was not an easy undertaking that Sir Percy grappled with, and his knowledge of railways and how best he applied this knowledge to achieve what he wanted or failed to achieve portrayed his failing that was also considered in this work. Another important consideration for the economic development of the colony was the question of land tenure. As to the latter, Sir Percy proposed and recommended the administration of land policy for settlement and farming by European settlers. His policy of land administration was a curious undertaking as the proposed amendment of the land ordinance had been on hold prior to Sir Percy's assumption of government of the EAP. The revision of Lord Elgin's land regulation was on, as it was not fully applied by Sir Percy's predecessor, Sir James Hayes Sadler. Instead, Sir Percy, on assumption of government, introduced his own regulations, in addition to Elgin's regulations that complicated land administration in the EAP. His land grants vis-à-vis land regulations left a lot to be desired and portrayed unhealthy land administration which could not be judged to be an effective land administration policy. This policy suggested the limit or otherwise of Sir Percy's land administration to European settlers, as well as difficulties it occasioned to prospective immigrants into the colony.

Another important question relating to Sir Percy's land policy was the removal of the Maasai and the question of compensations to displaced European farmers. The failed attempted removal of the Maasai and displacement of some European settlers from their farms with a view to allocate Laikipia land to them is discussed. The failure to allocate Laikipia as a result of the failed Maasai move created two bodies of displaced persons. The compensation paid to European settlers for their suffering following the failed move, and the failure to afford compensation to the Maasai who were in the same situation suggests a clear shortcoming in Sir Percy's sense of justice in his administration of policy. The question of justice can also be seen in other aspects that bordered directly or indirectly on land question and compensation, and a commitment to fairness in his dispensation of government functions. The later aspects were reflected in Sir Percy's removal of the Maasai without recourse to the CO.

In addition to the removal of the Maasai was the appalling miscarriage of justice that characterized the court proceedings of Galbraith Cole and the CO's directives to deport Cole. These issues and the circumstances or policy application that brought them to light suggests a policy that portrayed a serious shortcoming on the part of his administration of justice and Sir Percy's unwillingness to comply with the CO's directives.[13] However, some of the issues could be debatable, as to whether or not such policy could be considered outstanding in view of the argument and counter argument that occasioned the deportation of Cole.

In the administration of the subject peoples of the Crown, the Crown administration lacked uniformity as exemplified in the administration of Kenya. Not all Crown agents are excellent administration. Crown lacked uniform defined policy of government administration as the colony was saddled with a succession of ineffective administrators, further complicated by settler insatiable demands on the relatively weak and poor administration. Despite lack of policy of administration, there was a defined policy of segregation in the administration of government resources and services as exemplified in land allocation, allocation of business premises, and a separate use of railway steamers between European and Indians.[14] It showed difficulty in administering mixed community.

The question of amalgamation, Maasai move and Cole case all suggests that the proconsuls were not administering based on Crown's directives to a large extent. Despite British expertise, Kenya proved a difficulty as four administrators had resigned as a result of altercation with the home government. It showed how influential private individuals could influence government policy in Kenya or how settler community could influence government policy especially when such settler community composed of persons of noble origin as exemplified by Delamere and Galbratith Cole, and Grogan among other settlers.

As to Kenya, it showed how the Kikuyu were displaced, their social formation altered when land ownership was, through legislation taken over from Kikuyu to the settlers, and the Maasai removed and gave way to settler farming and habitation, all in a desperate attempt to secure fertile land for European farmers. Kenya's prior existing social, political, and economic institutions were either marginalized or scrapped making a sustained development of such institution impossible. Life was never the same again. The autochthons became the subjects instead of governing their own affairs and the British became the masters and made the Africans a ready source of labor who had to work for wages on the European settlers farms, thereby losing freedom of action over their own affairs. This was the impact of imperialism and colonialism on the colonized subjects of the EAP.

This is important because no extensive research into Sir Percy's administration of Kenya has been done by scholars despite the fact that his tenure has proved to be one of the significant period in Kenya history, as the EAP was able to financed it budget despite the fact that it was not Sir Percy's policy that provided the relief to the colony. His period of administration was the time when Kenya was in a serious economic difficulty and he was brought to solve the problem but he failed to do so, despite his widely acclaimed competence. The nature of the colony's problem on the ground, the economic position of the colony and the need for direction for the colony all combined to suggests that a research problem exist which historians have not ventured to research, and it was based on such recognition that this work addressed such a research question. In this case, this research fills a vacuum in the political and economic history of Kenya in the period between 1909 and 1912, thereby contributing to historical knowledge in the field of Kenya's political and economic history. It is also a contribution to the understanding of the role of Sir Percy as Canadian serving as British proconsul and his place in the history of British Africa and British policy in Africa. As at the time Sir Percy left the colony, it was not better off. He had not been able to implement his policies either they were denied by the CO or he could not have time to implement them. In some issues, especially the Maasai, he caused altercations with the home government, which led to his premature removal from office.

Moreover, Sir Percy's was a failed governorship that happened at a critical juncture in Kenyan history. The EAP was indeed at a crossroads when he took over in 1909. The issues relating to land alienation for European settlement was still to be worked out in the form of legislation and administrative practice. Satisfactory administrative provisions had yet to be made for the diverse groups which constituted the EAP's population at the start of the second decade of the twentieth century. Most important of all, the basis of the protectorate's economic future had yet to be decided. Was it to be European farming or peasant production? In dealing with these and other issues at this time, Sir Percy Girouard seemingly possessed the skills and experience to move Kenya forward towards prosperity and progress. He was a hard working, strong personality, unlike two of his predecessors; the lazy and uninterested Stewart and the weak and vacillating Sadler. He began his administration with the support and goodwill of the CO as he moved quickly to assess the protectorates problems and needs.

Yet Sir Percy's performance during this crossroads period sent Kenya along a wrong path as he failed to deal with a thorny land issues, refused to pursue a balanced policy in dealing with diverse racial groups, and he ignored the prevailing economic reality that the economic viability of the EAP was based on the production of African peasants. In his preference for the interests of European settlers, he helped to shape Kenya's future in ways that proved disadvantageous for the majority of its population and for British policy in the East African dependency.

NOTES

1. A. H. M. Kirk-Greene, "Canada in Africa: Sir Percy Girouard, Neglected Colonial Governor," *African Affairs*, Vol. 83, No. 331 (April. 1984), 208–209.

2. G. H. Mungeam, *British Rule in Kenya, 1895–1912: The Establishment of Administration in the East Africa Protectorate* (Oxford: Clarendon Press, 1966), viii–ix, 268.

3. M. P. K. Sorrenson, *Origins of European Settlement in Kenya* (London: Oxford University Press, 1966), 129.

4. Lotte Hughes, *Moving the Maasai: A Colonial Misadventure* (London: Palgrave Macmillan, 2004), 70. Cole was an influential European settler in the protectorate. He was a son of the British Earl of Enniskilin. He arrived in the protectorate in 1903 as a settler. He was also a brother in law to Lord Delamere, an influential leader of the European settlers in the protectorate. Also, see Sorrenson, *Origins of European Settlement in Kenya*, 129. Mungeam, *British Rule in Kenya*, 268. Robert M. Maxon, *Struggle for Kenya: Loss and Reassertion of Imperial Initiative, 1912–1923* (Cranbury: Associated University Press, 1993), 41. George Bennett, *Kenya, A Political History: The Colonial Period* (London: Oxford University Press, 1963), 33.

5. A. H. M. Kirk-Greene, "Canada in Africa," 208–209.

6. Ibid., 223.

7. Sorrenson, *Origins of European Settlement in Kenya*, 129.

8. Maxon, *Struggle for Kenya*, 31. Also, see Bruce J. Berman, *Control and Crisis in Colonial Kenya* (Athens, Ohio University Press, 1999), 55. Mungeam, *British Rule in Kenya*, 220.

9. Maxon, *Struggle for Kenya*, 31.

10. Sorrenson, *Origins of European Settlement in Kenya*, 129. Also, see Cosmo Parkinson, *The Colonial Office from Within* (London: Faber & Faber, 1947), 27. Also, see Maxon, *Struggle for Kenya*, 41.

11. Parkinson, *The Colonial Office from Within*, 9.

12. Lord Lugard, *Dual Mandate in British Tropical Africa* (London: Archon Books, 1965), 96–97.

13. Maxon, *Struggle for Kenya*, 41.

14. Sorrenson, *Origins of European Settlement in Kenya*, 168.

Chapter 2

Sir Percy and the East Africa Protectorate

SIR PERCY'S EARLY LIFE AND CAREER

Sir Percy Girouard or Sir Edouard Percy Cranwill Girouard, K.C.M.G., D.S.O., R.E. (1867–1932), was a French Canadian, Roman Catholic, whose ancestors had settled in Quebec in the early eighteenth century. He was born to the family of Desire Girouard, an eminent Montreal attorney, justice of the Canada's Supreme Court, Member Federal Parliament, and Canada's Deputy Governor General.[1]

Sir Percy's mother, whom he lost in 1879, when he was 12 years old, was a daughter of an Irish doctor. Three months later, in September 1879, Sir Percy and his elder sister moved to boarding schools. Sir Percy went to College St. Joseph at Trois Rivieres, on the banks of the St Lawrence River in Quebec. Sir Percy attended a seminary college headed by "a radical conservative bishop whose message of faith depended upon the preservation of the French language, and culture that had been imported to French Canada in the time of Louis XIV."[2]

On completion of his college, Sir Percy enlisted in the Royal Military College at Kingston where he pursued engineering as his course of study. Upon his graduation at the age of 19, with a diploma in engineering, he joined the Canadian Pacific Railway, as a surveyor, and worked from 1886 to 1888.[3] In the Pacific Railways, Sir Percy was preoccupied with the task of surveying, mapping and "fixing the final stages of the Pacific of Railways west of Winnipeg."[4] Sir Percy was interested in the latter as Williams wrote, "Girouard loved nothing better than the sight of virgin land to be laid bare, levelled trammelled and tracked."[5] It was at this point of his career that his actual interest and practice of railway construction began.

In 1888, Sir Percy decided to move to Britain to enlist in the British Royal Army. On the heels of his departure to Britain, his father, having objected to Sir Percy's enlistment into the military, refused to pay for Sir Percy's trip and uniform fee of one hundred pounds. Sir Percy's auntie gave him the money, and the journey began, leaving Canada behind.[6] Upon his entry, he advanced a coastal defense theory rooted in the railway. He proposed that a railroad could be constructed to the coast, machine guns mounted on railway steamers, so as to move past to confront the enemy.[7] The officials of the British Royal Army College welcomed his idea but it was not put into practice. It showed how creative he was in proposing defense by railway, which earned him respect and he became an enviable military engineer.[8]

After a successful completion of his military training, he made his way to the Royal Arsenal at Woolwich. In 1888, Sir Percy received a commission in the British Army Royal Engineers, and by 1890, he attained the rank of Second Lieutenant in the Royal Army engineering corp.[9] His engineering knowledge, especially on railway construction, became very important in his career and in his future appointments in the colonial service. This was clearly demonstrated when he was called upon by the Sirdar of the Egyptian army to help construct a railway for a military campaign.

SIR PERCY'S TOUR OF DUTY IN THE SUDAN

In the Sudan, there were developments that necessitated a military campaign against the Mahdist forces of the Khalifah of the Sudan, which had murdered the governor of the Sudan, Sir Charles Gordon.[10] The death of the latter would not go unpunished as the Sirdar of both the Egyptian and the Sudan's armed forces, General Horatio Herbert Kitchener, was preparing to confront the Mahdists.[11] Kitchener was hampered by the lack of a railway from Khartoum to Dongola so that he could move his troops.[12]

On the question of construction of the railway, Sir Percy was introduced to Kitchener in July 1895, and he invited Sir Percy to join his army and help construct the railway to confront the Mahdists, by advancing from Egypt south to the Sudan. But there was hesitation on the part of Sir Percy who, according Williams, wrote in his unfinished memoir of his life that he felt the end has come.[13] The War Office did not approve his deployment to the Sudan on the spot. The War Office's objection might have been informed by Sir Percy's hesitation to accept Kitchener's invitation. But when Sir Percy heard that Kitchener was preparing to advance to Dongola to confront the Mahdists, he cabled Kitchener, asking him if he could join him in the expedition.[14]

Sir Percy arrived in Sudan and discovered a 33 miles unfinished railway toward the south, from Khartoum to Wadi Halfah, abandoned due to lack of funds by Egypt's Khedive Ismail.[15] Sir Percy took over the abandoned railroad and construction began in earnest. Despite the difficult terrain characterized by rock and sand, dust storms, heat files and lack of equipment, Sir Percy constructed this desert railroad from Wadi Halfah; to the Berber; north of Khartoum.[16] Sir Percy worked a minimum of a mile a day for 250 miles. Having completed the railway, he joined Kitchener's expeditionary forces in the Dongola campaign against the Mahdists in 1895. He won a prestigious medal for his outstanding performance in the expedition.

The medal was the Distinguished Service Order (DSO). The Dongola expedition against the Mahdists made Sir Percy famous and popular and was significant in his future assignment in the Transvaal. Following the successful completion of the Dongola campaign and the Nile expedition in 1897. Sir Percy was called upon to work for the Sudan railways, and by 1898, he was appointed president of the Egyptian Railway Board at the age of 31.[17] His railway skill became an asset in his progression to the top echelon of the colonial service. The latter was the last position he held until his redeployment to the Transvaal and Orange River Colonies, on the heels of the Anglo-Boer War, so that he could construct another railway, from the Transvaal to Bloemfontein, to confront the Boer rebellion against the British authorities.[18]

SIR PERCY'S TOUR OF DUTY IN THE TRANSVAAL

There was the need for a railway to confront the Boer rebellion, but the deployment of Sir Percy from the Sudan to the Transvaal might have been informed by his knowledge of railway engineering within the CO. The deployment of Sir Percy to the Transvaal was requested by the Transvaal, Sir Percy having had a prior acquaintance with the Governor of the Transvaal and Orange River colony, Lord Milner.[19] At the time of the construction of the Khartoum to Wadi Halfah railway, Milner worked under the British Consul General at Cairo, Lord Cromer.[20]

Sir Percy arrived the Transvaal in 1899 and assumed dual responsibilities of the construction of the railway and control of the South African Field Force. This was at the time of incessant bombing and guerilla sabotage by the Boers.[21] In view of the increasing hostility of the Boers and the urgent need of the railroad, Sir Percy laid eighty miles of track in forty-eight hours.[22] The British War Office queried his estimate for the construction of the railway, but he ignored the query and went over to the Secretary of State for the Colonies, Joseph Chamberlain, and resolved the issue.[23] Sir Percy completed the construction of the railroad, and the Boers were confronted and defeated. The railway that Sir Percy constructed used electricity to illuminate the road, making travel in the night possible. It was a great engineering work never seen anywhere in Africa. With the end of the Boer War in 1902, Sir Percy was knighted and appointed railway commissioner of the Transvaal and Orange River colonies.[24] Thereafter, in the lull that followed the Boer War, Sir Percy met his future wife in Pretoria.

It was in the house of the Attorney General and Lieutenant Governor of the Transvaal, Sir Richard Solomon, and his wife, Elizabeth, that Sir Percy, at the age of 36, met their 21-year-old daughter, Gwendolen, who became his wife.[25] Gwendolen, Williams wrote, was, "slim, dark-haired and shy; she was their much-loved only child."[26] Gwen's father, Solomon, and his wife, Elizabeth, "were children of non-conformists missionaries, having grown up among the Griqua."[27] They were compassionate, religious, and kind. In fact, Williams described Solomon as "known for his principles and liberal sympathies for the black and dispossessed."[28]

Despite the humble orientation that Gwen had from her parents, Sir Percy caused her to comment on some of his conception about life. Gwen, while listening to a discussion between Sir Percy and members of his railway board relating to costs of running the railway, and "having trouble trying to persuade hard bitten members of his railway board in Johannesburg-owners of gold companies and hostile Afrikaners to agree to the costs of running the railways."[29] The railway freight was an important aspect of the Transvaal economy as the cost of freight was seen to have been the main cause of the rising cost of living in the Transvaal. But in spite of the interwoven nature of the economy being tied to the railway receipts, Sir Percy did not care to state what was in his mind. However, Gwen disagreed, and the following day, she wrote to Sir Percy, "I am only a child in some ways, and you are a very clever man, but…you told me last night that no-one in this world cares whether you live or die, or whether you do well or badly. Never think that again because there is one person who cares more than a little and who would give a great deal to be able to help a little… ."[30]

The wedding of Sir Percy and Gwen was held on 10 September 1903 in the cathedral at Pretoria massed with tropical palms and arum lilies. Thereafter, they proceeded to London for their honeymoon. On their visit to Canada, Gwen told his father in Montreal. "We meet some interesting people but they talk of nothing in the world but this Fiscal Question, till one gets quite tired of it."[31]

After successful completion of the railway, Sir Percy was charged with the administration of the Transvaal railway as its Commissioner. But he could not stay long to administer the railway as disagreement between him and Milner ensued. The basis of their disagreement stemmed from the fact that Sir Percy introduced low railway rates on goods and passengers on the Transvaal railway. But Milner was concerned that he had subscribed to a £35 million loan for the construction of the railways for the two colonies, and as the Transvaal could not balance its fiscal expenditure from its receipts, it would incur a deficit, annually.[32]

Therefore Milner wanted to raise the cost of freight rates so that he could repay the loan. He told Sir Percy to raise railway rates on goods so that Transvaal would have more receipts to be able to balance its annual expenditure and to contribute its share in loan repayment. Milner argued that doing so would help the colonies offset the debt and invest profit accruing elsewhere to reduce dependence railway receipts. Sir Percy disagreed, believing that low rates were the means to secure more shipments and more receipts. The latter position became the source of disagreement between Sir Percy and Milner who was the president of the inter-colonial council, and called for its intervention.

The council had the responsibility of administering the two colonies, with Milner as its president, and its decision was final. The moment Sir Percy and Gwen returned to South Africa in December, he was immediately summoned to the Cape to discuss railway finances. The council deliberated on Sir Percy's disagreement with Milner on the railway rates, and in the ensuing discussion of the council, there were altercations between the council members and Sir Percy, on the administration of the Transvaal railway. The council wanted to harmonize the disjointed and chaotic railways for effective administration as well as to revisit costs of freight. But Sir Percy refused to give away, insisting on low rates on freight, frustrating efforts of the council. Milner could not hold back his frustration. He told Sir Percy, "With every recognition of your great service and your eminent ability in your army line, I do not think [finance and general business] are your strong points."[33]

The council insisted on Sir Percy's resignation, but Milner placed him on a compulsory leave with pay for six months. At the end of six months, his official tour of duty ended, and he moved out of the Transvaal.[34] Sir Percy was redeployed back to London at the end of 1904 as he resigned from railway commissionership and returned to regimental duties in England, much decorated with a K.C.M.G and there were three mentions in dispatches from the South African war, in addition to his Sudan war D.S.O.[35]

In the Transvaal, Sir Percy succeeded in accomplishing his mission as he constructed the needed railway that could be used to transport the army to confront the Boer rebellion. The railway was constructed to the satisfaction of the colony and became instrumental in defeating the Boers. The railway could be used for both civilian and military purposes.[36] In spite of his disagreement with Milner, his tour of duty was considered successful...mission accomplished.

Upon retirement from South Africa, in December 1904, Sir Percy sailed for England grimly determined to lobby for something more than the "regimental grind" as a staff officer he had been offered at Chatham. Already, Gwen was pregnant with their first child. Sir Percy had been promoted to brevet

Lieutenant Colonel before leaving Africa. There was also speculation that Sir Percy might perhaps stand for election to the Parliament.[37] His resignation did not go unnoticed. During a Parliamentary debate, Secretary of State for the Colonies, Alfred Lyttelton, was asked whether he could make a statement as to the change in railway policy proposed by Milner which led the resignation of Sir Percy. Lyttelton replied that Milner had informed him that in consequence of the debate and resolution of the International Council, Sir Percy had tendered his resignation of the office of railway commissioner.[38]

SIR PERCY BACK TO THE REGIMENTAL LIFE IN ENGLAND

Sir Percy was posted to HQ Eastern Command at Chatham, Kent, where he served as staff officer to the Chief Engineer. Shortly thereafter, Gwen's parents also moved to London. Solomon was appointed High Commissioner for South Africa in London. He settled in a house at Studland Bay in Dorset; Sir Percy stayed in London during the week, commuting home to see them at weekends.[39] He was subsequently appointed Hon. Lieutenant Colonel of the 18th Regiment of Canadian Infantry, the Franc-Tireurs de Saguenay, and granted the freedom of the Ironmongers' Guild of London.[40]

In 1906, Sir Percy was transferred to HQ Western Command at Chester (he himself lived at Hartford) where he acted as Assistant Quarter-Master General. In 1906, the Secretary of State for the Colonies, The Earl of Elgin, on the recommendation of the Parliamentary Undersecretary of State for the Colonies, Winston Churchill, selected Sir Percy for appointment as High Commissioner for Northern Nigeria.[41] It was possible that Elgin had taken into consideration the railway skill Sir Percy had demonstrated in appointing him to head the colony, so that he could speed the rail construction in Northern Nigeria, so desperately needed to speed up communication and combat rebellion.[42] The railway was the single most important factor in Elgin's decision to appoint Sir Percy to the job. In appointing Sir Percy, Elgin instructed Sir Reginald Laurence Antrobus[43] to write to Sir Percy, "In deciding to offer you this employment, Lord Elgin has been influenced by the consideration that your experience of railway construction would assist him in coming to a conclusion with regard to a project for light railway from Baro on the Niger which has been put forward by Sir F. Lugard."[44]

SIR PERCY'S TOUR OF DUTY IN NORTHERN NIGERIA

The appointment of Sir Percy as High Commissioner of Northern Nigeria, following Lugard's resignation, underlined the need for the construction of the railway. The railway was needed in view of Lugard's experience in crushing the Satiru rebellion. Lugard, before his resignation, sought and obtained the consent of the CO for the railway from Northern Nigeria to Southern Nigeria. Lugard's campaign against the Satiru revolt was hampered by lack of a railway to move troops quickly to crush the rebellion. Lugard constructed a railway from Zungeru to Zaria and to Sokoto, transported his troops, and crushed the rebellion.[45]

Lugard's difficulty in moving troops to crush the revolt informed the CO's decision to consider a Baro to Kano railway, which they believed, with the recent Satiru revolt, was indispensible.[46] Thus what really informed the appointment of Sir Percy was the need for railway for Northern Nigeria. Lugard had laid down an effective administration and, now the question of railway was the single most important aspect that was being envisioned for the north. It was widely believed that Sir Percy was the right person for the job. Sir Percy initiated the rail line that connected the important commercial center of Kano to the seaport so that shipping in and out of commodities as well as movement of peoples could be relatively eased.

Now, the main reason for the Baro to Kano railway was, in addition to defense, the need for communication and transportation.[47] On initiating the railway, Sir Percy changed the direction of the railroad. Instead of from Northern Nigeria to Southern Nigeria, he directed it to Lagos in the west. Sir Percy directed that the railway should run from Baro to Kano, instead of Kano to the Southern Nigeria.[48] He supported his change to Baro, stating that the river Niger would provide easy navigation of ships to upload the train goods from both directions, Kano or Lagos, and that Baro was the most suitable meeting point of both Kano and Lagos railways, citing professional consideration as the main factor for the Baro rather than the former.[49] The post of High Commissioner was upgraded to that of Governor, following the commissioning of Sir Percy, in 1908. Sir Percy served in Northern Nigeria as governor and perfected some of the policies introduced by Lugard, especially African land, taxation, and education. In all the latter three, Sir Percy departed from Lugard's, perspectives as to their application. Sir Percy considered that Africans should have control over their landed property rather than the crown. Africans should govern the local treasury as a native treasury, allowing Africans to have control over their landed property, finance and revenue.[50] On Lugard's return to Northern Nigeria, Sir Percy left for his vacation to London in April 1909.

In Northern Nigeria, Sir Percy's tour of duty could be clearly seen in the construction of the Baro to Kano railway, implementation of the indirect rule method of administration, which allowed land control under African chiefs with limited interference by the colonial officials. Sir Percy's remarkable successes in Northern Nigeria were not only on the construction of the railway; he succeeded in ensuring that Africans were allowed to govern their own affairs. These were significant successes in the execution of policies of administration bequeathed to him by his predecessor. Following Lugard's return from Hong Kong, Sir Percy was appointed governor of the EAP. While Sir Percy was still on his vacation in April 1909, the Secretary of State for the Colonies, Lord Crewe, concerned with the economic stagnation of the EAP, intimated to Sir Percy whether he could be transferred to the EAP, despite the fact that Churchill wanted Sir Percy to remain governor of Northern Nigeria.[51]

Colonial, cavalier and cautious, Sir Percy replied to Crewe that he would defer the question of his transfer from the west to the east to public interest.[52] The transfer to the EAP might not have been in the very best interest of Sir Percy, as he was reported to have told his father his comfort in the exercise of his power and authority in Northern Nigeria, when he was on vacation in Canada. Sir Percy told his father, in Northern Nigeria, other than the hold of the Secretary of State, he was a little independent king.[53] His statement suggested Sir Percy's own colonial ambition, and his desire for self-esteem, power, and relevance.

By August 1909, Sir Percy was bound to Mombasa, EAP, in a German boat. Disgusted, Sir Percy wrote that the British don't have it own line. Sir Percy's statement as to the lack of British line to the EAP further suggested the British government's lack of interest in the EAP or insignificance of the EAP to the British government. Upon his assumption of government in mid September 1909, he found the condition of the administration of the protectorate in a sorry state and recommended major reform of government policy of administration and development on his assumption of government of the EAP in September 1909.

CONDITION OF THE BRITISH EAST AFRICA PROTECTORATE ON SIR PERCY'S ASSUMPTION OF GOVERNMENT

The British East Africa Protectorate was conceived in uncertain circumstances and born into a chaotic situation, outstripped initial problems that led its emergence as a protectorate. The declaration of a protectorate in 1895 and the assumption of administration by a diplomat was a clear departure from the established norm of British imperial administration, especially in Africa. On assumption of government, the protectorate was saddled with the problem of a lack of a policy of colonial administration and lack of income.

The protectorate continued, in the short run, to be administered by the Foreign Office (hereafter, FO), in its pioneer years. In the midst of these problems, the protectorate, unwittingly, had a succession of incompetent governors whose tour of duties was punctuated by altercations with the FO and CO, leading to the resignation of governors. The administrative staff members were not any better, having been taken over from the Imperial British East Africa Company (hereafter, IBEA) or Uganda administration, which was in a healthier economic and political condition than the EAP. Despite the relatively developed condition of the Uganda Protectorate, these staff members were untrained in colonial administration and most of them lacked a university education.

There was also a neglect of the protectorate by the imperial authorities, as it was never considered of any significance to the overall British interest in East Africa and the Indian Ocean. The protectorate was also poor relative to the Uganda, as it could not fund costs of administration and development, thereby, deferring responsibility to the British Treasury, which annually supported the protectorate with a grant-in-aid to fund administration and development. The inhabitants of the protectorate were multi ethnic communities, living in scattered areas, who, on the introduction of the colonial rule, had little knowledge of agricultural production for export and economic development, other than their usual annual production for subsistence.

The entry of European planters, their demands for agricultural land for cultivation, as well as Indian demands for equal rights and treatments with the Europeans, caused competing demands between the two, altered the course of events that made weak local authorities unable to administer the protectorate effectively. The politics between the two and settler interest in fertile agricultural land interfered with African reserves, causing rebuke from the British authorities, and provoking resignations.

The EAP came into existence in unusual circumstances in 1895, when the British Consul General to the Zanzibar government, Sir A. H. Hardinge, on the instruction of the British government, declared a protectorate over an area, between Mombasa and Uganda, as the EAP.[54] On the declaration of a protectorate, Hardinge retained the infrastructure of the IBEA and its staff members as pioneer administrators of the protectorate.[55] Since then, not much had been done to accelerate political and economic developments of the protectorate.

As at the time of Sir Percy's assumption of government of the protectorate in 1909, there was near absence of a defined policy of government administration and economic development.[56] The latter were occasioned by developments on the ground, in the protectorate that accentuated difficulty in its administration. The difficulty in the administration of the protectorate was not uncommon to Sir Percy's predecessors and would be a potent factor in Sir Percy's difficulty in placing the administration of the protectorate on a policy that could mitigate its troubled policy of administration and accelerate its economic development.

Moreover, the protectorate administration was characterized by a succession of incompetent governors who could not define the protectorate's government policy of administration and economic development. The latter produced a condition where the protectorate's policies of administration and development were almost absent.[57] Therefore, the confused state of the protectorate's administration was attributed to a succession of weak governors. Such incompetency of Sir Percy's predecessors had not been in doubt as the CO was fully aware of the protectorate's predicaments. The CO pointed out that on Sir Percy's assumption of government, he was startled with the contrast between the EAP and Northern Nigeria.[58] The CO staff realized that, in Northern Nigeria, Sir Percy had a clean slate as Lugard had worked out a defined policy of government administration. On the other hand, in the EAP, there was a succession of weak governors.[59]

Some of the earlier governors had difficult times in handling the affairs of the protectorate or in dealing with the imperial authorities. For example, the protectorate's second commissioner, Sir Charles Eliot, had difficulty in dealing with the FO, on the protectorate's land question, and resigned, prematurely.[60] Stewart succeeded him, but he died soon after taking office. Stewart's successor, Sir James Hayes Sadler, was said to be incompetent to handle the affairs of the protectorate.[61] Sadler had not been able to administer the protectorate effectively and the continued economic stagnation of the protectorate had been a source of concern to the CO.[62] The CO transferred him to the Windward Islands, and appointed Sir Percy whom they believed was competent governor who could solve the protectorate's problems.[63]

Many of the staff members of the protectorate were also incompetent. The staff members were untrained colonial administrators; they were former IBEA staff members, inherited by the protectorate or staff of the Uganda administration.[64] When the British government took over of the administration of the protectorate, the IBEA, having relinquished its charter to the British government, closed its door to further business in the protectorate.[65] Among those staff members; few had university degrees and, as Sir Percy maintained, they lacked social connections and social graces. These unqualified staff members became pioneer administrators of the protectorate and had been seen as part of the difficulty of the protectorate. The staff members were not trained in public administration, as they were company officials that the protectorate inherited rather than trained colonial administrators. Therefore, the unsuitable staffing of the protectorate also became a difficulty in the administration of the protectorate.[66]

In view of a succession of weak governors and poor staff members that the protectorate inherited from a commercial company, there was a near absence of a defined policy of government administration and economic development from which Sir Percy could take up the task of administration and development.[67] The administrative condition of the protectorate was in a sorry state and execution of government function was left to personal originality of each individual official. This position of the protectorate had contributed to the difficulty of successive administrations in coming up with a defined policy of administration and development. The latter had not been without its influence in the complex nature of the administration that challenged Sir Percy's predecessors, and could also have challenged any governor the CO could appoint to the protectorate. Another problem was the position of the EAP relative to Uganda. To Britain, the EAP was not an important protectorate; economically, the EAP was poor, it lacked the significance of Uganda for Britain. Uganda was taken over in 1894 by Britain, earlier than the EAP, taken over in 1895.[68]

In the EAP, the African people were culturally diverse and lived in scattered areas; most had little connection to the world economy prior to colonial rule. The latter condition was further compounded by multiracial character of the protectorate and the problems created by Eliot's decision to encourage European farmers to settle. This had several consequences; the first produced the protectorate's land question. Another was the fundamental contradictions of accumulation and control. It was expressed during the first years of the protectorate as, Lonsdale and Berman expressed it, as competition over "the surplus product of African labour power." It pit African peasant production against that of settler farmers.[69]

Upon the entry of European farmers, land became an important resource as the European settlers took to agricultural production. Therefore, the question of how to make land available and accessible to European farmers and also protect the interest of the colonial state became further difficulties in the administration of the protectorate. As at the time of European entry, the protectorate lacked a clearly defined land policy.[70] Lord Elgin's land regulations being enforced had not been without its shortcoming; therefore, the question of a clearly defined land policy had to be addressed to ease difficulty in dispensing Crown lands, as well as secure income for the protectorate from increased land value for the future welfare of the protectorate.[71]

The amendment of the land ordinance that could have included the Elgin regulation would have resolved the question. But disagreement between Sir Percy's predecessor and the CO, and between the CO and Sir Percy, failed to provide the desired land ordinance for dispensing Crown lands.[72] The absence of the land ordinance and the refusal to enforce certain sections of the regulations had produced speculation and dummying in land dealing. The lack of a defined policy of dispensing Crown lands afforded wealthy and influential settlers in concert with local authorities to take advantage of the situation, by having easy access to land, but at prices exorbitant to poor and prospective immigrants. The latter had more or less discouraged the flow of immigration into the protectorate, causing some of the settlers to move back to South Africa and never return to the EAP.

Land dispensation was one of the problems that an administrator of the protectorate had to deal with, and it had been a cause of disagreement and altercations between the FO and Eliot, causing Eliot's resignation. The difficulty associated with land dealings alone was enough trouble to occupy and misguide any administrator of the protectorate. The CO expected that, while land would be made accessible to the settlers, it made it clear that the question of protection of African land rights in the reserves, against encroachment by syndicates and interest groups, would be complied with.[73] The CO's expectation that land in African reserves must be safeguarded for the Africans was another difficult responsibility that the local authorities had to enforce in a protectorate that settlers cast their eyes on any fertile lands; crown or African lands notwithstanding.

The local authorities and the CO could not prevent the desire for fertile land, and encroachment on land in African reserves by influential settlers. For example, the Maasai nominal grazing reserve was to have been granted to three South African brothers, by Eliot, and that became the cause of his disagreement with the FO, and his eventual resignation.[74] But in the FO, the Secretary of State for Foreign Affairs, Lord Lansdowne, went around Eliot, and granted thc same nominal Maasai grazing reserve to a London-based South African Syndicate, over Eliot's head.[75]

There was also Lord Delamere's reclaims over his Laikipia compensation on the eve of Sir Percy's arrival, and on his assumption of government, he granted Delamere's request, thereby, falling into the protectorate's troubles by removing the Maasai from Laikipia to the extended southern Maasai reserve.[76] There was also the Indian quest for land in the highlands; settlement reserved for the European settlers only. Indians quest for equality with the European settlers, especially in grants of land in the highlands, was rejected by all the governors and the CO.[77] The Indians, believing that they had better rights in the protectorate than the settlers, took their campaign to London.[78] The Indians demanded that they should be granted land in the white highlands, further immigration of the Indians into the protectorate should be allowed, similar Indian trial by jury as was the case with the Europeans, equal opportunities with the Europeans in government, land grant in the strategic place in Nairobi should be extended not only to the European but also them, and equal treatment between Indian and European in the railway steamer. The Indians further contended that because of their economic contribution to the protectorate and their cultural influence in the protectorate, the EAP should be made a vassal state of the Indian Viceroy. The Indian campaign caused indignation in both the protectorate and the CO, causing the India Office and the All Indian Muslim League to request for investigation. Despite the investigation of such grievances with Indian representatives present, the Indians were not accorded the equality they believed they deserved.

In fact, it was only on the question of land grant in the highlands that the Indians were given a definite answer. The Indians were told that the CO had reserved the highlands for the settlers only, and also, the CO, other than the highlands, had no objection to grant being made to subject of the Crown elsewhere, in the protectorate.[79] This ended the Indian search for equality that did not happen, and the inequality and mistreatment of the Indians continued.

As a result of the settler question, the protectorate was saddled with both the land question and racial politics that made it difficult for any administrator to secure cooperation and support in carrying through these responsibilities. The local authorities could not fulfill their responsibilities to the satisfaction of the multiracial groups, thereby creating disquiet for policy formulation and administration that became a difficulty in further complicating the administration of the protectorate. Some of these settlers had aristocratic connections; these big men came to dominate politics in the protectorate; the presence of wealthy, influential, and aristocratic settlers in the protectorate, capable of directly obtaining a decision from London, over the head of the governor, was no less a problem to the governor's exercise of authority over the protectorate's affairs.[80]

Settler demands for easy access to land and political representation in the protectorate, had caused some of them to make their way over the head of the governor. Competing demands of both the Europeans and Indians for opportunities in government and land, and equality in treatment between the two, could make the evolution of a defined policy of administration for the protectorate difficult. Settler demands was another difficulty in the administration of the protectorate, and some of the governors were not unaware of the influence of the settlers and the extent they could go to obtain satisfaction over the head of the governor.[81] Therefore, it was possible that some governors would have treaded carefully in dealing with the settler demands, not unmindful of the consequence that could arise against the governor, should he object to the wishes of the European settlers.

While on the other hand, most of the settlers were poor and thus wanted land for free and labor at low cost. This problem of sourcing labor for settler cultivation had taken its toll on both the government and the settlers on how best they could source labor for agricultural development. It had not been without its impact on the performance of European cultivation. Therefore, the entry of the European settlers could not be relegated in the factors making for the difficulty in the protectorate's administration, as their entry had accentuated the difficult position of the administration of the protectorate.[82]

A common source of labor in the protectorate was slaves, and with the abolition of a legal status of slavery, Arab plantation estates at the coast that had depended on slave labor reverted to waste land.[83] Competing title claims between the Arab Sharia land holding and the Mijikenda land tenure further complicated the question of demarcation of these abandoned Arab estates for grants to prospective European planters.[84] The Arabs had no knowledge of the boundaries of their estates and the former slaves who knew these boundaries had been dispersed by the abolition of the slavery.[85] Therefore, the competing title claims, abolition of slavery and the dispersal of the former slaves produced a difficult position for any governor to resuscitate the deteriorating coast economy. The slaves knew these boundaries but as slavery had been abolished and the slaves dispersed, it became a problem for government to delineate these estates for the development of the coast's economy.

With the abolition of slavery, the Arab economy deteriorated and their lifestyle ruined. Compensation paid to them by the British government failed to alleviate their sufferings. Therefore, the rebooting of the coast economy became another question that had to be addressed. The coast's poor economic condition that demanded action was further compounded by the protectorate's poor economic condition that depended on grants-in-aid from the British Treasury.[86] The protectorate's negative economic situation, as it had not been in a healthy financial position to balance its budget, was a huge challenge. Since the British declaration of a protectorate over the EAP in 1895, the protectorate depended on grants-in-aid from the British Treasury to fund administration and development.[87] This had been a serious problem to the protectorate as it was not in a position to generate revenue to fund administration and development.

CONCLUSION

Sir Percy's arrival in the EAP was the result of a successful tour of duty elsewhere in Africa. He distinguished himself as a railway builder in the Sudan and South Africa. These successes earned him positions of leadership in railway administration in Egypt and the Sudan as well as in the Transvaal and Orange River colonies. His resignation over a disagreement to railway rates with Milner did not hold back Sir Percy's rise in the service of the British Empire. After a brief stay in Britain, he received a major promotion as he was chosen by the CO to take over the governorship of Northern Nigeria.

In that post, Sir Percy succeeded in constructing the Baro to Kano railway as well as governing the colony effectively. He implemented policies in the interest of the African population, especially in the area of land, taxation, and education. With this success in Northern Nigeria, the CO appointed him governor of the EAP with a view that he could fix that protectorate's economic and administrative problems.

However, the EAP was quite different from Northern Nigeria. The absence of a well-grounded policy of administration, the EAP's different social composition on the ground, and the poor policies of his predecessors complicated Sir Percy's governorship. The CO's expectation that Sir Percy would provide strong and effective leadership for the EAP in working out policies for effective administration and the promotion of economic development was thus complicated by the earlier history of the EAP.

The condition of administration of the protectorate on the eve of Sir Percy's arrival was not in any satisfactory condition to afford effective administration. The government policy of administration was almost absent so that any administrator would have to navigate the administration based on his own individual idiosyncrasy. The succession of ill-equipped governors had accentuated the difficulty of administration as there was not a well-defined policy put in place by the previous governors, having little time in office due to the controversial nature of the protectorate, which most often engaged governors and the CO, in altercations, or the governor and the settlers or local colonial officials, causing a governor's resignation.

The staffing of the protectorate had not helped ease the difficult position of the protectorate. The staff members were taken over from the IBEA, when the IBEA liquidated its administrative charter over Uganda in 1895, and prompted the declaration of a protectorate over an area between Mombasa and Uganda, which came to be known as the EAP. Some of these staff members were not trained for colonial administration nor do they have university education, indeed a matter that compounded the difficult administration of the protectorate. In addition, there was the multiracial question and the hasty in rush of European planters into the protectorate. These races of the protectorate had to be protected and their rights safeguarded, but the European planters entry brought forth the question of their access to land which had been not been settled by 1909.

Grants of land to settlers were complicated, especially on the coast, where the abolition of slavery also ended Arab plantation estates. The latter produced a shortage of labor for the Arabs and the European planters and as there was no solution in sight, planters were left to their own individual devices. The labor problem compounded the productive output of the protectorate, if compared with the days when slaves produced. Having opened up the protectorate to planters, there was also the question of safeguarding the rights of other races, especially the Africans and the Indians, which had not been effectively carried through. The Indians, despite their early presence in the protectorate and their contribution in the development, trade, and commerce in the protectorate, were not afforded equal rights with the European settlers.

The Indian frantic search for equality had not been a less important factor in engaging the attention of the local authorities' energies in finding a way to avoid Indian demands, which continued, unresolved and remained one of the colony's problems. As to the question of land, the right to exclusive possession and use of land by Africans within their own reserve had not been safeguarded. Reserves were encroach upon, especially land relating to the Maasai nominal grazing reserve prior to Sir Percy's assumption of government. What had been accepted as a final solution of the Maasai reserve was reopened shortly after Sir Percy arrived. His handling of the issue was in many ways the defining aspect of his administration. As in several other key challenges faced by Sir Percy, it proved to be one that he failed to adequately deal with. One of the most pressing and demanding challenges that confronted him, on his assumption of government, was the absence of a clearly defined policy of administration of the protectorate. In this, he recommended for a defined policy of government and the strengthening of the machinery of government.

NOTES

1. John Mwaruvie, "Kenya's 'Forgotten' Engineer and Colonial Proconsul," *Canadian Journal of History*, 41 (Summer/Spring 2006), 3.
2. Stephanie Williams, *Running the Show: Governors of the British Empire 1857–1912* (London: VIKING an imprint of Penguin Books, 2011), 362.
3. Mwaruvie, "Kenya's 'Forgotten' Engineer," 2.
4. Williams, *Running the Show,* 362.
5. Ibid.
6. Ibid.
7. Mwaruvie "Kenya's 'Forgotten' Engineer," 3.
8. Ibid.
9. Ibid.
10. Fergus Nicoll, The *Mahdi of Sudan and the Death of General Gordon* (Stroud: Sutton Publishing Limited, 2004), 109.
11. Williams, *Running the Show,* 362. Field Marshall Horatio Herbert Kitchener, KG, KP, GCB, OM, GCSI. In 1899 he became famous in the British imperial history, having won the battle of Omdurman and brought Sudan under his control. He earned himself the title of Lord Kitchener of Khartoum; as Chief of Staff in 1900–02.
12. Kirk-Greene, "Canada in Africa," 214.
13. Williams, *Running the Show,* 362.
14. Ibid., 363.
15. John P. Dunn, *Khedive Ismail's Army* (New York: Taylor and Francis, 2005), 40.
16. Williams, *Running the Show*, 363.
17. Kirk-Greene, "Canada in Africa," 214; Mwaruvie "Kenya's "Forgotten" Engineer," 3. The Anglo-Boer War was fought between the British imperial forces and the Afrikaans speaking Dutch settlers of South Africa who has had two independent republics; the Transvaal Republic and Orange Free State. The British were

victorious in the war and it brought the two republics under the Union of South Africa that became a British dominion in 1910.

18. Williams, *Running the Show,* 362. Boer is Dutch and Afrikaan word for a farmer. It is used to refer to Dutch colonists or descendant of a Dutch colonist in South Africa [Afrikaans, from Dutch, *farmer*, from Middle Dutch gheboer, *peasant*; see bheu in Indo-European roots.] (Descendant of any of the Dutch or Huguenot colonists who settled in South Africa, mainly in Cape Colony, the Orange Free State, and the Transvaal) Also referred to a white native of Cape Province who is a descendant of Dutch settlers and who speaks Afrikaans.

19. Edgar Andrew Collard, "Sir Percy Girouard: The Jolly Engineer," *Montreal Gazette* (May, 15 1971), 16. Alfred Milner, 1st Viscount Milner, KC, GCB, GCMG, PC, British High Commissioner to the Union of South Africa, He played an influential role in the British formulation of both domestic and Foreign policies between 1890s and early 1920s, and had been a key leading figure in the build up to and after the Boer War, 1899–1902.

20. Ibid. Evelyn Baring, 1st Earl of Cromer, GCB, OM, GCMG, KCSI, CIE, GB, PC, FRS was British Controller General in Egypt in 1873 as head of Egypt's financial management after its mismanagement by Khedives. He also served as British Consul General at Cairo during British occupation of Egypt that was prompted by the Urabi Pasha revolt.

21. Williams, *Running the Show,* 363.

22. Ibid.

23. Ibid. Joseph Chamberlain was Secretary of State for the Colonies. He presided over the Anglo-Boer War.

24. Ibid.

25. Ibid., 364. Solomon (18 October 1850–10 November 1913) KCMG, CB, KC, MLC, was a Member of Parliament and the Attorney General of the Cape Colony and of the Transvaal, and Lieutenant Governor and Governor of the Transvaal. Solomon also served as legal advisor to Lord Kitchener during the Boer War and then to the Transvaal administration, and South Africa's High Commissioner to the United Kingdom. Solomon was part of a large and influential Cape family, of St Helenan Jewish descent. Solomon's family were involved in cape politics but were physically extraordinarily tiny in stature, but included some of the greatest legal minds in southern Africa. The famous and popular Cape Colony politician Saul Solomon was Sir Richard's uncle, and his brother; Edward Philip Solomon was the Transvaal politician.

26. Williams, *Running the Show,* 364.

27. Ibid.

28. Ibid.

29. Ibid.

30. Ibid.

31. Ibid.

32. Kirk-Greene, "Canada in Africa," 217.

33. Williams, *Running the Show,* 364.

34. Ibid.

35. Kirk-Greene, "Canada in Africa," 217 & 219.
36. Ibid., 219.
37. Williams, *Running the Show*, 362.
38. Great Britain, *Parliamentary Debates* (Commons) 5th Ser., 4 (1904), 819.
39. Williams, *Running the Show*, 365.
40. Kirk-Greene, "Canada in Africa," 219.
41. Ibid.
42. Ibid.
43. Mungeam, British *Rule in Kenya*, 137. Antrobus was one of four Assistant Secretaries in the Colonial Office. He was the head of the West Africa Department in the CO and responsible for the West African Frontier Force.
44. William Neville William Montgomery Geary, *Nigeria Under British Rule* (London: Frank Cass & Co., Ltd. 1965), 168.
45. Ibid.
46. Ibid.
47. Ibid.
48. Ibid.
49. Ibid.
50. Kirk-Greene, "Canada in Africa," 223.
51. Williams, *Running the Show*, 363.
52. Ibid., 365.
53. Ibid., 366.
54. A. H. Hardinge, *Diplomatist in the East* (London: Fisher T Unwin, 1928), 80; Mungeam, *British Rule in Kenya*, 1. Hardinge was British government's political agent and consul general at Zanzibar in 1895 when the British government declared a protectorate over an area between Mombasa and Uganda.
55. Mungeam, *British Rule in Kenya*, 10; William Mackinnon, *Imperial British Eat Africa Company* (London: Fisher T Unwin, 1930), 229; C. W. Hobley, *Kenya From Chattered Company to Crown Colony: Thirty Years of Exploration and Administration in Africa* (London: Frank Cass & Co., Ltd. 1970), V.
56. Mungeam, *British Rule in Kenya*, 10; Bennett, *Kenya*, 30.
57. Mungeam, *British Rule in Kenya*, 210; Sorrenson, *Origins of European Settlement in Kenya* (London: Oxford University Press, 1968), 117–8.
58. Mungeam, *British Rule in Kenya*, 210.
59. Ibid.
60. Sir Charles Eliot, *The East Africa Protectorate* (London: Fisher T Unwin, 1905), IV & 103.
61. Bennett, *Kenya*, 30; Sorrenson, *Origins of European Settlement in Kenya*, 117–18.
62. Sorrenson, *Origins of European Settlement in Kenya*, 117–18.
63. Mungeam, *British Rule in Kenya*, 210.
64. Ibid., 210–11.
65. D. K. Fieldhouse, *Economics and Empire*, 1870–1930 (Ithaca, NY: Connell University Press, 1973), 379.
66. Mungeam, *British Rule in Kenya*, 210–11.

67. Ibid., 210.

68. Mackinnon, *Imperial British Eat Africa Company*, 186–7; Hobley, *From Chattered Company to Colony*, 39.

69. John Lonsdale and Bruce Berman, "Coping with the Contradictions: The Development of the Colonial State in Kenya, 1895–1914," *Journal of African History* 20 (1979): 491.

70. Sorrenson, *Origins of European Settlement in Kenya*, 118.

71. Bennett, *Kenya*, 30–31.

72. Ibid.

73. Mungeam, *British Rule in Kenya*, 210–11.

74. Ibid.

75. Hughes, *Moving the Maasai*, 32.

76. Sorrenson, *Origins of European Settlement in Kenya*, 129; Mungeam, *British Rule in Kenya*, 214.

77. Sorrenson, *Origins of European Settlement in Kenya*, 168–9.

78. Ibid.

79. Ibid.

80. Bennett, *Kenya*, 31–2.

81. Ibid.

82. Ibid.

83. Mungeam, *British Rule in Kenya*, 240–1.

84. Ibid.

85. Ibid.

86. Great Britain, *East Africa Protectorate Report for 1908–9* (London: HMSO, 1910), 4.

87. Ibid.

Chapter 3

Policy of Administration

Sir Percy assumed the governorship of the EAP on 16 September 1909, and had, in pursuit of his desired policy, appraised the existing policy of the government, and proposed reforms in a manner he believed would be consistent with the administration of Crown colonies. Sir Percy deplored the lack of any defined policy of administration and development compared with Northern Nigeria, and the Transvaal. Sir Percy became very critical of government policy of administration, especially taxation, the records of administration, the large size of administration staff, the government departments, and the almost complete absence of a general policy of administration.

Sir Percy proposed that a well-defined policy of administration would engage the staff with specific responsibilities. Sir Percy added that government departments would be reorganized in a manner consistent with the needs of the administration; the required departments for the administration of policy would be retained while those with duplicate functions or redundant would be merged or phased out. Therefore right from the onset, Sir Percy criticized the existing policy, and proposed reforms in the government policy of administration.

Sir Percy proposed the reorganization of government departments, African policy, European and Indian policy, land policy, agriculture, trade and commerce, the police and the military affairs. The appraisal and reform that Sir Percy considered for the protectorate were common in crown colonies, especially in Northern Nigeria where he had been governor. In the EAP, by contrast, he found that there was an absence of government policy of administration. The absence of policy was not only evident in government circulars, political memoranda, staff and government departments' organization for effective administration and taxation, but it was common in all areas of government function.

APPRAISAL OF POLICY OF ADMINISTRATION

Upon his assumption of the governorship, Sir Percy planned a tour of the country so that he could acquaint himself with the protectorate so as to be able to report on land and agricultural subjects.[1] But after his perusal of official documents on the workings of the protectorate's successive governments, he deferred his tour, and reported on the general policy of the administration of the protectorate.[2] Sir Percy observed and reported the deplorable condition of administration of the protectorate to the Secretary of State for the Colonies, The Earl of Crewe.[3]

In both his confidential dispatch of 13 November 1909 and his Interim Report, Sir Percy told Crewe that the protectorate lacked "any defined policy of administration."[4] Sir Percy also told Crewe that his Interim Report was out of his own general knowledge of the protectorate, which he learnt after "as close a study of the records," consultations and enquiry from executives, and a series of meetings with the provincial commissioners, whom he had assembled for such purpose.[5]

Also, Sir Percy, in his review of the condition of administration, held discussions with other individuals he "deemed advisable and necessary," especially Lord Delamere, leader of the European settler community, and the unofficial members of the Legislative Council.[6] Sir Percy added that he also gathered information on the affairs of the protectorate from the meeting of the Legislative Council and that of heads of departments during the consideration of the 1910–11 proposed annual estimates.[7]

Therefore, Sir Percy had, after perusal of all documents that could be laid before him, and through which he obtained knowledge of the protectorate, in addition to his meetings with the officials of the protectorate and consultations with individuals he deemed desirable, told Crewe, "I was reluctantly forced to the conclusion that there was an utter absence of any defined policy, where I could take up the work of my predecessor and ensure continuity of effort and direction."[8] Sir Percy added that there was no compilation of records of administration, service regulations, and it was "hardly necessary to state those steps are being taken to remedy the situation."[9]

Sir Percy also told Crewe that the situation was unlike Northern Nigeria, where a "clearly well-defined and printed policy of government" existed.[10] In Northern Nigeria, Sir Percy told Crewe, such policy was covered in "series of admirable political memoranda and a thoroughly worked out and published series of government standing Orders."[11] However, Sir Percy was quick to point out that the Nigerian situation may not be applicable to the EAP in its entirety. In the case of the latter, Sir Percy admitted that there were great differences between his Nigerian policy experience and his attempt to grasp the EAP's policy of the past, through a perusal of the secretariat's files and annual departmental reports.[12]

In view of the latter state of the administration, Sir Percy deplored the near absence of any policy. Sir Percy further pointed out that the only available laws of the protectorate were "set forth in seven printed books and each law may be spread over the whole series, to which there was no general index."[13] The latter situation of the laws suggested to Sir Percy that "No attempt whatsoever appears to have been made to consolidate the statutes, and combined with the above legal labyrinth there are Indian laws to the number of twenty-seven, upon such subjects as Lunacy, Penal offences, whipping, succession, Posts, Divorce, evidence, contract, Criminal & Civil Procedure, Railway, &c."[14] Out of the seven volumes, Sir Percy collated the laws of the protectorate, and deleted those laws that had been repealed, which successive governors had not done.[15] Sir Percy, in concluding his recommendations, requested for a speedy approval of his proposals and threatened to resign should the CO delay approval or deny latitude in the application of the approved recommendations.[16]

In the CO, Sir Percy's observations on these matters were the cause of much interest and comment. Before F. G. A. Butler could embark on Sir Percy's comment on the absence of policy, he cautioned that in the EAP, Sir Percy went to a government that was totally different from that which he administered in the Northern Nigeria Protectorate.[17] However, Butler agreed that there was the need to strengthen the administration of the colony, suggesting that Sir Percy was "evidently somewhat startled and shocked by the contrast, a contrast, which in reality is quite intelligible."[18] Butler added that his "Predecessor in Northern Nigeria, Sir F. Lugard, had a clean slate on which to write. He had the molding of the administration and of the government policy from the very start, and he used his opportunity with excellent effect."[19]

In contrast, Butler stated, "in East Africa, on the other hand, we have had a succession of Governors who, if not actually unsatisfactory, have been ineffective."[20] Other than unsatisfactory administrators being posted to the colony, Butler stated that "For various reasons, there has been, in addition, the grave complication of the perhaps over-hasty rush of white settlers, buoyed up by extravagant hopes and correspondingly discontented when progress was slow."[21] Butler stated, "it is only fair to Sir Percy to say that he recognizes these reasons for the difference."[22] But at the same time, Butler stated, "it is only fair to him also to point out that his record shows that he is not merely a new broom."[23]

Butler pointed out that in Northern Nigeria Sir Percy "followed most loyally and minutely in the footsteps of his predecessor. He was a strong admirer of and supporter of Sir F. Lugard's policies in every respect, as I know from personal experience in the West African Department."[24] Butler added that Sir Percy was following Lugard in Northern Nigeria, kept Lugard informed of his progress along the lines laid down by Lugard.[25] Therefore, Butler suggested that as drastic as Sir Percy's proposals in respect of the EAP might be, they should not be dismissed on the ground that he was "keen to strike out a new line for himself and is suffering from the usual inclination of a new governor to reverse the acts and policy of his predecessor."[26]

Despite his commendation of the proposals, Butler expressed his doubts as to the originality of the report, stating that they should be cautious in their responses.[27] Butler viewed that it would not be possible for Sir Percy to produce such reports within two months of his assumption of government, in view of the fact that he would have to attend to the affairs of the government while at the same time writing a report.[28] This was another reason for careful study and a delayed response by the CO.

In a reply to Sir Percy's Interim Report in a telegram of 7 January 1910, the Secretary of State for the Colonies, The Earl of Crewe, agreed to Sir Percy's proposed strengthening of the administrative staff with a view to enhancing government policy of administration. Therefore, Crewe asked Sir Percy to transmit details as to the proposed strengthening of the administration of the colony.[29] Thus Sir Percy, in a telegram of 19 February 1910, requested action on his proposed staff reform.[30] Butler commented that there was the need for Sir Percy to provide detailed information by dispatch on how he wanted to carry through his reform.[31] H. J. Read agreed and stated that Sir Percy should be asked to transmit full details of the process of his reform.[32] Sir G. V. Fiddes pointed out that there must be a detailed presentation on the question before action could be taken. Fiddes warned that the proposed reforms should not be made in piece meal by telegram.[33] Crewe told Sir Percy that nothing could be done until he transmitted a full report by dispatch.[34] In a reply to Crewe's request for more details, Sir Percy transmitted, two months later, his secret dispatch covering his Main Report Upon the East Africa Protectorate of 26 May 1910, recommending far-reaching reforms. In this, he recommended the retirement of certain officials from service and the abolition of certain departments so that efficiency and strengthening of the machinery of government could be possible.[35] But nothing was done on this aspect as the CO refused to rely on his recommendations in effecting these reforms.

As to the question of provincial administration, Sir Percy recommended, in his Main Report, for the merger of the three coast provinces of Jubaland, Tanaland, and Seyyedie, under one provincial administration headquartered at Seyyedie.[36] Sir Percy recommended further that Lieutenant Governor Frederick Jackson, if not transferred to Uganda as governor, be appointed provincial commissioner of the newly reconstituted coast province. But if he was transferred, C. W. Hobley should be appointed as provincial commissioner.[37]

However, the request for the merger of the provinces was refused, as the existence of each province was considered significant in controlling the ethnic formations within its boundaries.[38]

This suggested that Sir Percy had not appraised the rationale for the existence of the three provinces before transmitting his request for their merger. In this case, Sir Percy could not secure the approval of Crewe for the merger of provinces as their separate existence out weighted the advantages of merger.[39] Therefore, the CO expressed its hesitations that the proposed merger of the coast provinces could not be put into operation immediately and it was deferred. The question was never revisited up to the time when Sir Percy resigned and left the colony.[40]

Other than the question of provincial administration, Sir Percy appraised the method of tax collection in the colony, which he noted not only varied with individual idiosyncrasy but he also noted that it was chaotic and would have to be reformed. Sir Percy pointed out that the protectorate lacked a uniform method of tax collection and recommended that there was the need of a unified method of tax collection to be adopted. Sir Percy decried the near absence of records of government activities, especially government standing orders, which he suggested must be put in place in order to organize efficient and effective administration. There was a lack of government records and where they existed they were vague, especially at provincial and district headquarters. Where such records existed, they were disorganized and lacked a clearly defined description of function. The absence of policy, Sir Percy stated, had created a body of staff without any defined role other than backstabbing among themselves.

Therefore, Sir Percy proposed, in his Interim Report, the introduction of John Ainsworth's method of tax collection in the Nyanza Province, as the most effective means of tax collection throughout the colony.[41] Ainsworth, who became the Provincial Commissioner of Nyanza Province in 1907, had successfully evolved an effective method of tax collection. Ainsworth directed the district officers to collect taxes and to be assisted by chiefs and headmen, and they should use registers where a list of eligible payees was recorded, and records of defaulters made. It was this method that Sir Percy considered the most effective means of tax administration and, therefore, sought to introduce it throughout the colony. In this regard, Sir Percy made a significant effort in the introduction of the said method but he was not able to introduce the method throughout the colony up to the time he left the protectorate. He was able to make certain progress in the administration of taxation, but he had not successfully introduced the method of tax collection throughout the colony. Therefore, the question of carrying through an effective means of taxation had to be deferred to his successor, Sir Henry Conway Belfield.

AMALGAMATION BETWEEN THE EAST AFRICA PROTECTORATE AND THE UGANDA PROTECTORATE CONSIDERED

The question of Uganda's administration and its potential amalgamation with the EAP occupied the attention of Sir Percy at the time he was compiling his Interim Report. The question of amalgamation came forth as a result of Crewe's direction to Sir Percy, some two weeks after the latter assumed office, to report on the administration of Uganda.[42] On receipt of Crewe's telegram, Sir Percy made interim recommendations on the question of amalgamation in his confidential dispatch of 13 November 1909, stating that he favored that Uganda be amalgamated to the EAP.[43]

He gave his reasons and provided recommendations to carry it into effect. Sir Percy added that he was persuaded of the necessity of strengthening the East African administration and inclined toward amalgamation of the two protectorates.[44] Sir Percy reiterated that the Uganda Protectorate should be amalgamated with the EAP in his Interim Report of the same date.[45] Sir Percy added that the amalgamation of Uganda would afford it the opportunity to develop in the same way the EAP developed. Sir Percy argued that if Uganda were amalgamated the administration of the protectorate would be strengthened.[46] Sir Percy argued that the amalgamation of Uganda and the EAP would be in the very best interest of Uganda and that it would not accentuate its difficulties but lessen them.[47]

Sir Percy wrote a report on the administration of Uganda following a brief visit to that protectorate. He completed the report and included it with his Interim Report on the East Africa Protectorate of 13 November 1909. A significant part of the Uganda report was Sir Percy's recommendation that Uganda should be amalgamated with the EAP. He did this despite the fact that his report on Uganda clearly indicated that Uganda was in a healthier administrative and economic condition than the EAP. Sir Percy considered that the merger, or at least a fusion of government departments of the two protectorates, was imperative.[48]

Sir Percy's recommendation on amalgamation engaged him and the CO in a long drawn argument on the desirability, or otherwise, of the amalgamation of the two protectorates. The argument clearly demonstrated knowledge of colonial administration and policy, the developed and underdeveloped conditions of both protectorates, and how, according to Sir Percy, the underdeveloped condition of Uganda could be mitigated by its amalgamation to the EAP so that it could experience all the developments similar to that of the EAP.[49]

Sir Percy, in his Uganda Report, told Crewe that he considered that amalgamation would bring benefits of economic development and the strengthening of the administration of the amalgamated colonies. Sir Percy told Crewe, in both his Interim Report and Uganda Report, that Uganda would benefit from the proposed amalgamation. It was, he asserted, uneconomical to allow Uganda to look for services and development that the EAP could afford her.[50] In his report upon the condition of administration in the Uganda Protectorate, Sir Percy reported to Crewe that, "of the two protectorates Uganda appears to be in a healthier administrative condition, though certain departments would be the better for new blood, and the provincial administration is languid for the same reason."[51] Sir Percy also pointed out that other than the land question, Uganda as an African state presented fewer complications.[52] The land position that Sir Percy was referring to was the Buganda Agreement of 1900; an agreement that provided "that waste and uncultivated land, and land occupied without prior gift, was to be vested in His Majesty's government."[53]

Sir Percy also reported to Crewe that the former governor, H. H. Bell, had however pointed out that Uganda was not unsuitable country for planter life, and that the question of settler entry into the country should be expected to come forward at any time.[54] Sir Percy stated that when the latter issue came up, there would be "much criticism of the government land policy, which would require the soundest possible judicial and legal assistance to avoid pitfalls we have practically dug for ourselves."[55] As to the condition found in the EAP, Sir Percy observed and reported in his Uganda report, that "it would have been impossible to conceive that the East Africa Protectorate would have been on an even sounder basis today, had it not witnessed the somewhat hurried introduction of white settlement."[56]

Sir Percy criticized previous administrators of the EAP, especially Sir H. H. Johnston and Sir A. Hardinge, for the protectorate's administrative problems, stating that the latter two failed to provide adequate infrastructure that could have supported the entry and settlement of Europeans in the protectorate, despite the fact that they were aware of the planned European immigration in to the protectorate. Sir Percy added that the absence of any arrangement for settler entry into EAP, a colony organized purely for African populations, had complicated the administration of the protectorate and forced Africans into conditions suitable for white settlers.[57] Sir Percy suggested that in spite of the cost that might be involved in the setting up those departments and the Uganda land question, that they should be hurriedly established.[58] With regard to the land question, Sir Percy also reported that it was fortunate that as far as the Uganda chiefs were concerned, the land question would not present any difficulties in the event of white settler entry.[59]

As to the prevailing administrative difficulties occasioned to the EAP, Sir Percy stated that such problems, which authorities in the Uganda Protectorate might think that Uganda was spared the trouble of the EAP, would have happened in any colony organized for purely African administration.[60] He suggested that should Uganda witness planter immigration, the difficult situation that occasioned to the EAP, on the entry of European planters, would also manifest itself in the Uganda Protectorate, if not more.[61] Sir Percy, therefore, pointed out that the settler entry into the EAP had been accomplished and that their presence should be seen in a broader view. This was in reference to Uganda, which he believed was suitable for the habitation of European planters and that the CO should have a broader view of the white entry into Uganda. Sir Percy also pointed out that the settlers were their own kith and kin who would have wished applications for their entry into Uganda, would have been well received.[62]

Sir Percy added that it would be unfair to allow Uganda to reap all the benefit that EAP could afford her, and, in return, the EAP would be compensated only from receipts of the Uganda railway. Therefore, Sir Percy recommended, "If by amalgamation the Colonial Department can be strengthened in East African administration and policy without impeding Uganda's progress and development, fusion of some kind should take place."[63] Sir Percy pointed out that the general benefits that would accrue to both protectorates would be the strengthening of the machinery of government and development of the Uganda Protectorate and its economy.

In the CO, before they could embark on reviewing Sir Percy's recommendations, officials sought and obtained comments on Sir Percy's Uganda Report, from a senior government official in Uganda, Stanley Tomkins. Tomkins examined Sir Percy's Uganda Report, and expressed his views to Crewe, in an "undated Memorandum Containing Rough Notes for a Dispatch to the Secretary of State upon the question of Amalgamation between the Uganda Protectorate and the East Africa Protectorate."[64]

Tomkins, in his comments, opposed Sir Percy's recommendations on the administration and the proposed amalgamation of the Uganda Protectorate to the EAP. Tomkins, drawing from Sir Percy's Uganda Report, wondered why Sir Percy considered Uganda's amalgamation with the EAP, when Uganda was more advanced and prosperous than the EAP, would still be to the benefit of Uganda.[65] Tomkins opined that it was the latter that would be amalgamated to the former, in view of its less developed condition.[66] He therefore stated that the prosperous colony of Uganda should be separate from the EAP.[67] On the question of the legality or otherwise of amalgamation that was raised by Sir Percy, in his Uganda Report, Tomkins "questioned whether it was legally possible" which he felt it was not.[68]

Tomkins observed that the Commissioner of Uganda, A. Boyle, concurred in the proposals as to amalgamation, but Tomkins also observed that Boyle had subsequently modified his views. Tomkins stated that he was not convinced of the facts that the EAP had something beneficial to offer for the development of the Uganda. Tomkins also disagreed with Sir Percy's view that if Uganda were amalgamated, its difficulties would be mitigated, and instead, told Crewe that the difficulties of Uganda would be accentuated, if the proposed amalgamation would be considered.[69]

In this regard, Tomkins pointed out the difficulty in intercommunication between the headquarters in Nairobi and Uganda, which could cause delays in making a decision on any issue relating to Uganda. Tomkins stated that the distance and communication between Nairobi and Uganda would delay a decision on any issue of Uganda that would have to be transmitted to London via Nairobi where, before a decision could be reached, it would take no less than three weeks of back and forth and thereafter, the decision would be referred to London for approval.[70]

Tomkins stated further that whatever advantages Sir Percy considered would accrue to Uganda as a result of its amalgamation to the EAP, it "would not have been otherwise than detrimental to the best interests of the Uganda."[71] In this regard, Tomkins believed that in spite of Sir Percy's report, which clearly showed that Uganda was more advanced and more prosperous than the EAP, Sir Percy should not recommend the amalgamation of Uganda and instead, he should have recommended the amalgamation of the EAP to Uganda. Therefore, Tomkins disagreed with the proposed amalgamation as Sir Percy failed to convince him of the expediency of the amalgamation.

The officials of the CO were equipped with Tomkins's view on the administration of Uganda and the proposed amalgamation when Crewe sought their comments on Sir Percy's Uganda Report. Butler, in his minute on Sir Percy's Uganda Report, stated, "since Sir Percy was authorized to go to Uganda and report on the question of amalgamation, circumstances have changed considerably, it has been found necessary to designate Captain Cordeaux as Governor of Uganda for a period of two years, which will expire, so far as can be seen at present, about the middle of 1912."[72] Butler added, "There can, therefore, be no question of immediate amalgamation even of the partial kind advocated by Sir Percy Girouard."[73]

However, the question of amalgamation was left open when Butler pointed out that "Fortunately Sir Percy has the foresight to make recommendations which are applicable to EAP whether amalgamation is decided or not."[74] Butler added, "we can therefore consider them on their own merits undeterred by the fact that amalgamation is for the present out of the question."[75]

Read, who commented on the question of white penetration into the Uganda Protectorate, if amalgamation of Uganda to the EAP was decided, complemented Butler's minute. Read, in his minute, opposed the proposed amalgamation of Uganda with the EAP, stating: "Personally I think it would be unwise, at any rate for the present, to amalgamate Uganda with the EAP. In addition to the objections of Mr. Tomkins, it seems to me that the EAP with its numerous problems is likely to require all the attention of Sir P. Girouard for some time to come. Further, Sir P. G. is evidently paving the way for giving a larger share in admin. to the white settler of the E. A. P. and I do not think that a purely native country like Uganda would be likely to benefit by the arrangement."[76] He went on: "There is, however, an amalgamation which seems to be desirable in itself & which would throw but little additional work on Sir P. G.—the amalgamation of Zanzibar with the EAP."[77] Read added, "Sir P.G. would probably like to have his command in this direction & with this additional responsibility; he might be less keen about the Uganda amalgamation."[78] Read clearly believed that Sir Percy's recommendation for the amalgamation of Uganda to the EAP was not based on account of conditions found in Uganda, rather it was based on his own desire to have a large area under his command.

Fiddes also commented on the question of white penetration into Uganda should the CO agree to amalgamate the two colonies. He complemented Butler when he minuted: "one thing seems to me to stand out clearly: viz that on no ground of public advantage is amalgamation desirable at present."[79] Fiddes, moreover, pointed out the enormous task involved in running the two colonies when he stated: "the governor will have enough and more than enough to absorb all his energies in dealing with all the problems of the eaP [sic]."[80] Fiddes also stated that Sir Percy "practically recognizes that Uganda is in a better position administratively than the eaP [sic]."[81] Fiddes cautioned that Sir Percy suggested that this would not be the case if a white element came into Uganda; but if this happened it would afford an additional reason against amalgamation, as it would make "it more than ever necessary that the head of the govt. should be on the afot [sic]."[82] As to the land agreement between the Baganda chiefs and His Majesty, Sir Percy observed and reported that if the proposed amalgamation would be implemented, it would relegate the relevance of the land agreement to the back seat.[83] In the two latter cases, Fiddes disagreed with Sir Percy's observation on the benefits that could accrue to the Uganda as a result of its amalgamation with the EAP and stated, "The Baganda have recently given several striking proofs of their capacity for development and—apart from our agreements with them that cannot be disregarded–we owe it to them to give them a chance of development such in this we have to keep them aloof from the disturbing white influence of the eaP [sic]."[84] Fiddes also minuted that Sir Percy should be told in a telegram that "the S of S has thought it advisable to recommend the apt of a new Gov. for Uganda for a short term of office during wh. [sic] time the question of amalgamation will receive further constion [sic]."[85] Fiddes refused to agree with Sir Percy's recommendations that the amalgamation would be to the benefit of the Baganda, stating that the Baganda were capable of developing by themselves, having proven that earlier. Fiddes thus concluded that the Baganda should be left free of white entry. Fiddes also suggested that amalgamation might produce difficulty in the administration of Uganda similar to that of the EAP.[86] To avoid a repeat of the situation, Fiddes suggested that a new Uganda governor should appointed for a term of office within which the issue would be considered fully. Therefore, Fiddes's recommended to Crewe a telegram to Sir Percy, intimating to him the decision to appoint a new governor.

Parliamentary undersecretary of State J. B. Seeley accepted the advice of the civil servants and called attention to another issue. Seeley minuted that, "on the whole I should be disposed to telegraph as Mr. Butler proposes. Sir P. Girouard's talk of resignation unless he gets a free hand is the result of the unaccustomed altitude on a highly energetic temperament."[87] Butler proposed that Sir Percy's threat of resignation if he was not given a free hand or his work delayed should be disregarded so that it would not distract them from the merit of his report. Seeley stated that when Sir Percy "gets used to living 9000 feet above sea level the energy will remain and the tendency to hurry will vanish. In the meantime, we may well support and encourage him as far as possible. It is a good thing to have in our service a man so full of energy and enthusiasm for his work."[88] Seeley believed that Sir Percy was yet to get accustomed to the influence of the environment which would make his head lighter and less determined in view of the altitude of the new environment where he found himself. But the tendency to hurry would still remain, the change in the altitude notwithstanding. Crewe noted that, "for some reason our relations with Sir P. Girouard are delicate and I concur in Col. Seeley's view of the situation."[89] Despite Butler and Seeley's comments that Sir Percy's threat of resignation should be ignored, the officials at the CO treaded cautiously in dealing with Sir Percy's recommendations. Sir Percy threatened to resign if approvals of his recommendations were delayed or latitude in their application denied. This had been the cause of the CO's caution, and Crewe also described their relationship with Sir Percy was delicate. This threat of resignation suggested the cavalier nature of Sir Percy, and difficulty in dealing with him, keeping in mind his earlier run in with Milner, perhaps a portrait of the man is coming together that is not so commendable as some suggest.

Therefore, Crewe replied to Sir Percy, in a telegram of 7 January 1910, stating, "as to amalgamation, circumstances which I will explain to you separately have made it necessary to designate a new governor of Uganda for a period of not more than two years."[90] Crewe stated further: "Full amalgamation therefore is not practicable at the present, but I am much impressed by your arguments in favor of amalgamation of some kind, and I shall not cease to consider the question more closely during the period of office of the new Governor."[91] However, Crewe added that, "in the meantime, your report on Uganda will be extremely valuable to me particularly in the matters of the land question, communications, and military policy."[92]

This ended the question of amalgamation in the short run, but Crewe was willing to review the question on amalgamation at an appropriate time with a view to appraise the position fully. Despite the intimation transmitted to Sir Percy on the position of the CO on the question of amalgamation, the CO continued to deliberate on the question, which did not produce an outcome other than the suggestion made by Read, that Zanzibar could be amalgamated to the EAP rather than Uganda.

However, the main factor that could inform any decision on Sir Percy's proposed amalgamation of the two colonies was the expediency of the scheme, which the CO was open to consider. Nevertheless, Sir Percy was faced with the most daunting task of convincing the CO of the expediency of amalgamation that informed his recommendations, which the CO would also consider at length before they could decide whether or not amalgamation would produce the desired strengthening of the machinery of government. In the interim, it was clear from Crewe's reply that Sir Percy could not from the very beginning convince the CO of the need to amalgamate Uganda to the EAP. The latter situation had informed the CO decision in the interim, pending full appraisal of the position before a final decision on whether or not amalgamation would be considered.

All that the CO wanted was to be convinced that the proposed amalgamation would produce development of the protectorates and strengthen the machinery of government as Sir Percy had recommended to Crewe. The CO, having considered Sir Percy's proposed amalgamation, came to a clear conclusion that Sir Percy's arguments on the desirability of the amalgamation were not convincing. The CO opined that Uganda was more advanced and more prosperous than the EAP and therefore, Uganda would remain as a separate protectorate from the EAP.[93]

This suggested that Sir Percy refused to advise based on the existing conditions, and, instead, reported out of his own personal interest; that of placing Uganda under his command.[94] His Uganda report was based on facts in most instances, but in other instances, his report was marred with misapprehension on certain issues especially on the staff of the Uganda Protectorate. Sir Percy might have wanted to have a large area under his command, which would extend his power as well as his control over a large expanse of land. It could be recalled that Read, in a minute on Sir Percy's Interim Report and the Uganda Report, stated that Sir Percy might be interested in having a large expanse of area under his command, which might have informed his amalgamation scheme, rather than the need of amalgamation based on public advantage as Uganda was in a better state of administration and development than the EAP.

The fact that Sir Percy stated that the provincial staff of Uganda was weak clearly demonstrated that his recommendations were unfair, as he was only in Uganda for two weeks, which might not be enough to assess all the provincial staff of Uganda. It could be recalled that he made a similar statement on the staff of the EAP, in his Main Report Upon the EAP of 26 May

1910. [95] From all indication, personal interest might have informed his report on Uganda, as his recommendation contradicted what he reported as to the status of Uganda's administration and state of development. This was an indication that Sir Percy's proposed amalgamation was informed by personal political prestige rather than real knowledge and expertise on administration. It also suggested that Sir Percy was willing to sacrifice Uganda administration and development to enhance his political authority.[96] The CO objected and pointed out his bias, rather than administration expediency, and refused to budge on the idea of amalgamation.

The question of whether he could convince the CO of the desirability of amalgamation clearly demonstrated that Sir Percy had not fully appraised the conditions of administration of the two protectorates to warrant his recommendation for the amalgamation. Sir Percy did not avail himself of knowledge of the two administrations sufficiently to convince the CO of the expediency of amalgamation. Despite the CO's interest on the question of amalgamation of the two colonies, they declined to approve of the policy, as there were no merits for such amalgamation based on Tomkins's memorandum.

From Sir Percy's report and the reaction of the CO staff, another interesting view which Sir Percy raised was the question of white penetration into Uganda, and it was not illogical from his own view that the placing of Uganda under the EAP would afford him the opportunity of opening up Uganda to the white settlers, a view that Fiddes rejected outright. Fiddes viewed that the whites would penetrate into Uganda if amalgamation was decided and it would afford additional reason against the amalgamation so that Uganda would not be thrown in a similar problem that the EAP has had.[97]

Therefore, Sir Percy's recommendations were informed by his desire to have a large expanse of area under his command rather than advantages that would accrue to the colonies and the CO. This situation left a lot to be desired on the personality of Sir Percy, as he was more interested in the promotion of his own personal political interest by having a large area under his command rather than advancing the course of the two colonies based on public interest. This case of amalgamation, and its resolution by the CO, suggests that Sir Percy was not be an administrator devoted to the promotion of ideals based on the best interest of advancing the course of the colonies and the interest of British government of effecting economy in colonial administration.

APPRAISALS OF THE EXECUTIVE, LEGISLATIVE, AND JUDICIAL BRANCHES

The executive, legislative, and judicial arms of the colony were appraised in Sir Percy's Interim Report. He recommended that they should be reorganized.

As to the executive council, Sir Percy reported to Crewe, in his Interim Report, that lack of a strong colonial secretary had been the cause of the secretariat disabilities in many respects. Sir Percy added the absence of the latter had caused the governor to be preoccupied with minor affairs that would have been attended to by a strong colonial secretary. The effect of this preoccupation, Sir Percy stated, caused the governor to devote less time to the question of the evolution of both political and administrative questions.[98] In short, lack of a strong colonial secretary and the weakness of the executive council in numerical strength as well as in debate caused Sir Percy to recommend the reorganization of the council.

As to the legislative council, Sir Percy reported in his Interim Report that from his experience of one meeting with the legislative council, it appeared to be "an invertebrate body, and requires strengthening both officially and unofficially."[99] Owing to the number of departments in the protectorate, many had no direct representation in council, which Sir Percy viewed as a very grave disadvantage in debate.[100] Sir Percy also pointed out "the government element not infrequently divides on subject of importance, and there has been wanting a strong lead. It is not politic to my mind that this lead should in council come from the President himself. In a community such as I gauge this one to be, this line of action might create a situation in which the governor could not allow himself to be placed."[101]

Therefore, Sir Percy recommended that the policy must come from the governor and his executive council, and what was desired was a strong exponent of these views in the legislative council, a colonial secretary.[102] Sir Percy recommended that what he expected in council were elements who share the views of the governor and who could advocate such views in the council debates, especially the colonial secretary. Sir Percy added that the only possible solution to such weakness was to appoint a competent colonial secretary who could take the work seriously. Also with regard to the legislature, Sir Percy recommended for more European unofficial as members of the legislative council, so that they could be heard.[103]

With regard to the judicial and legal affairs, on the other hand, Sir Percy was very critical as to the competence of the judiciary when he told Crewe, in his Interim Report, that "the Bench as a body is I fear somewhat discredited."[104] Sir Percy observed that there was the need "for strengthened and even leavening the Judiciary."[105] However, Sir Percy told Crewe that he gained experience of the principal judge, Judge Barth's, competence when he was compiling his Interim Report.[106] Sir Percy added that Judge Barth impressed him as an able conscientious justice who would be of assistance.[107]

The law department, in Sir Percy's view, was none too strong for the many difficult tasks before the colony. The senior officer was a charming person, but had no extensive colonial experience; his junior was said to be incompetent.[108] Neither judiciary nor law department appeared "to have done any serious work in the very necessary codification of the laws or in the removal of the anomalous situation created by the application of Indian enactments unsuited to the white or indigenous inhabitants."[109]

In the CO, Butler commented that Sir Percy stated that the reorganization he proposed would involve no increase in the estimates but will be met by his savings from the proposed annual estimates.[110] Therefore, Butler continued, "on this understanding, I think that the appointment of a Chief Justice, a Colonial Secretary, and an Attorney General is in itself desirable."[111] Butler added, "we should have to consider the question further in the light of the difficulty of dealing with the present holders of appointments which have virtually taken the place of these, viz: - The Principal Judge, the Lieutenant Governor, and the crown advocate."[112]

Therefore, Butler summarized Sir Percy's requests for reform as to the executive, legislative and judicial branches that Sir Percy recommended for the appointment of chief justice, a colonial secretary, and an attorney general. Butler added, "Sir Percy sketched his idea on the distribution of work between the various departments, and proposed his idea of the composition of the executive and legislative councils."[113] Butler added that Sir Percy had clearly made "out a preliminary case on all these points, but of course detailed consideration must follow."[114] Butler recommended that if there were a colonial secretary there should be no lieutenant governor and "the Colonial Secretary would naturally replace the treasury on both councils."[115] Butler also stated that there was no need for both the attorney general and the crown advocate to be in the councils, the attorney general could replace the crown advocate.[116]

As to the agriculture and lands departments, Butler recommended that the merger of the two departments "would make unnecessary the presence of the Director of Agriculture on the Legislative Council."[117] Butler went on to describe the important alterations suggested in the legislative council. The alterations suggested for new appointments or rearrangement of departments were the removal of A. C. Hollis, Secretary for Native Affairs (henceforth a part of colonial secretary's department), the making of the commissioner of public works an ex-officio instead of an official member and the addition of two unofficial members. The net result would be to have eight ex-officio in the legislative council, one of whom is the governor, face to face with seven unofficial in the legislative council. The present council had six ex-officio members, three official, and five unofficial members. The margin against a vote adverse to the government, Butler observed, "is thus considerably narrowed."[118]

Butler added, "This is an inevitable accompaniment of giving the people of the Protectorate more voice in their own affairs, but I should be inclined not to let the number of unofficial members exceed 6 at present."[119] Butler added that Sir Percy's recommendation of having the Attorney General and the Solicitor General in the Legislative Council appeared to be "a little odd as there was no other department that was doubly represented."[120] Butler stated, however, the need to discuss legislation in the council might require the presence of both the Attorney General and the Solicitor General.[121] Therefore, Butler, in continuation of his comment on the proposed reforms of these branches of the government, recommended that the immediate "necessary thing is to intimate to Sir Percy the sympathy and interest with which the Secretary of State has received this report and the value he attaches to it, and to show him that he is secure of full support within reasonable limits."[122]

Butler stated further that it should be made clear to Sir Percy that he must expect "a certain amount of criticism, and that it is not possible to swallow all the proposals which he puts forward without examination."[123] Butler added "a telegram conveying all this would be a lengthy and expensive affair, but I think it is justified by the circumstances."[124] In spite of Butler's indisposition to reply by telegram, he recommended that the telegram was the most appropriate as it had been found urgently necessary to inform Sir Percy that there would be a new governor for the Uganda Protectorate for a certain period of time.[125] But such intimation, Butler suggested, should go along with the general sympathetic attitude of Crewe in other aspects of his report.[126]

Without sympathetic expression of Crewe on his report, Butler added, "I am afraid that Sir Percy might think, very naturally, that he had not been well treated by the appointment of a governor immediately on the heels of instructions to him to report on the question of amalgamation."[127] Therefore, Butler recommended to Crewe to send a telegram to Sir Percy as a reply. Read expressed concurrence with Butler's recommendations. He minuted: "Mr. Butler has dealt so fully & ably with this interesting desp: that it is scarcely necessary for me to add anything."[128] However, Read observed that they may differ in opinion as to Sir Percy's proposed reforms especially in "the weeding out of inefficient officials."[129] Read added, some of these officials did an excellent job in the early pioneer days of the protectorate and "we naturally hesitate to cut them adrift without some sort of provision."[130]

Read added that the older staff remember the colony during its early years and had interest in the protectorate and the big game and there were no trouble with questions which white settlement had raised and they might not be enthusiastic about modern development.[131] Fiddes complemented Read's comments, when he minuted on Sir Percy's proposed reform in the legislative council. Fiddes recalled Sir Percy's consideration that unofficial members would be equal in number to the officials (members of the government). Fiddes minuted, "it seems to me that if he wanted to produce trouble this is exactly the way to do it." Fiddes pointed out that the governor's casting vote will be required and if the governor's representative or the commandant were away, the government will be in a minority position.[132] In this situation, Sir Percy wanted to have a lead over the council by having more voting unofficials in the council so that he could have overriding votes for his agenda to pass through. In an equal vote or if the legislators are in majority, Sir Percy might not get his way out. Despite this potential difficulty, this was one of many issues that indicated Sir Percy's desire to curry favor with the European settlers.

Nevertheless, he could not implement the proposal, as the CO could not approve some of the recommendations in view of their being detrimental to the colony. Thus his policy failed. Crewe, in a reply to Sir Percy, in a telegram of 7 January 1910, wrote that it was necessary to consider them in connection with the men, the office of the principal judge, lieutenant-governor, and crown advocate, and asked Sir Percy to submit detailed recommendations on the said subject.[133]

Sir Percy, in a reply to Crewe's request for more information on the proposed reorganization, addressed a telegram of 19 February 1910, requesting the consideration of his proposed reforms he transmitted in his Interim Report.[134] In the CO, Butler minuted that Sir Percy should transmit a detailed explanation of how he wanted the reforms carried out in a dispatch.[135] Read also emphasized the need for detailed information in a dispatch.[136] Fiddes, in his comment on Sir Percy's request for action on his proposed reorganization of the executive, stated that Sir Percy's piecemeal requests for a policy formulation by means of a telegram could lead to complications in the future and cautioned against similar requests.[137] Crewe thus replied to Sir Percy, in a telegram of 2 March 1910, and directed Sir Percy to transmit full detail of his request by dispatch.[138]

In a reply to Crewe's telegram, Sir Percy transmitted another report, which he titled Main Report. There he reiterated his request for the abolition of the post of lieutenant governor and, in its place, a new post of a colonial secretary should be created.[139] In a covering secret dispatch, Sir Percy recommended that Jackson should be transferred to "a purely native country."[140] This was a veiled reference that Jackson should be transferred to Uganda. Sir Percy stated that he admired and respected Jackson and that he commanded respect within the community and had qualities for the administration of a purely African state, but he lacked requisite qualities for a developing mixed community like the EAP.[141] Sir Percy added that Jackson did not control the legislative council as speaker or leader, nor could he control the secretariat, which got out of control.[142] Sir Percy recommended the Treasurer, Bowring, as the colonial secretary for his ability, popularity, success, tact, and urbanity in handling council.[143]

In reply to Sir Percy's requests for the reorganization of the executive, legislative and the judiciary, a decision was not made until early 1911.

With regard to Sir Percy's request for the abolition of the post of lieutenant governor and the creation of a post of a colonial secretary in its place, the CO approved the abolition of the post of the lieutenant governor, and the post of a colonial secretary was created. Bowring, the treasurer of the colony, was appointed colonial secretary. Jackson, who was the lieutenant governor, was promoted and transferred to the vacant post of governor of the Uganda Protectorate. In fact, Jackson elevation's was made possible by Read who insisted that Jackson's past service should be recognized and it was in consideration of Read's appeal that Jackson was elevated.[144] As to the legal department, the CO refused to make any reorganization of staff of this department.[145]

These reorganizations were necessary, as Sir Percy had indicated that other than the absence of a clearly defined policy of government administration, the colony's machinery of government must be strengthened to carry through his proposed reforms. Lack of policy was responsible for many of the disabilities of the colony, especially government standing orders, which Sir Percy stated had caused the presence of a body of staff without a defined role.[146] Therefore, Sir Percy believed that his proposed reforms would provide the desired policy reform that would strengthen the executive to carry through his reforms.

But of Sir Percy's proposed reforms at the executive level, other than the two changes mentioned; lieutenant governor and colonial secretary, nothing had been altered. The CO was reluctant to affect a sweeping reform that could have a dire consequence on the administration, believing that Sir Percy must not have appraised the condition of the administration sufficiently to inform his proposed reform. Therefore, his reforms at the executive level failed as he failed to convince the CO of the necessity of the sweeping reforms. This suggested that Sir Percy failed to examine the condition of administration fully before he could recommend for the changes, a situation that an effective administrator would always desist from effecting inconsequential reforms.

SIR PERCY'S VIEWS ON THE PROVINCIAL POLITICAL STAFF

Another part of Sir Percy's assessment of the EAP's administration was his evaluation of individual staff members in his Main Report. In that document, he assessed the staff members and passed very uncomplimentary statements on them. He claimed that his comments were guided not just by his own observations, but also reflected the opinion of some of the provincial commissioners. Sir Percy told Crewe, in the Main Report, that in the opinion of the commissioners, some of the senior staff were "hopelessly incompetent."[147] There were some of the staff whose grade had been reduced, and there were also two other staff that were known to have been "habitual drunkards."[148] Sir Percy also reported on other separate cases of two staff; one had already been transferred to Nyasaland for circumstances that Sir Percy refused to disclose and the conduct of the other staff member was under investigation for circumstances that he "could not believe possible in a British colony or protectorate."[149] Sir Percy lamented the very deplorable conduct of the staff but declined to condemn them, reiterating that he was impressed favorably by the provincial commissioners.[150]

In spite of lack of defined policy of administration, which made it difficult for Sir Percy to highly praise the staff, Sir Percy, in his Main Report of 26 May 1910, told Crewe that the commissioners had been long without any defined policy of administration, and had become "hopelessly self-satisfied or supine."[151] Sir Percy stated that the former was not a matter of moment with capable men; "but of such we only have Ainsworth, and he is probably leaving the Protectorate service."[152] Sir Percy added that Hobley was "mistrusted and unpopular; he has undoubted ability which tends towards assuming all possible functions he can lay his hands on: he has been at one and the same time Acting Lieutenant-Governor, Provincial Commissioner, President Municipal Committee, and President, Education Board."[153] Sir Percy in perusing reports and correspondence on the activities of the protectorate noted the excellent qualities of some individual officers in the service of the protectorate, he deplored the lack of loyalty and *esprit de corps* of the entire staff:

> I have been struck, in perusing reports and correspondences, with the sprite of factious rivalry and even disloyalty which animates some of its [i.e. staff's] members. Some changes are imperative, but, above all, continuous policy must be established and harmony and cooperation engendered.[154]

With such attitudes Sir Percy found it difficult to let go. He advised Crewe that winnowing was imperative, and should be "ruthlessly carried out."[155] At the same time, Sir Percy suggested that the most important consideration was that "continuous policy must be established, and harmony and co-operation engendered."[156]

At this point, Sir Percy, upon the counsel of the executive, became increasingly critical on some of the senior officials of the administration when he recommended for their retirement from service.[157] Sir Percy also told Crewe that his criticism of the political staff was informed by the views he sought and obtained from the Lieutenant Governor and provincial commissioners in council, as to the general weaknesses or incompetence in the administration.[158] The commissioners offered frank advice without allowing their "personal feelings to actuate them in tendering their advice."[159] Distance however was great, and it was not for some time that, "I thoroughly realized the efficiency in working of both the administrative and judicial machines and the suitability of the executive policy."[160]

Just as in the Interim Report, Sir Percy also criticized what he viewed as a lack of general policy that was characterized by little action to collate laws or set out proper administrative regulations. But it was his staff criticism that was most striking. That the staff situation was not pleasing to the governor may be seen when he told Crewe "the situation will demand much close attention and pruning knife."[161]

Two senior members of the provincial staff who came under Sir Percy's critical assessment were H. L. Hinde and C. R. W. Lane. Sir Percy described Hinde as "lazy and unreliable" and stated that Lane was "self-satisfied, pig-headed and highly unpopular."[162] Sir Percy also told Crewe that Lane "came to me unsolicited to deny that 'he was drunk in a public bar and making use of disloyal utterances as to Government and myself.' I had heard from the best of sources that he was talking a great deal too much, nothing else; and Mr. [sic] Jackson was asked by me, as a friend of his, to caution him."[163] Despite Sir Percy's admonition to Jackson on Lane, Sir Percy "was mortified and astonished to hear Mr. Lane repeat this accusation of drunkenness, and told him it was quite unnecessary to have explained. Had I heard of any such conduct I would have at once required him to clear his character."[164] In addition to this inappropriate behavior, Sir Percy put forward another factor in his negative views of officers such as Lane. This was that most provincial commissioners lacked the social qualifications necessary for the entertaining of a white community. Only the now retired S. S. Bagge had the desirable "social qualifications fitting him for a Provincial Commissionership."[165]

Sir Percy also reported that Mr. Reddie was a newly appointed staff at 58 years of age, and Sir Percy was of the opinion that Reddie was "desirous of pension."[166] There was also Mr. McClellan whose appointment was the last to have been made in the protectorate. Sir Percy told Crewe that other than McClellan, none of these officers had the "social qualifications necessary for the handling or entertaining of a white community."[167] This was very unfortunate and Sir Percy stated, it had been a "potent factor in accentuating the situation."[168]

Sir Percy also took a negative view of many senior district commissioners. Among these was a Mr. Foaker who had been passed over for promotion and no provincial commissioner would have him in his province. The governor considered him an obstacle to administration. Sir Percy added that he was "indeed a bitter and disappointed man, with a quite impossible wife who stirs up dissension wherever she goes," and "He should undoubtedly be pensioned at once."[169] There was Mr. Gilkison who had been pensioned but he was still in the service of the protectorate, and a "reason for his continued retention in the service I cannot fathom-the results were deplorable."[170]

Sir Percy also pointed out two senior assistant district commissioners, Farrant and Mayes, as similarly unsuitable officers. The two were " useless as officials,"[171] and such a state of affairs, Sir Percy maintained, "demands more than ordinary remedies."[172] Thus he called for the immediate retirement of men like Farrant and Mayes. Provincial and district commissioners, in his view, must be men of ability, social position, and good education.[173]

Despite Sir Percy's strong demands for the retiring and firing of staff, the CO recognized that there would be problems in carrying out Sir Percy's recommendations. In his response to Sir Percy's Interim Report, for example, Read had minuted that there would be difficulty in carrying through Sir Percy's staffing recommendations. He pointed out that some of the staff had done an excellent job in the early days of the colony and London would naturally hesitate to cut them adrift without some sort of provision.[174] He added that in giving a retiring allowance the Treasury does not offer any assistance, having taken an uncompromising attitude in the matter. In the EAP, Read stated that practically all the IBEA employees were taken over by the protectorate, with the result that the protectorate was saddled with various officials who were unable to keep pace with the development of Uganda and the EAP.[175]

Crewe followed up Read's December minute in a telegram of 7 January 1910. As to the question of retirements, the Secretary of State advised Sir Percy to work out separately the circumstances of each staff member in respect of his retirement, or possible transfers of present heads of departments, and submit such proposals to the CO for further consideration.[176] Crewe added that in forwarding the said proposal, Sir Percy should take into consideration the adjustments of claims of officers now at the heads of separate departments by some means other than dispensing with their services, unless "absolute inefficiency can be maintained against them."[177]

But such a request from Crewe was not clearly honored as Sir Percy followed up these requests in his Main Report with harsh criticism of staff. The CO refused to approve of him effecting any changes, as it had not been found necessary to make alteration in the provincial staff.[178] The CO believed that the position of staff should be left alone, conceding to Sir Percy's proposal would jeopardize the administration and place the staff in difficulty. There was no provision for pensions being made in that year by the colony. Again, sourcing for replacement or promoting junior staff to take up senior positions would further entail financial costs to a colony depending on annual grants-in-aid from the British Treasury. Therefore, not much alteration was done in respect of the staff. In this case, it could be argued that Sir Percy had not appraised the competence of the staff to even warrant his recommendations. It could be learnt from the Uganda Report, where he stated that the staff members in Uganda were weak, having spent only a fortnight in Uganda at the headquarters of the administration.[179] There were objections on the latter view by Tomkins who stated that Sir Percy was in Uganda for only weeks which was not enough to appraise the position, if at all he met all the staff of the protectorate. Therefore, his appraisal of the staff in the EAP might have been done under misapprehension in a similar manner to that of the Uganda Protectorate. In this case, Sir Percy had not carried through an objective assessment of the situation to warrant the approval of his recommendations. The fact that the CO refused to approve his recommendations for firing and retirement meant that he had failed to effect the sound administration he had proposed to carry through for the development of the EAP.

REORGANIZATION OF GOVERNMENT DEPARTMENTS AND STAFF REDEPLOYMENT

In the reorganization of government departments and senior staff redeployment, Sir Percy proposed the merger of certain departments which he believed were either redundant or duplicating functions of other departments or they should not have been there in the first place. In this reorganization, Sir Percy wished to trim the size of government departments and the weeding out ineffective staff members with a view to ensure that the machinery of government was strengthened to carry through his proposed reforms. In carrying through his reforms, Sir Percy recommended to the CO, in his Main Report, that the eight provinces of the colony should be reduced to four provinces. A chief commissioner who would be reporting to the central government would head each of the four provinces.[180] At a district level, Sir Percy recommended that there would be senior district commissioners to administer the fifteen districts."[181]

For the proposed chief commissioners, Sir Percy recommended that one should be located in Nyanza and proposed Ainsworth should be appointed to the position. In a situation where Ainsworth retired, Sir Percy proposed that Lane should be appointed to the position. In the white highlands, Boyle would be transferred from Uganda to take charge. For the Northern Province, McClellan was recommended for the job while the fourth office was to be at the coast with Jackson proposed for the job, or Hobley in case Jackson was transferred to Uganda.[182] If the latter arrangement failed to take off, Hobley would be transferred to Uganda to replace Boyle. Hinde and Reddie were to be retired, as there were no senior positions for them to fill. Sir Percy made it clear in his report that he wanted to see some of the changes. It was his concern to placate and promote good feelings with the European settler community. He wanted Hobley out of the protectorate, for example, as he would not work well with the white community of the highlands.[183] If amalgamation was approved, Sir Percy would transfer him "to a purely native province in Uganda."[184] Sir Percy's desire to transfer Boyle to the EAP had a similar motivation. The governor felt that Boyle would "get on well with both the white and native community."[185]

In the CO's response to Sir Percy, Crewe asked him to submit detailed proposals. This suggests that by mid-1910, the CO was wary of Sir Percy's condemnation of officials and calls for wide ranging reorganization. The officials had good reason to be. Sir Percy failed to submit further recommendations on retirements, transfers, and adjustment of claims on all the staff members regarding whom he had made recommendations.[186]

Therefore, his failure to follow up on the issue of staff reorganization ended his proposed reorganization. Other than Jackson, who was transferred to Uganda as governor, and the treasurer, Bowring, who was appointed to the newly created post of a colonial secretary, nothing had been affected. For the heads of departments he recommended for retirement, it was agreed that they should retire on the expiration of their terms of office. Other than the latter two, nothing had been achieved in his proposed restructuring of staff. These recommendations were informed by his knowledge of Northern Nigeria. He hoped to see that a similar administration was established in the EAP. But the different conditions of the EAP and Northern Nigeria, and a lack of evidence to support some issues he raised, complicated his proposed reforms.

Therefore, Sir Percy's assessment of the situation was not carried through in a manner that would afford improvement on the conditions found as it was haphazardly done. He had not invested sufficient time and learned of the condition in the colony to enable him put forward those recommendations. An administrator considered to be sound would carry through all his assignments in a manner that would afford progress and development, but Sir Percy's recommendations on these subjects would have created shortages of staff and difficulty, which suggests that Sir Percy either lacked knowledge of the outcome of his action or he ignored the outcome. These were not the qualities that could be associated with an outstanding administrator, as they would have caused embarrassments to the CO.

In this regard, Sir Percy's administration came under critical scrutiny by historians of East Africa, especially Mungeam, who argues that Sir Percy had been a force to be reckoned with in the administration of Kenya as he had given the administration a sense of direction by putting official circulars in place, hitherto almost absent.[187] While this success may be acknowledged, it is still clear that Sir Percy's achievements in the area of the administration of policy and staff matters were far from satisfactory. He failed to implement most of the recommendations discussed in this chapter, and this revealed a failing of his governorship. Sir Percy also failed to convince his superiors in the CO of the rightness of his policy recommendations, which without London's backing and approval, he thus had limited success.

Contrary to Mungeam's assessment, going by Sir Percy performance in policy, which he stated was absent, Sir Percy could have been considered to provide a sense of direction to the colony's policy as far as the official circulars of the colony were concerned. On the contrary, and administration was characterized by individual idiosyncrasies of each of the senior officials of the protectorate.

CONCLUSION

The administration of policy recommendations became a very critical aspect of Sir Percy's administration but not much had been achieved, other than a political memorandum guiding officials in the discharge of their functions, improved record keeping, and taxation had improved to a certain degree. But the relative improvement had not been as successful as he had proposed in his policy recommendations. This is very clear from his failed attempt to introduce his proposal for applying Ainsworth's method of tax collection throughout the colony.

On the question of merger of the three coast provinces of Jubaland, Seyyedie, and Tanaland, the CO refused to approve of the merger. As to amalgamation between the East Africa and the Uganda protectorates, the CO, having studied Sir Percy's Uganda Report and the Interim Report, opined that Sir Percy was under misapprehension for recommending Uganda to be amalgamated to the EAP. Uganda was more advanced and prosperous than the EAP. Therefore, Uganda continued as a separate protectorate, and the question of amalgamation was dropped.

As to the executive, legislative and judicial arms of administration of the colony, Sir Percy's recommendations for reform had not been approved. Other than the appointment of Bowring as a colonial secretary, the transfer of Jackson to Uganda, and the increase of members on the legislative council, nothing had been approved. On the provincial political staff, the CO took no measure of reform. However, Sir Percy was advised to treat the staff with respect so that there will be harmony engendered in the colony.

With respect to his recommendation on termination of appointments of some officials, Sir Percy was advised to wait until the expiration of their terms of office so that they would be relieved of their functions and their offices could be merged as he had recommended. In this case, Sir Percy secured the termination of the position of the commissioner of lands, public works, and conservator of forests upon the expiration of their terms of offices. On the merger of their departments and elevation of their juniors to take control of the departments, Sir Percy was told to provide details on how to carry through the reforms, considering adjustment in pay and payment of pension to retiring officials. However, Sir Percy never transmitted such detail to the CO, and the proposed reform remained in abeyance. Therefore, his proposed policy of establishing government standing orders, record keeping and taxation had improved but had not been as proposed for introduction in the colony. The question of reforms in the executive, legislative and judiciary as well as provincial political staff and government departments had not been achieved to a degree that could be considered a successful introduction of policy.

By the time he left the colony, not much satisfaction had been achieved in the evolution and development of government policy of administration as he had proposed in both his Interim and the Main reports. This failing was spectacular in the areas he had proposed to reform, and as he could not do so, the administration of policy had not been successful and Sir Percy had not succeeded in his task of administration worthy of being an outstanding colonial administrator. Also, there was an increasing tension between the government and the two immigrant races (European settlers and Indians), and this compounded the problem of governance in a protectorate where policy of administration was almost absent.

NOTES

1. Sorrenson, *Origins of European Settlement in Kenya,* 117–18.
2. Mungeam, *British Rule in Kenya*, 210–11.
3. G. H. Mungeam, *Kenya, Select Historical Documents,* 1884–1923 (Nairobi, Kenya: East Africa Publication House, 1978), 111; Sorrenson, *Origins of European Settlement in Kenya,* 117–18.
4. Sir Percy to Crewe, confidential, 13 November 1909, CO 533/63; Sir Percy to Crewe, Interim Report Upon the East Africa Protectorate (hereafter, Interim Report), confidential, 13 November 1909, CO 533/63; Mungeam, *British Rule in Kenya*, 210–11; Sorrenson, *Origins of European Settlement in Kenya,* 117–18.
5. Sir Percy to Crewe, Interim Report, confidential 13 November 1909, CO 533/63; Mungeam, *British Rule in Kenya*, 210–11; Sorrenson, *Origins of European Settlement in Kenya,* 117–18.
6. Sir Percy to Crewe, Interim Report, confidential, 13 November 1909, CO 533/63; Mungeam, *British Rule in Kenya*, 210–11.
7. Mungeam, *British Rule in Kenya*, 210–11; Sorrenson, *Origins of European Settlement in Kenya,* 117–18.
8. Sir Percy to Crewe, Interim Report, confidential, 13 November 1909, CO 533/63; Mungeam, *British Rule in Kenya*, 210; Sorrenson, *Origins of European Settlement in Kenya,* 117–18.
9. Sir Percy to Crewe, Interim Report, confidential, 13 November 1909, CO 533/63; Mungeam, *British Rule in Kenya*, 210-Sorrenson, *Origins of European Settlement in Kenya,* 117–18.
10. Sir Percy to Crewe, Interim Report, confidential, 13 November 1909, CO 533/63; Mungeam, *British Rule in Kenya*, 211; Sorrenson, *Origins of European Settlement in Kenya,* 117–18.
11. Sir Percy to Crewe, Interim Report, confidential, 13 November 1909, CO 533/63.
12. Ibid.; Mungeam, *British Rule in Kenya*, 210–11.
13. Ibid.
14. Ibid.

15. Mungeam, *Kenya, Select Historical Documents,* 1884–1923, 111.

16. Sir Percy to Crewe, confidential, 13 November 1909, CO 533/63.

17. Minute by Butler to Read, 14 December 1909, on Sir Percy to Crewe, confidential, 13 November 1909, enclosure, Interim Report, confidential, 13 November 1909, CO 533/63.

18. Ibid.

19. Ibid.

20. Ibid.

21. Ibid.

22. Minute by Butler to Read, 14 December 1909, on Sir Percy to Crewe, confidential, 13 November 1909, enclosure, Interim Report, confidential, 13 November 1909, CO 533/63.

23. Ibid.

24. Ibid.

25. Ibid.

26. Ibid.

27. Ibid.

28. Ibid.

29. Crewe to Sir Percy, telegram, 7 January 1910, CO 533/63.

30. Sir Percy to Crewe, telegram, 19 February 1910, CO 533/71; Mungeam, *British Rule in Kenya,* 212.

31. Minute by Butler to Read, 23 February 1910, on Sir Percy to Crewe, telegram, 19 February 1910, CO 533/71; Mungeam, *British Rule in Kenya,* 212.

32. Minute by Read to Fiddes, 24 February 1910, on Sir Percy to Crewe, telegram, 19 February 1910, CO 533/71; Mungeam, *British Rule in Kenya,* 212.

33. Minute by Fiddes to Crewe, 24 February 1910, on Sir Percy to Crewe, telegram, 19 February 1910, CO 533/71; Mungeam, *British Rule in Kenya,* 212.

34. Crewe to Sir Percy, telegram, 2 March 1910, CO 533/71; Mungeam, *British Rule in Kenya,* 212.

35. Sir Percy to Crewe, secret, 26 May 1910, CO 533/74; Sir Percy to Crewe, Main Report Upon the East Africa Protectorate, confidential, 26 May 1910, CO 533/74.

36. Ibid.; Mungeam, *British Rule in Kenya*, 216.

37. Ibid.

38. J. A. L. Montgomery, Report of the Department Lands, East Africa Protectorate, confidential, 9 May 1910, CO 533/73.

39. Ibid.

40. Mungeam, *British Rule in Kenya,* 214–15.

41. Ibid.

42. Crewe to Sir Percy, confidential, 24 September 1909, CO 533/63.

43. Sir Percy to Crewe, confidential, 13 November 1909, CO 533/63.

44. Ibid.

45. Sir Percy to Crewe, Interim Report, confidential, 13 November 1909, CO 533/63.

46. Ibid.

47. Ibid.

48. Sir Percy to Crewe, confidential, 13 November 1909, enclosure, Report Upon the Uganda Protectorate (hereafter, Uganda Report), confidential, 13 November 1909, CO 533/63. In fact, Sir Percy actually signed the report on 15 November 1909. Since it was included in the same file with the Interim Report of 13 November 1909, the 13 November date is used here. Also, in Sir Percy to Crewe, confidential, Interim Report, confidential, CO 533/63.

49. Ibid.

50. Sir Percy to Crewe, Uganda Report, confidential, 13 November 1909, CO 533/63.

51. Ibid.

52. Ibid.

53. Ibid.

54. Ibid.

55. Ibid.

56. Ibid.

57. Ibid.

58. Ibid.

59. Ibid.

60. Ibid.

61. Ibid.

62. Ibid.

63. Ibid.

64. Stanley Tomkins to Crewe, Memorandum Containing Rough Notes for a Dispatch to the Secretary of State upon the question of Amalgamation between the Uganda Protectorate and the East Africa Protectorate, confidential, undated, 1909, CO 533/63; D. A. Low, *The Mind of Buganda Documents of the Modern History of an African Kingdom* (Berkeley and Los Angeles: University of California Press, 1971), 41–2.

65. Ibid.

66. Ibid.

67. Ibid.

68. Ibid.

69. Ibid.

70. Ibid.

71. Ibid.

72. Minute by Butler to Read, 14 December 1909, on Sir Percy to Crewe, confidential, 13 November 1909, enclosure, Uganda Report, confidential, 13 November 1909, CO 533/63.The normal procedure in the CO was for officials to write minutes to their superior, making clear their observations and recommendations for a response to dispatches and telegrams.

73. Minute by Butler to Read, 14 December 1909, on Sir Percy to Crewe, confidential, 13 November 1909, enclosure, Uganda Report, confidential, 13 November 1909, CO 533/63.

74. Ibid.

75. Minute by Read to Fiddes, 14 December 1909, on Ibid.
76. Ibid.
77. Ibid.
78. Ibid.
79. Minute by Fiddes to Crewe, 8 January 1910, on Sir Percy to Crewe, confidential, 13 November 1909, enclosure, Uganda Report, confidential, 13 November 1909, CO 533/63.
80. Ibid.
81. Ibid.
82. Ibid.
83. Ibid.
84. Ibid.
85. Ibid.
86. Ibid.
87. Minute by Seeley to Crewe, 1 January 1910, on Sir Percy to Crewe, confidential, 13 November 1909, enclosure, Uganda Report, confidential, 13 November 1909, CO 533/63.
88. Ibid.
89. Minute by Crewe to Seeley, 2 January 1910, on Sir Percy to Crewe, confidential, 13 November 1909, enclosure, Uganda Report, confidential, 13 November 1909, CO 533/63.
90. Crewe to Sir Percy, telegram, 7 January 1910, CO 533/63.
91. Ibid.
92. Ibid.
93. Tomkins to Crewe, confidential, undated, 1909, CO 533/63.
94. Sir Percy to Crewe, Uganda Report, confidential, 13 November 1909, CO 533/63.
95. Sir Percy to Crewe, Main Report Upon the East Africa Protectorate, confidential, 26 May 1910, CO 533/74.
96. Minute by Fiddes to Crewe, 8 January 1910, on Sir Percy to Crewe, confidential, 13 November 1909, enclosure, Uganda Report, confidential, 13 November 1909, CO 533/63.
97. Ibid.
98. Sir Percy to Crewe, Interim Report, confidential, 13 November 1909, CO 533/63.
99. Ibid.
100. Ibid.
101. Ibid.
102. Ibid.
103. Ibid.; Bennett, *Kenya,* 29.
104. Ibid.; Mungeam, *British Rule in Kenya*, 214.
105. Ibid.
106. Ibid.
107. Ibid.
108. Sir Percy to Crewe, Interim Report, confidential, 13 November 1909, CO 533/63.

109. Ibid.

110. Minute by Butler to Read, 14 December 1909, on Sir Percy to Crewe, Interim Report, confidential 13 November 1909, CO 533/63.

111. Ibid.

112. Ibid.

113. Ibid.

114. Ibid.

115. Ibid.

116. Ibid.

117. Ibid.

118. Ibid.

119. Ibid.

120. Ibid.

121. Ibid.

122. Ibid.

123. Ibid.

124. Ibid.

125. Ibid.

126. Ibid.

127. Ibid.

128. Minute by Read to Fiddes, 17 December 1909, on Interim Report and the Uganda Report, confidential, 13 November 1909, enclosures on Sir Percy to Crewe, confidential, 13 November 1909, CO 533/63.

129. Ibid.

130. Ibid.

131. Ibid.

132. Minute by Fiddes to Crewe, 1 January 1910, on Sir Percy to Crewe, confidential, 13 November 1909, enclosures, Interim Report and the Uganda Report, confidential, 13 November 1909, CO 533/63.

133. Crewe to Sir Percy, telegram, 7 January 1910, CO 533/63.

134. Sir Percy to Crewe, telegram, 19 February 1910, CO 533/71.

135. Minute by Butler to Read, 23 February 1910, on Sir Percy to Crewe, telegram, 19 February 1910, CO 533/71.

136. Minute by Read to Fiddes, 24 February 1910, on Sir Percy to Crewe, telegram, 19 February 1910, CO 533/71.

137. Minute by Fiddes to Crewe, 25 February 1910, on Sir Percy to Crewe, telegram, 19 February 1910, CO 533/71.

138. Crewe to Sir Percy, telegram, 2 March 1910, CO 533/73.

139. Sir Percy to Crewe, Main Report, confidential, 26 May 1910, CO 533/74.

140. Sir Percy to Crewe, secret, 26 May 1910, CO 533/74; Mungeam, *British Rule in Kenya,* 213.

141. Ibid.; Sir Percy to Crewe, Main Report, confidential, 26 May 1910, CO 533/74.

142. Sir Percy to Crewe, Main Report, confidential, 26 May 1910, CO 533/74.

143. Mungeam, *British Rule in Kenya,* 213.

144. Ibid.

145. Ibid.
146. Sir Percy to Crewe, Main Report, confidential, 26 May 1910, CO 533/74.
147. Ibid.
148. Ibid.
149. Ibid.
150. Ibid.
151. Ibid.
152. Ibid.
153. Ibid.
154. Ibid; Mungeam, *British Rule in Kenya,* 215.
155. Ibid.
156. Ibid.
157. Sir Percy to Crewe, Main Report, confidential, 26 May 1910, CO 533/74.
158. Ibid.
159. Ibid.
160. Ibid.
161. Ibid.
162. Ibid.; Mungeam, *British Rule in Kenya,* 216.
163. Sir Percy to Crewe, Main Report, confidential, 26 May 1910, CO 533/74.
164. Ibid.
165. Ibid.
166. Ibid.
167. Ibid.
168. Ibid.
169. Ibid.
170. Ibid.
171. Ibid.
172. Ibid.
173. Ibid.
174. Minute by Read to Fiddes, 17 December 1909, on Sir Percy to Crewe, confidential, 13 November 1909, enclosures, Interim Report and the Uganda Report, confidential, 13 November 1909, CO 533/63.
175. Ibid; Mungeam, *British Rule in Kenya,* 212.
176. Crewe to Sir Percy, telegram, 7 January 1910, CO 533/62.
177. Ibid.
178. Mungeam, *British Rule in Kenya,* 222.
179. Tomkins to Crewe, confidential, undated, 1909, CO 533/63.
180. Sir Percy to Crewe, Main Report, confidential, 26 May 1910, CO 533/74.
181. Ibid.
182. Ibid.
183. Ibid.
184. Ibid.
185. Ibid.
186. Mungeam, *British Rule in Kenya*, 222.
187. Mungeam, *British Rule in Kenya*, 244–5.

Chapter 4

The Creation of White Supremacy

The CO and Sir Percy recognized the EAP as a multiracial colony. By 1909 the territory was inhabited by a majority of African ethnic groups as well as three others recognized at the time as belonging to distinct racial groups: Arabs, Europeans and Indians (also referred to as Asians). A challenging aspect of Sir Percy's administration was the often-competing claims of the European settlers and the Indian residents of the EAP for political influence. Even more than his predecessors, Sir Percy's policy of administration was slanted to favor the European settlers in what would later be termed the Indian question in Kenya's history. He helped to provoke deepening tensions between those two racial groups that emerged within a decade to become a major issue confronting the British government. His failure to balance the competing claims of the Indians and the Europeans, as in the case of his failure to reform the protectorate's administration, thus left huge problems unresolved at the end of his governorship.

INDIANS AND EUROPEAN SETTLERS POLITICAL DEMANDS

The Indians were also conscious of their political aspirations since the beginning of their immigration into the colony. The Asians demonstrated this in the formation of an association in order to coordinate among Indians and as a means of protest against what they could conceive as unjust.[1] Therefore, the Indians formed their first political association, the Mombasa Indian Association, in 1900, which was led by L. M. Savle.[2] In 1906, the Indians formed a similar association in Nairobi that became a leading organization for Indian politics in the colony. The Indians also formed other associations, especially after World War I, in Kisumu, Naivasha, Eldoret, Fort Hall, and in other urban centers of the colony.[3]

The Indians political voice was first heard from the colony in 1906 notably by the formation of Mombasa Indian Association, which protested against European settler exclusive possession of the highlands for settlement. The Indians sent a deputation to the CO, demanding fair treatment against what they described as unequal treatments between them and the settlers.[4] By 1907, the Indians had formed a broad based association, the British East Africa Indian Association, which addressed Churchill during his visit to the colony on the question of the highlands. But Churchill told the Indian deputation that the highlands would be reserved for the settlers. After Churchill's tour, however, he recommended that the colony be made more suitable for the Indians.[5]

The time coincided with the Liberal government of Herbert Asquith who sought to implement Churchill's recommendations that the EAP was more suitable for Indian colonization. In March 1909, Crewe appointed a parliamentary committee to investigate Indian migration and recommend the most useful area where it could be encouraged.[6] The committee chaired by Lord Sanderson was also asked to recommend on the desirability of Indian colonization of the protectorate. Sanderson's recommendations were not considered, and by 1909 Sir Percy was appointed governor of the colony.[7] He demonstrated an anti-Indian bias in his administration, especially when he demanded the removal of A. M. Jeevanjee from the legislative council.[8] But it was not long before Jeevanjee aired his grievances against the administration while on a vacation in London. The Indian grievances came up when Jeevanjee was granted an interview to the press on Indian disabilities in the colony. What could be seen as an outburst from Jeevanjee to the *Daily Chronicle*, which was, later on, publicized in the media and newspapers throughout Britain, caused indignation in the colony and caused the settlers to unite as a political force with a view to counter Jeevanjee's position.

Jeevanjee alleged preferential treatment of the settlers by the colonial state against the Indians in the interview with the *Daily Chronicle*. Jeevanjee told the *Chronicle* that there were no equal rights or equal opportunities between the settlers and the Indians. He added that there were restrictions on Indian acquiring land in the highlands, favoritism to the settlers in the award of contracts, unfair use of the immigration laws, prohibition against Indians using the European market in Nairobi, discriminatory treatment on the railway, and refusal to allow Indians trial by jury.[9] The Indians were discontented with the preferential treatment being accorded to the settlers, and the general disabilities under which they lived.[10]

As the news filtered into the protectorate, there was indignation among the settlers as his interview brought about a renewed feeling of unity among the settlers.[11] Even though such disabilities were not the making of Sir Percy, he compounded them, in view of his open anti-Indian stand as demonstrated in his opposition to Jeevanjee's appointment on the legislative council soon after his arrival in the protectorate.[12] Therefore, the settlers asked Sir Percy to travel to London to represent their grievances, as well. Sir Percy sought and obtained permission, in August 1910, to travel to London to represent the settler's view.[13]

Before Sir Percy traveled to London, the settlers who had entered the colony and settled there since 1903 had formed a well-established ideological political organization as well as set their eyes on the agriculturally fertile Nyanza basin.[14] In a counter to the Indians press interview, the European settlers organized a dinner in November, in Nairobi, to mark his departure.[15] During the dinner, in November, Delamere, in his address, told the crowd that recognized itself with the name of convention of associations, on the very first day of its meeting that since the assumption of government of Sir Percy, division between the settler and the local authorities had disappeared.[16] Captain Ewart S. Grogan was elected Chairman of the convention, and in his address, he replied to a toast, when he described himself as "the baddest and the boldest of the bold bad gang."[17] The association brought the settlers together so that they could ventilate their grievances to the government. The settlers became a united force in countering what they said was a fabricated interview that Jeevanjee granted to the press. These allegations and counter allegations were part of the struggle of the Indians for equality and the European search for supremacy in which Sir Percy sided with the cause of the Europeans and ignored the Indian cause. This was also part of the problem that had accentuated racial division and portrayed Sir Percy's bias toward the settlers that had made it difficult for him to evolve a fair and just policy for the administration of the races. While Sir Percy was at the CO representing settler opinion on Jeevanjee's interview to the press, the India Office was also responding to Jeevanjee's interview by demanding an explanation from the CO. Sir Percy and Read represented the settlers view in a meeting with the India Office representatives and two members of the Council of India. It was noted that all the grievances boiled down to two points; the land question in the highlands with the Indians not allowed to have a grant, and also a grant of land in some parts of the townships. Sir Percy and Read were able to convince the meeting that there was nothing to worry about.[18]

Sir Percy told the meeting that it was Lord Elgin who decided that the highlands should be reserved for the whites and in that regard; he should not be accused of bias, and, more importantly, the highlands were not suitable for Indian agriculturalists. As for grants in the townships, Sir Percy stated that in view of the sanitary condition of the Indians, he decided to limit grants to Indians in certain parts of the townships.[19]

But that was not the end of it, as Sir Percy fought back against Jeevanjee's renewal of his tenure in the council. Sir Percy became very critical of him, and told Crewe, in a confidential dispatch of 19 October 1910, that Jeevanjee's statements were "fabrications and falsehoods," which have "caused much indignation here."[20] Sir Percy criticized Jeevanjee, whom he claimed could neither read nor write, and was refused permission to have his secretary in the legislative council.[21] He added that Jeevanjee had plenty of opportunities to ventilate his grievances in the council, but except on small matters had not done so. Sir Percy recommended to Harcourt, on the expiration of Jeevanjee's term of office in September 1911 that it should not be renewed.[22] Harcourt agreed to Sir Percy's request that Jeevanjee's appointment would not be renewed immediately. Harcourt opposed a complete termination of Jeevanjee's appointment but was disposed to delay the renewal of Jeevanjee's appointment.[23]

The Indians, nevertheless, continued to suffer, as they had no equal rights and opportunities with the settlers. Despite these disabilities associated with the Indians and their resolution, Sir Percy refused to do so, and instead turned against Jeevanjee by suspending his tenure on the council and renewing the tenure of the unofficial settler members regularly.[24] Sir Percy's bias in this case was clearly a manifestation of his favoritism toward his kith and kin which was further demonstrated when he supported and advocated for the European course, especially during the formation of their umbrella organization; the convention of associations.

The convention of associations convened in February 1911, for its first convention in the colony, where it passed a motion for the protectorate's representation and Eliot was nominated as their representative at the fourth imperial conference. The meeting had a grandiose idea of the protectorate's representation. In view of the conference, the settlers were talking of responsible government being "almost within a hand reach."[25] In August, the convention of associations convened for a second conference, where it voted unanimously for elective representation to the legislative council. Thereafter, a delegation met Sir Percy, at different times, to press for elective representation, but Sir Percy told them that the CO would turn down their request.[26]

This was the first time for Sir Percy to turn down the request of the settlers, without making reference to the CO. His past dealings with the CO might have informed his renewed sense of duty, that it was not all for the settlers, and the settlers must be run-on in certain instances, in the best interest of fairness and justice especially, when Harcourt, in December 1910, refused to consent to his proposed land reform and also rejected the April 1909 land ordinance.[27]

Nevertheless, the settlers were increasingly becoming interested in participating in the government of the protectorate so that they could be part of any decision affecting their lives.[28] Not only were the settlers conscious of the latter, even the Indians were aware of it and interested in being part of the government, so that they be would be part of any decision affecting their lives. This was clearly demonstrated by Jeevanjee's interview to the press in London, in 1910, where he exposed the politics and the competitions between the Indians and the settlers, and how the former were relegated to the back door, in the politics and policy of government.[29] The settlers were politically conscious and were working toward the formation of political associations and unions that would lead their struggle for self-government.[30]

The settlers believed that colonization of the protectorate and, more especially the white highlands, was a possibility.[31] The settler's worldview as to colonization was that they would establish a purely white settlement and a government side by side with an African state, and each would govern their own affairs. The settlers were determined to make Kenya their permanent home, not as a place where they could make wealth and quit.[32] Sir Percy supported the settler's quest for self-government and worked to achieve that through piecemeal policy initiatives. But the settler desire for self-government was rebuffed.[33]

Despite this eventual outcome, the European settlers considered Sir Percy's administration as the best, and most promising. The settlers considered Sir Percy an advocate and defender of their interests. This view was held by Elspeth Huxley, who considered that Sir Percy had provided a gateway for the development of the settlers and the colony by allowing unhindered settler access to land for the development of the colony as the Africans were unwilling partners in production for development. Huxley concluded that Sir Percy was an outstanding administrator who left Kenya, much revered by settlers.[34] However, Maxon disagrees with Huxley, pointing out that Sir Percy's administration of the races was detrimental to other races especially the Indians, as he adopted an unfavorable disposition toward them and opposed all their political aspirations for fairness in the colony.[35]

In view of his anti-Indian stand that was more like a continuation of a policy of his predecessors, Maxon suggested that his administration accentuated racial prejudice between the Europeans and the Indians, instead of providing the desired quiescence administrative environment for both races to achieve their political aspirations. With this performance, Maxon contends that Sir Percy performed below the expectations of the CO, and cannot be considered an outstanding administrator, considering his failure to fairly administer a multiracial colony.[36]

LEGISLATIVE COUNCIL

Sir Percy, within the first week of his assumption of government, told Crewe, in a telegram of 23 September 1909, that Lord Delamere, leader of the European settlers should be appointed to the legislative council, as the settler representative.[37] Earlier on, Delamere had been appointed to the legislative council, but he resigned his appointment in May 1909, about four months before Sir Percy's assumption of government.[38] In his telegram, Sir Percy also urged Crewe to postpone the appointment of the Indian representative to the legislative council, A. M. Jeevanjee, made on 25 August 1909, until he had been able to "fully appreciate the position."[39]

Sir Percy pointed out that the appointment of Jeevanjee might lead to a "legitimate demand" on the part of Arabs and the Swahili community, "who are our oldest native subjects, and who outnumbered the Indians by two to one."[40] Sir Percy went further as to Jeevanjee's appointment, when he told Crewe that even the term "Indian was an embarrassment to thousands of Goanese who were not British subjects."[41]

In the CO, Butler minuted that Sir Percy should be told by telegram that steps might be taken to appoint Delamere to the council.[42] As for the postponement of Jeevanjee's appointment, Butler minuted, "unfortunately it was announced in the gazette of the 21 September 1909 that the King had been pleased to give direction for the appointment, so that postponement is impossible."[43] Butler minuted, "we had better tell the Governor by telegraph, the question of appointing a representative for the Asiatic was carefully considered, and the intention was public property for a year before the notification appeared in last Tuesday's gazette."[44]

Fiddes agreed and pointed out that Delamere had done a lot of work in Kenya.[45] Sir Francis Hopwood, Permanent Undersecretary of State, agreed, and stated, a full explanation by a telegram should be transmitted.[46] Crewe agreed, and asked them to go ahead and work on the appointment of Delamere. Crewe, in reference to Delamere's appointment, stated they should go on as proposed. He added: "by the way, talked a great deal, with insufficient knowledge," referring to Delamere.[47] In the interim, Crewe replied to Sir Percy, in a telegram of 2 October 1909, that the appointment of Delamere will be favorably considered, but regretted that he could not postpone Jeevanjee's appointment as it had been announced in the gazette of 21 September 1909.[48]

Therefore, Crewe, in order to convince Sir Percy, directed him to a confidential dispatch, dated 14 July 1908, which detailed that the "question of appointing Jeevanjee as an Indians representative in the legislative council was carefully considered, and that the decision to appoint a representative for the Indians was made public for more than a year."[49] Therefore, Sir Percy was told that the appointment of Jeevanjee would not be postponed. In this regard, Sir Percy failed to persuade the CO to drop Jeevanjee from the legislative council.

On the other hand, Sir Percy succeeded in convincing the CO to approve Delamere's appointment as settler's representative on the legislative council. His Majesty the King approved Delamere's appointment on the legislative council on 16 November 1909.[50] Thus, Sir Percy succeeded in convincing the CO to appoint Delamere to the legislative council, as a settler representative, which was a great stride in the implementation of his policy recommendations.

On the other hand, he was unsuccessful in his effort to convince the CO to postpone Jeevanjee's appointment, in view of the fact that the appointment of Jeevanjee had already been made. It could not be withdrawn as His Majesty's government had already consented to his appointment.[51] Sir Percy's anti-Indian stand mainly informed his opposition to Jeevanjee's appointment, as he had not supported his opposition to the appointment with any convincing evidence as to whether Jeevanjee's was incompetent to represent the Indians residents of the protectorate, on the legislative council. Again, as to the number of the Indians, they certainly outnumbered the settlers and if the settlers could be allowed representation, why not the Indians.

Therefore, his anti-Indian stand informed his opposition to the appointment of the Indian representative rather than any policy consideration. This also suggested his open support for the settlers' interest and against the Indian interest. In considering the question of policy of administration on the Indians, Sir Percy proposed that the Indians should not be represented on the legislative council, in view of their insignificant numerical strength relative to the Arabs and the Swahili.[52] With such a tendency in the administration of government, Sir Percy failed to demonstrate fairness in his dealings with the Indians, which could not be considered a fair, sound administration of government.

Moreover, Sir Percy ignored that the numerical strength of the whites, who were represented on the council, were less than that of the Indians. But Sir Percy pressed further his anti-Indian stand when he told Crewe, in a confidential dispatch of 5 May 1910, that Jeevanjee might be preparing to table before the legislative council demands for the appointment of Indian juries. The Indians wish to be tried by jury as it was the case with the settlers.[53] Despite the Indians persistent demands for participation in the administration of the colony, Sir Percy refused to give way, and instead continued to block each move the Indians could make for participation in the colony's political life.

POLICY OF ADMINISTRATION

In dealing with the European settlers and the Indians, Sir Percy adopted a different method of handling their respective affairs, conferring preferential treatments on the settlers over the Indians. In the administration of European settlers, Sir Percy proposed a separate area for their settlement, participation in county and local government, more voice in the legislative council, and service as advisers in agricultural matters of the colony.[54] Yet Sir Percy did not propose any policy for the administration of the Indians other than accentuating their difficulties.[55]

The Indians experienced disabilities even before the arrival of Sir Percy to the colony, and upon his assumption of the administration of the colony, he had not mitigated the difficulty of the Indians and instead, adopted an unfavorable stand against them. There were shortcomings in dealing with these races, which became instrumental in his failure to evolve an effective policy of administration over them. His proposed settler policy usually resulted in accentuating racial divisiveness and prejudices between the settlers and the Indians.[56] In this regard, Sir Percy's recommendations as to the general policy of settler administration were a sharp contrast to that of the Indians, which showed a clear partiality toward the settlers and a disregard toward the Indians.

Upon his assumption of government, Sir Percy noted that the protectorate lacked a well-defined policy of administration. The absence of policy not only impacted the settlers and the Indians but also on every aspect of government administration.[57] Therefore, Sir Percy proposed in his Main Report the establishment of an exclusive area for a settler habitation, which would be independent of any province within the protectorate.[58] Sir Percy's proposed policy of administration on the settler was to afford him participation in government so that he could be part of decisions affecting his life.[59]

In carrying through some of his favorable policies toward the settlers, some of these eventually produced difficulty for the settlers. Despite his favoritism toward the settlers, other than a few influential individuals, policies designed to accelerate settler politics resulted in accentuating their difficulty.[60] Part of the difficulty was the favorable stand that he had adopted toward the settlers, causing competing demands from the Indians. This development caused the CO to refuse approval of any policy it deemed would accentuate the racial divide between the settlers and the Indians.[61]

The introduction of suitable policies of administration for these races had been a difficulty as both settlers and Indians were competing for an active political participation in the colony's administration, which contributed to the widening racial divide. The latter was reinforced by Sir Percy's favorable disposition toward the settlers and his racial prejudices against the Indians, which complicated his administration of policy and ultimately produced unsuitable policies, resulting in an unsuccessful administration. The lack of success was not only on the Indians but it also affected these settlers as succeeding paragraphs clearly demonstrate his view and vision that occasioned his failure to administer the races with an even hand.

SETTLER POLICY OF ADMINISTRATION

The European settler was considered the most favored not only during Sir Percy's tour of duty but right from the commencement of European settlement in the colony. As noted in the previous chapter, Sir Percy, in his consideration of a settler policy, told Crewe, in his Interim Report of 13 November 1909, that previous governments of the protectorate lacked a defined policy of administering the European settlers. Sir Percy added, the settler never knew how he was being governed and neither was there any policy that would promote his active political participation in the government of the colony.[62]

To remedy this, Sir Percy recommended to Crewe, in his Interim Report, that the government should produce "a more clearly defined area devoted to the settler separate settlement."[63] As for the outlined map of the existing white settlement, Sir Percy told Crewe that it had "the appearance of the patches on an old fashioned crazy-quilt," which Sir Percy believed, lent themselves to amalgamation of the eastern province of Uganda to the EAP in 1902.[64] Nevertheless, the area devoted to the European settlers was standing on its own, as the area was not part of any of the provinces of the protectorate.[65] Sir Percy added that a clearly defined area for the settlers should take into consideration further expansion without affecting areas defined as African reserves. As to the area of settler habitation, Sir Percy suggested that the highlands could foster a conducive habitation for the settlement and that it should be devoted exclusively to settler habitation only.[66]

As to the question of government policy over the settlers, Sir Percy recommended to Crewe, in his Interim Report, that it was not only essential but it was in all interests to allow active participation of the settler in the government of the protectorate.[67] Sir Percy added that to expect the settler to know how he was being governed by "a perusal of the existing book of law would be to demand a virtue young colonists do not seem to be possessed of, lasting patience and deep research."[68] This was in reference to what was described in chapter four as Sir Percy believed in the colony's lack of a clearly defined policy of administration other than the only available books of law from which an administrator could infer as to what was supposed to be the right course of action for the administration of the colony. Sir Percy pointed out that the absence of a clearly defined policy for a settler administration had made it difficult for the settler to know how he was governed.

Sir Percy recommended further, in his Main Report, that they should be held in confidence as to the policy, which would be approved. However, Sir Percy observed that the presence of the settlers at the moment was not of great financial assistance, but they will demand full recognition and it should be accorded to them. Sir Percy also told Crewe that the settlers should not be kept in the dark as to the financial position of the protectorate or the aims of the government. If the latter was to be the case, Sir Percy told Crewe that would "only be productive of grossly exaggerated figures as to their financial weight as a community and perverted statements of the policy of the government."[69] Sir Percy, however, told Crewe that all the European associations have vied with each other, in giving him every possible assistance. Sir Percy added that the missionaries of all denominations were too anxious to assist him in any government-defined policy.[70]

Sir Percy went on to tell Crewe that it had been his aim to "show no favour to individuals or communities, but to try and act in the best interest of all and in accordance with your instruction."[71] To the latter, Sir Percy did not prove good to his word when he supported the settlers' quest for political participation and denied the same to the Indians. The latter case was, in part, what led to his unsuccessful policy of administration of these races.[72]

Not surprisingly, he recommended in his Main Report of 26 May 1910 that the European settlers should be actively involved in the administration of the country.[73] Sir Percy reiterated to Crewe that with the question of the type of administration policy to be established for the white community, they should be held in confidence by the government and due recognition should be given to them, where they needed it. The settlers, Sir Percy observed, "are quite reasonable in their attitude, and Lord Delamere himself, as a votary of leasehold, will I trust be of assistance."[74]

Moreover, Sir Percy told Crewe, in the same report, "I do not consider the European community an unreasonable one, and, except for a few, they constitute a body of settlers of unusual education and social standing."[75] Therefore, Sir Percy recommended to Crewe that if his recommendations for settler policy could be approved, "it will be possible to give the inhabitants more duties in purely local government."[76] Sir Percy pointed out that with the introduction of the justice of the peace ordinance, an indication of a start in that direction was being made. There was the need to go further by the introduction of divisional councils or some other bodies. Sir Percy further suggested that if the urban population could be allowed more active participation in local government, it was highly desirable that the settlers should also be allowed to feel the difficulties associated with the administration of government, as well as the "weight of the Courts in the revision of J. P. ordinances."[77] Therefore, to achieve the latter, Sir Percy recommended that the settlers should be given more duties in their county or local government, legislative council, and be part of an agricultural advisory committees.[78]

In this circumstance, Sir Percy's policy recommendations as for the Europeans suggested that the settlers would be participating in the administration of the protectorate, establish a separate settlement, and it is possible to suggest from his proposed policy recommendations that the settlers would be able to participate in the county and local government administration.

With the latter, the settlers would have been in a position to push for self-government, a desire which most of the settlers viewed as within their reach. But Sir Percy's proposals did not amount to anything, as he had not push further to actualize his proposed policy and neither did he pushed for the settler political ambition when he noted Harcourt's reservation over his support for settler opportunities were beyond what the CO could approve.

As noted earlier, Sir Percy recommended to Crewe, in his Interim Report, that other than their participation in local government, the settlers should be given the opportunity, especially for those who intended to make a home in the protectorate, to have more voice on the legislative council.[79] Sir Percy cautioned Crewe, "Like all other young colonies, concealment in any sense can do no good whatever, and on the other hand-as has been patent from the past here can do an infinity of harm."[80] On the question of the legislative council, Sir Percy told Crewe in his Main Report that he needed more representation from the settlers so that they could participate fully in the government of the country.[81] His request for more participation of the settlers in the government, in his both his Interim and the Main report, was in support of his request for the appointment of Delamere to the legislative council, which had already been transmitted to Crewe, a week after his assumption of government.[82] In addition to the latter, Sir Percy desired more unofficial representatives on the legislative council.

In the CO, his recommendations for the participation of settlers in government contained in his Interim Report were favorably accepted. Butler, in his minute, expressed his general agreement with Sir Percy's recommendation, as to more active participation of white settlers in county or local government. More voice on the Legislative Council, and facilities for giving advice in agricultural matters were accepted. Therefore, Butler urged that Sir Percy's recommendations be accepted as a general outline of policy, but a more detailed explanation on how he intended to carry out his recommendations on each subject was necessary.[83] Butler minuted that Sir Percy's recommendation was "on the right line, but of course it will be necessary to go slowly and consider carefully the detailed proposals made under this head."[84] Read, in his minute, stated that Sir Percy was planning to give a larger share in administration to the settlers of the EAP and "I do not think a purely native country like Uganda would be likely to benefit by this arrangement."[85] Read referred to Uganda in view of the proposed amalgamation, if carried out, would not produce any benefit as Uganda was purely an African country.

In Crewe's reply to Sir Percy, in his telegram of 7 January 1910, the Secretary of State expressed his concurrence with the proposal. Crewe told Sir Percy, "it is desirable to encourage a more active participation of the white settlers in county or local government and in agricultural matters."[86] The latter approval as contained in the telegram paved the way for the participation of the white settlers in the government of the EAP. By such approval, it was left to Sir Percy to give more details of how he should carry out the process through which they will be involved in the administration of the protectorate. But Sir Percy failed to follow up on the participation of the settlers in the county and local governments of the protectorate.

In this aspect of his policies, other than securing additional unofficial members that should not exceed six unofficial members in the Legislative Council, he had not done much to see to the realization of his proposed settler involvement in county and local governments. The latter recommendations were informed by Sir Percy's consideration that the settlers should be allowed to govern themselves and be part of government decisions affecting their lives. This would empower the settlers politically and might led to the settler colonization of the protectorate.[87]

CONCLUSION

The most challenging aspect of the administration of these competing races was the question of balancing the quest for equality between the European settlers and the Indians. The more the Indian demands for equality, the further the settlers objected to their being on the same footing. The participation in the legislative council was the first instance where the CO sought to balance the equilibrium, when it directed for the appointment of Delamere and Jeevanjee on the Legislative Council as representatives of their respective races. When Sir Percy assumed government, he requested for the removal of Jeevanjee and wondered why the Indian was represented while the settlers were not.

He therefore, sought the removal of Jeevanjee and the appointment of Delamere. The CO accepted his request for the appointment of Delamere but refused to approve of his request for the removal of Jeevanjee. In his consideration of a settler policy, he recommended for their participation in government but other than the appointment of Delamere and the increase of unofficial to six, nothing had been achieved in respect of their participation in county and local government, and in agricultural matters. As to their settlement, he had not succeeded in establishing a distinct European settlement as he had envisioned in his Main Report.

As to the Indians, he had not been able to come up with any defined policy other than his unfavorable disposition to their demands. The Indians, despite their struggle for a fair treatment by the administration, had achieved nothing. In fact, Jeevanjee was removed from office, even though the CO reinstated him, because of his criticisms of the administration's unfair treatment of the Indians in comparison to the way the settlers were treated. In spite of the favorable treatment Sir Percy afforded the settlers, he had not been able to push for their demand for electoral representation.

His failings in this regard, resulted from the CO's refusal to allow the settlers to have their way in everything. This clearly demonstrated their hesitations on how Sir Percy advocated for settler insatiable demands, which might provoke racial division and empower the settlers politically which would be to the detriment of the Indians. This could be seen from Sir Percy's trip to the CO to represent the settler position on Jeevanjee's press interview. Sir Percy also extended a similar attitude toward the Africans whom he proposed to govern separately and indirectly. Sir Percy proposed African chiefs and elders should govern the affairs of their own people and that they should be placed under the trustees to safeguard their land.

Despite his recommendation of the latter, Sir Percy, as will be seen in the next chapter, sacrificed the interest of the African reserves to the Europeans, allowing the Europeans to have unhindered access to land. He also attempted to remove the Maasai from their Laikipia settlement to the southern reserves with a view to allot Laikipia land to the European settlers. Sir Percy could sacrifice the interest of any of the races of the colony to satisfy the European settler interest. Sir Percy further demonstrated this, in his attempt to establish African administration policy, especially when he compromised land regulations and African reserves. His favoritism for the settlers over the Indians was thus not an isolated issue.

NOTES

1. Robert Gregory, *Quest for Equality: Asian Politics in East Africa,* 1900–1967 (New Delhi: Orient Longman Limited, 1993), 31.
2. Ibid., 32.
3. Ibid.
4. Robert Gregory, *India and East Africa: A History of Race Relations Within the British Empire,* 1890–1939 (London: Oxford University Press, 1971), 83.
5. Ibid.
6. Ibid., 82–3.
7. Ibid., 88–9.
8. Ibid., 89.
9. Sorrenson, *Origins of European Settlement in Kenya*, 168. European settlers had the right of trial by jury.
10. Sorrenson, *Origins of European Settlement in Kenya*, 168–9.
11. Bennett, *Kenya,* 30.
12. Sir Percy to Crewe, telegram, 23 September 1909, CO 533/62; Bennett, *Kenya,* 30.
13. Sir Percy to Crewe, telegram, 16 August 1910, CO 533/76; Bennett, *Kenya* 31–2.

14. Bruce Berman & John Lonsdale, *Unhappy Valley: Conflict in Kenya and Africa: Book One: State and Class* (Athens: Ohio University Press, 1992), 88–9.
15. Bennett, *Kenya,* 31.
16. Ibid.
17. Ibid.
18. Sorrenson, *Origins of European Settlement in Kenya*, 169–70.
19. Sir Percy to Crewe, confidential, 19 October 1910, CO 533/77; Sorrenson, *Origins of European Settlement in Kenya*, 171.
20. Ibid.
21. Minute by Cox, 26 April 1910, on Sir Percy to Crewe, confidential, 8 April 1910, CO 533/72; Sorrenson, *Origins of European Settlement in Kenya*, 171.
22. Mungeam, *British Rule in Kenya*, 224–5.
23. Ibid.
24. Sir Percy to Harcourt, telegram, 4 October 1911, CO 533/91; Sorrenson, *Origins of European Settlement in Kenya,* 171.
25. Ibid.
26. Bennett, *Kenya,* 32.
27. Ibid., 32–33.
28. Sir Percy to Crewe, Main Report, confidential, 26 May 1910, CO 533/74.
29. Sorrenson, *Origins of European Settlement in Kenya*, 167.
30. Bennett, *Kenya,* 30; Major Archibald Church, *East Africa: A New Dominion, A Crucial Experiment in Tropical Development and Its Significance to the British Empire* (West Port, CT: Negro University Press, 1970), 37; Espeth Huxley, *Whiteman's Country: Lord Delamere and Making of Kenya,* 1870–1914 (New York: Praeger, 1967), 261–2.
31. Church, *East Africa,* 37; Bennett, *Kenya,* 32.
32. Church, *East Africa,* 37.
33. Bennett, *Kenya,* 32.
34. Huxley, *Whiteman's Country,* 269.
35. Maxon, *Struggle for Kenya*, 37.
36. Robert M. Maxon, "Judgment on a Colonial Governor: Sir Percy Girouard in Kenya," *Transafrican Journal of History*, vol. 18, (1989), 91–2.
37. Sir Percy to Crewe, telegram, 23 September 1909, CO 533/62; Huxley, *Whiteman's Country*, 262.
38. Bennett, *Kenya*, 30.
39. Sir Percy to Crewe, telegram, 23 September 1909, CO 533/62.
40. Ibid.
41. Ibid.
42. Minute by Butler to Read, 24 September 1909, on Sir Percy to Crewe, telegram, 23 September 1909, CO 533/62.
43. Ibid.
44. Ibid.
45. Minute by Fiddes to Hopwood, 24 September 1909, on Ibid.
46. Minute by Hopwood to Crewe, 25 September 1909, on Ibid.
47. Minute by Crewe to Fiddes, 30 September 1909, CO 533/62.
48. Crewe to Sir Percy, telegram, 2 October 1909, CO 533/62.

49. Ibid.
50. Crewe to Sir Percy, confidential, 16 November 1909, CO 533/62.
51. Bennett, *Kenya,* 30.
52. Sir Percy to Crewe, confidential, 5 May 1910, CO 533/ 73.
53. Ibid.
54. Sorrenson, *Origins of European Settlement in Kenya,* 118.
55. Bennett, *Kenya*, 31–32; Maxon, *Struggle for Kenya*, 37–38.
56. Ibid.
57. Sir Percy to Crewe, Interim Report, confidential, 13 November 1909, CO 533/63.
58. Sir Percy to Crewe, Main Report, confidential, 26 May 1910, CO 533/74.
59. Ibid.
60. Ibid.
61. Bennett, *Kenya*, 30–31.
62. Sir Percy to Crewe, Interim Report, confidential, 13 November 1909, CO 533/63.
63. Ibid.
64. Ibid.; BA Ogot, "Kenya Under the British," *Zamani: A Survey of East African History, New Edition*, B.A. Ogot ed. (Kenya: Longman, 1974), 252.
65. Sir Percy to Crewe, Interim Report, confidential, 13 November 1909, CO 533/63.
66. Ibid.
67. Ibid.
68. Ibid.
69. Sir Percy to Crewe, Main Report, confidential, 26 May 1910, CO 533/74.
70. Ibid.
71. Ibid.
72. Maxon, *Struggle for Kenya*, 37–8; Bennett, *Kenya,* 31–33.
73. Sir Percy to Crewe, Main Report, confidential, 26 May 1910, CO 533/74.
74. Ibid.
75. Ibid.
76. Ibid.
77. Ibid.
78. Ibid.
79. Ibid.
80. Ibid.
81. Ibid.
82. Sir Percy to Crewe, telegram, 23 September 1909, CO 533/62; Bennett, *Kenya,* 30; Sorrenson, *Origins of European Settlement in Kenya,* 119.
83. Minute by Butler to Read, 14 December 1909, on Sir Percy to Crewe, confidential, 13 November 1909, CO 533/63.
84. Ibid.
85. Minute by Read to Fiddes, 17 December 1909, on Sir Percy to Crewe, confidential, 13 November 1909, CO 533/63.
86. Crewe to Sir Percy, telegram, 7 January 1910, CO 533/63.
87. Bennett, *Kenya,* 32–3.

Chapter 5

African Administration

Sir Percy viewed that the colony lacked a well-defined policy of government administration and sought to reform the policy as to African administration. Sir Percy concluded that the Africans were administered in a manner that was inconsistent with the administration of the crown subjects of the empire. He therefore proposed to provide a well-defined policy for the administration of Africans in their reserves. Sir Percy accused the High Court of interference in the administration of Africans and sought to change it with a system of indirect rule, similar to that Lord Lugard introduced in Northern Nigeria. His proposed policy was welcomed by his provincial commissioners who sought for the same policy for the colony, even before Sir Percy's arrival.

But the High Court refused to give way on its interference, citing an Order-in-Council, 1902, as its basis of involvement in African administration and stating that the order must be repealed or amended before Sir Percy could introduce a new African policy of administration. The position of the two had been a source of discord, but there wasn't much variation as to their position that could cause friction. Both sides insisted that they had rights to govern the Africans. However, through administrative reforms, Sir Percy was able to introduce his African policy of administration, which defined the role of chiefs and elders and the function of European officers assigned to deal with the administration of African reserves.

It also provided a common action in dispensing government functions by provincial commissioners and district officers as against the former position occasioned by individual idiosyncrasy of government officials. This brought in Africans to govern their people under the direction of European officials, as was the case in Northern Nigeria. Despite his administrative reform, the application of the indirect rule method in the East Africa Protectorate was not as elaborate as Sir Percy proposed to introduce. Even then, he failed to effectively end the court's control in certain areas, especially where Africans, European, and Indians interacted. The success was too little and too late to have been considered an outstanding performance in affecting defined policy of African administration.

BASIS OF SIR PERCY'S AFRICAN POLICY

Sir Percy's African Policy was designed so as to provide a better means of administration for the Africans in their own reserves as well as to establish safeguards against infringement on their land within their reserves.[1] Sir Percy proposed the administration of the Africans by their chiefs and elders as the most desirable means of governing the affairs of the Africans.[2] In his proposed African policy, Sir Percy recommended the introduction of an indirect rule method of administration that was similar to what Lord Lugard introduced in Northern Nigeria Protectorate.[3] The latter would allow the Africans to be administered by their chiefs where they existed, and where they do not, community elders would be allowed to govern the affairs of their people.[4]

The African chiefs would be supervised and guided by a British official designated as a Resident. Under this arrangement, the African chiefs would have a relative freedom of action over their own affairs but subject to the guidance of the Resident, in matters of government policy and administration.[5]

While the British officials will be deployed to serve as Resident officers supervising, advising and guiding African rulers to conform with the policy laid down by His Majesty's government, they would, as well, avoid imposition of certain policies considered repugnant to African norms and values.[6] Sir Percy's decision to introduce the policy was informed by what appeared to have been a near absence of a defined policy of administration.

Under this method, Sir Percy proposed to allow African chiefs and elders as well as headmen where they existed to administer, and where they never existed, community elders would be appointed to take control of their people.[7] Sir Percy's proposed Africa policy was a replica of Lord Lugard's indirect rule method of governance that he successfully introduced in the Northern Nigeria Protectorate. Sir Percy, equipped with the Northern Nigeria's experience of indirect rule, sought to introduce the same in the EAP. Prior to Sir Percy's arrival into the colony, a similar African policy of administration had been proposed in a memorandum coauthored by two provincial commissioners, Ainsworth and Hobley, dated 2 October 1908.[8] But the provincial commissioners proposed African policy of administration could not be introduced, as it would have conflicted with the role of the High Court of the protectorate, in the administration of African reserves. This conflicting position could not allow the application of African policy, unless the order was amended or repealed.

Other than the role of the High Court, was the question of placing the Africans under trustees as guardians of the African people. The question of trustees had in 1907 been contemplated, but the British government refused to give way to trustees to serve as guardians of the Africans. Sir Percy's proposed introduction of the trustees in the administration of African reserves might have been outweighed by government's apprehension of complications that might occasion His Majesty's government by the introduction of private persons in the administration of the subjects of the empire. There was also the question of African land within the African reserves, which Sir Percy proposed to safeguard exclusively for the Africans and against capitalists' encroachment into African reserves with a view to grab African land within the African reserves. The safeguard of African land became a challenge to Sir Percy, in view of increasing European demands for fertile land, which caused Sir Percy to compromise his proposed African land safeguards, thereby jeopardizing his entire proposed African administration policy. In considering his proposed administration policy and the challenge of the court's interference, Sir Percy opined that it would still be possible to establish effective methods of administration as opposed to the court's administration.

DIVERGENCE OF OPINION ON AFRICAN ADMINISTRATION POLICY

Sir Percy hoped to uphold his proposed African policy of administration, where African chiefs would be allowed to govern their people. The latter position was fully corroborated in a memorandum by his provincial commissioners who sought the introduction of the policy earlier on, before Sir Percy arrived into the colony but their proposal was defeated as the court was empowered to govern African areas.[9] Sir Percy, in his drive to institute his proposed policy, reported to Crewe, in his Interim Report, that there was a near absence of a policy of administration in the protectorate. Sir Percy also told Crewe that as to Africans, he proposed to introduce a method of administration, where African chiefs would be allowed to govern their people with a minimal supervision by British officials. Sir Percy's position and that of his provincial commissioners was in sharp contrast with the position of the court and despite the divergence of opinion, Sir Percy was determined to uphold his position against that of the court.

Sir Percy, therefore, reported to Crewe, in his Interim Report of 13 November 1909, of the desirability of introducing his proposed method of African administration. Sir Percy pointed out that as long as tribal groups were to be retained, therefore, the government should consider improvement in the administration of Africans, by their chiefs under the supervision of the British officials.[10] Under the latter, Sir Percy believed that the government would be successful, in gradually evolving and applying the most desirable African administration policy. In a situation that demanded appeals, it should take African law into consideration, rather than the British law, especially, in a case with greater political weights.[11]

With the latter, it was difficult to come to some understanding or to balance the appropriate method to administer justice between African law and custom and the method of the colony's judiciary, considering the fact that it was not the function of the judiciary to administer African policy. Sir Percy shared the view with Ainsworth and Hobley.[12] This was one reason Sir Percy advocated that his policy of using African chiefs and elders to administer their people using African law and customs, through customary courts, should be seriously considered.[13]

In addition, Sir Percy recommended for the introduction and application of British East African code, except in certain special circumstances where its application was considered inappropriate, and that civilian affairs should not be left to the "discretion of native courts."[14] With such a policy, Sir Percy believed that it would not only have the support of a larger section of people and influential bodies in Britain, but would also provide a strong safeguard against individuals or groups interested in jeopardizing the legitimate African interests and rights.[15] Sir Percy recommended that the best method of governing Africans would be to allow their chiefs to govern their own affairs with a minimal supervision by British officials.[16] Sir Percy pointed out that the position of the commissioners was in concurrence with African policy in British Crown African dominions, and the provincial commissioners, Sir Percy added, were experienced in colonial administration in both the EAP and Uganda and some these officials had 15 years of service.[17]

Therefore, the commissioners' memorandum on African policy of administration should carry weight, and he urged Crewe to take into consideration the position of the commissioners, in view of their long service experience in British African colonies.[18] Also, Sir Percy suggested that the memorandum had the same substance as those, which Sir F. Lugard adopted successfully in West Africa. The recommendations of the memorandum, Sir Percy pointed out "had the acceptance of every leading authority on native rule in Africa," and requested the CO to accept the memorandum for application in the EAP.[19]

Sir Percy believed that the involvement of the court was accentuated by their belief that if they administer British law, to all the Africans, it would make it easy for them to exercise full control.[20] Sir Percy dismissed the latter view and stated that Africans would have greater benefit and justice, less oppression, if the protectorate allowed the chiefs to govern their people and to be charged with the enforcement of reasonable native law and custom over their people.[21] Sir Percy further opined that such methods as the judiciary advocated would substitute the power and law that the Africans cherished and were accustomed to for with British or Indian law and at the same time employ the service of the native police.

In this regard, Sir Percy was advocating that the African policy should be moderated or synthesized with the British policy, so as to check the power of the chiefs. Also, the police who were charged with the enforcement of the law were "unacquainted with, and not expected to know native law and custom."[22] Sir Percy was confident that his proposed policy, which was in concurrence with the position of his commissioners presented to the court before his arrival, would produce the desired African policy of administration.

Sir Percy further stated that experience over the years suggested that the application of such policy especially in African countries, such as, West Africa and Uganda, was based upon the use of Africans and the application of African law and customs, as long as they were desirable to the people.[23] But Sir Percy was concerned that the native police charged with the enforcement of the law, would subject the application of purely a British law to abuse.

However, Sir Percy was concerned that the recruited African police, having "the thinnest European veneers with its attendant advantage," was bound to be ambitious in application of the British law, or British made law, which he was as well bound to compromise. However, Sir Percy opined that there was the tendency of the African police to use the British law as means of extortion and oppression, which was far more oppressive that the rule of the African chief under the supervision of a British Resident.[24] Sir Percy was attempting to establish a safeguard against the African police recruit exploiting the ordinary African, when he recommended full control of affairs of the Africans, by their chiefs, instead of the newly recruited African police who would be desirous of power and exploitation of the situation.

In spite of Sir Percy's support of the African chiefs, he stated that the African police might not be perfect in the dispensation of this policy. However, Sir Percy pointed out that, notwithstanding the shortcomings of the African chiefs, they were part of the Africans and could administer their "rough and ready justice," based on their own customs and traditions of their tribal formations that had been in existence over the years.[25]

In the memorandum of the provincial commissioners, coauthored by two provincial commissioners, Ainsworth and Hobley, "Memorandum on Native Policy," dated 2 October 1908, held that African chiefs and elders should administer African reserves, and where the latter were absent; there were recognized patriarchal systems of authority among all the tribal formations.[26] They recommended that in a situation where African chiefs never existed, a system of patriarchal administration, where community elder(s) would be responsible for the administration of his tribe within the tribal reserve, as earlier on, recognized by the protectorate, was also proposed in the said memo.[27] The Memorandum of the provincial commissioners was transmitted to the Principal Judge of the protectorate for his comment. Justice R. W. Hamilton in his comment in a Memorandum titled "Proposed Introduction of a Simple Code for Natives of 1 December 1908," objected to Ainsworth and Hobley's proposed "Memorandum on Native Policy." Hamilton was not only adverse to the views expressed by the provincial commissioners, but also very critical of the provincial commissioners. Hamilton made the position of the court very clear on the question of the legality of its interference in the administration of African areas that:

> His Majesty the King Order in Council 1902, constituted the High Court, and gave it full responsibility to supervise the administration of Justice in East Africa. For the last six years the High Court has been endeavoring to do its duty in that respect and it is not unnatural that its interference, where interference was before unknown, has led to some soreness of feeling; but unless your excellency is prepared to recommend the amendment of that order and the curtailment of the powers of the High Court the country must be permitted to develop on the lines laid down.[28]

Sir Percy did not agree with Hamilton's position. He strongly supported the position of the provincial commissioners in his Interim Report. He maintained that his provincial commissioners were men of a longstanding experience in colonial administration and that their views would be very valuable in the consideration of the policy.[29] Sir Percy also reported to Crewe, that the role of the High Court in the administration of African areas had produced difficulties and divergence of opinion in the administration of African reserves. Even though, the divergence of opinion was to a lesser extent because whenever provincial commissioners decided on a case, they were found to be in accord with the court's verdicts.

It was on a few incidences that the court had altered the decision of the provincial commissioners. Despite the latter instances, the provincial commissioners were unhappy with the court's interference, and Sir Percy, having served in Northern Nigeria, where indirect rule was well established, proposed his African administration policy which was fully supported by the memorandum of his provincial commissioners. Sir Percy also reported to Crewe that in the administration of African people, his position was the most accepted and widely used, citing northern Nigeria and Uganda as examples, and urged Crewe to approve his proposal for the introduction of the said policy.[30] To emphasize his stand Sir Percy enclosed Ainsworth and Hobley's Memorandum on Native Policy" and Hamilton's "Proposed Introduction of a simple Code for Native" as appendixes to his Interim Report.

In the CO, Sir Percy's recommendations were welcomed. Butler, in a minute on Sir Percy's proposed African administration, commented on the general interference of the Court in areas where the whites, Indians and Africans interacted and to inside the African reserves.[31] In view of such interference, Butler supported the proposed policy of administration of Africans by their chiefs and elders, stating that it was desirable for the Africans to be governed by their chiefs, and the use of native law and customs and native courts in African areas.[32] The latter would be applied "side by side with the gradual introduction of British East Africa law, when evolved, except in certain criminal and civil matters, which cannot even, at the outset, be left to the discretion of native courts."[33]

Butler recommended that Sir Percy's recommendations should be accepted in their entirety but he was, at the same time, concerned that Hamilton would oppose the policy, once it was introduced in the country.[34] Butler added, "we shall find a strong and determined opponent in Mr. Hamilton, the Principal Judge," whose memorandum of 1 December 1908, formed one of the appendices of Sir Percy's covering confidential dispatch to his Interim Report.[35] Butler added that the memorandum proposed and could be applied in the case for applying British or British-made law in minute detail all over the protectorate."[36] Butler added that his own sympathy, based on long experience, at any rate, from this end, of similar question in West Africa, was entirely with the provincial commissioners.[37]

Butler stated, "it seems absurd to me that, with our scattered officials set in enormous masses of native population, there could ever be any idea of applying our own system of law in detail and individually to the Africans. It is in fact impossible to apply a uniform British made laws throughout the protectorate," but he suggested that it could no doubt be possible to do so, in old established and highly organized districts. But in the further areas on the fringe of administration, and in the new areas hereafter to be occupied, Butler suggested that the only method of procedure is to lay sympathetic hands on the native machinery, which had existed. In order to transform African authority, both administrative and judicial, into "a tool suitable for the admitted purposes for which our administration in these protectorates exists."[38]

Butler also pointed out that there was the need for a careful discrimination to decide, where this system shall be followed and where "the Principal Judge's idea of absolute adherence to British or British made laws and procedure shall be adopted."[39] However, Butler expressed his confidence in Sir Percy, stating that, "it can be done, and I am sure that Sir Percy, with his experience of similar problems in Northern Nigeria, and with the aid of a political staff with whom he appeared to be in entire sympathy on this point, will be successful in handling the question."[40] However, Butler added, "Sir Percy made out a preliminary case on all these points, but of course detailed consideration must follow."[41] Butler was suggesting that Sir Percy had identified and proposed the desired policy of African administration but further detail was necessary on how he intended to carry his proposed scheme out. Also, Butler agreed with Sir Percy's recommendation that Africans be placed under the administration of their chiefs and headmen.[42]

Crewe, in his reply to Sir Percy's Interim Report, and reflecting on Butler's comments, addressed a telegram of 7 January 1910, expressing his concurrence to the desirability of placing the Africans under the administration of their chiefs, stating that, "I agree that native chiefs should be used in the administration of native reserves or states."[43] Crewe also requested Sir Percy to furnish further details on the procedure to be adopted in carrying through his proposed policy.[44] Therefore, Sir Percy's recommendations as to African policy were accepted despite objection from Hamilton.

It was up to Sir Percy to carry out his proposed reform by providing details of how he intended to implement his approved African administration policy. Therefore, the African policy would form one of his policies for implementation and subsequent events would determine the course of its implementation. The success or failure of the policy would depend to a large extent on the ability of Sir Percy to lay out an acceptable detailed process, by which African policy of administration could be implemented in the colony.

TRUSTEES AS GUARDIANS IN ADMINISTRATION

The question of involving trustees in the African administration had been contemplated in 1907, but Parliamentary Undersecretary State for the Colonies, Winston Churchill, rejected the idea outright. Sir Percy revisited the question of using the trustees as guardians of African reserves, when he sought to introduce a method of African administration.[45] Sir Percy reported to Crewe in his Interim Report that there was almost a complete absence of a defined policy of government administration and that he proposed to place the Africans under the administration of their chiefs.[46] Sir Percy was determined to safeguard African reserves, by making them independent of any interference from the government, individuals, and interest groups. In carrying out the latter, he considered the inclusion of appointing private individuals as trustees of the African people. Sir Percy told Crewe, in a secret dispatch of 6 May 1910, that he proposed to place the Africans under the administration of their chiefs and headmen, who would be supervised by private individuals as a board of trustees.[47]

Sir Percy told Crewe, in his secret dispatch, that the board would be independent and would be saddled with the responsibility of safeguarding the African reserves against interest groups who would want to seize lands within the reserves.[48] The trustees would be composed of the chief justice of the protectorate as chair, a high court justice, a bishop, and the secretary for African affairs, Sir Percy stated.[49] Sir Percy told Crewe that he would transmit a further intimation on the policy by dispatch.

The question of safeguarding the African reserves against land grabs by individuals and syndicates as well as the placing the Africans reserves under the supervision of a board of trustees formed an important policy consideration of Sir Percy. Sir Percy was determined to safeguard the reserves. The inclusion of the trustees was a departure from his initial recommendations on the administration of the reserves. In Sir Percy's African policy, for the introduction of a policy that was similar to that one introduced by Lugard, in Northern Nigeria. Therefore, the inclusion of trustees to safeguard the African reserves altered his initial proposed African policy of administration. In fact, it was the inclusion of the trustees as guardians of the African people that provoked Crewe's dissatisfaction, when Sir Percy, in his secret dispatch of 6 May 1910, told Crewe that, the Africans should be placed under the administration of their chiefs and headmen who would be supervised by private individuals as a board of trustees.[50]

The first Africans he considered for the policy were the Maasai who became a focal point of such policy, because they were occupying an agriculturally fertile land, much desired by the European settlers for agricultural cultivation. Therefore, Sir Percy proposed to remove them from their fertile Laikipia to the extended southern Maasai reserve so as to give way to European farmers.[51] As for the trustees, Sir Percy told Crewe, in his Interim Report, that the board would be independent and would be saddled with the responsibility of safeguarding the African reserves against interest groups who would want to seize lands within the reserves.[52] The inclusion of a board of trustees as part of the details of the policy became a source of concern to the CO, even though, Sir Percy told Crewe that he would transmit a further intimation on the policy, in his Main Report.

Prior to the transmission of further details, he had already initiated his first test case of placing the Africans on a separate settlement as reserve when, in his 6 May 1910 secret diapatch, he proposed the removal of the Maasai from Laikipia to the extended southern Maasai reserve. Sir Percy added that the Maasai would be placed under the administration of a board of trustees, in the first instance, but the CO refused Sir Percy's proposed board of trustees as administrators of African reserves. In a reply to Sir Percy's telegram of 6 May 1910, Crewe told Sir Percy, in his telegram of 12 May 1910, "I fear it is not feasible to place the Masai Reserves in the hands of trustees for reason which will be explained to you by dispatch. I am therefore not able to depart from the policy of making trustees the guardian of the African people."[53] Crewe reiterated his view in a further confidential dispatch of 31 May 1911, when he told Sir Percy, "I was unable to accede to your suggestion that the Masai reserve should be placed in the hands of private trustees as stated by Winston Churchill in the House of Commons on 22 July 1907."[54]

Crewe added that even if suitable persons could be found as trustees, the responsibility of administrating African people would in the long run, rest in the British government.[55] Crewe also told Sir Percy, in his dispatch of 31 May 1910, of Churchill's House of Commons debate of 22 July 1907, on the nature and extent of government commitment in safeguarding the African reserves.[56] The question of safeguarding African reserves and the possible involvement of trustees in the administration of reserves, in the EAP, had been brought forth, for consideration, but Churchill rejected it outright.[57]

Sir Percy revisited the question of using the trustees as guardians of the African reserves, when he sought the approval of Crewe to allow him to use trustees as custodians of African reserves.[58] But Crewe refused to depart from the policy of Lord Elgin and Churchill, and held that he would not approve of Sir Percy to appoint private individuals as trustees of the African people, which he viewed as an unnecessary complication.[59] Crewe rejected the proposal, having had no doubts of the presumed complications that the involvements of the trustees could produce, in the administration of African reserves, and thus, kicked against the proposed policy, once more. The British government would not consent to the trustees, as the question of government being the trustee of the African people became policy.

Therefore, Sir Percy's proposed African policy was refused, as it was not in consonance with the policy of the British government. Crewe's dispatch of 31 May 1910 ended further correspondence, in the short run, on the desirability of Sir Percy's proposed African policy recommendations. The development of the African institutions would have afforded the African chiefs and elders an opportunity to govern their people with minimal interference from the colonial authorities.[60] In the case of the EAP, what probably seemed to have raised doubt of its viability was the inclusion of the proposed board of trustees, which gave the impression that His Majesty's government was abandoning its responsibility to private individuals.

Crewe argued in his confidential dispatch of 31 May 1910 that the British government would not surrender its responsibilities to "a private board of trustees, even if suitable persons as trustees could be found, the responsibility of deciding whether the trust was being suitably administered, had in the last resort, to rest with the Government, and intermediaries would only be an unnecessary complication."[61] It was on the strength of the latter statement that

Crewe dumped Sir Percy's proposed African policy of administration, so as to avoid embarrassing His Majesty's government. The impression of the CO as to the involvement of trustees in the administration of Africans was that His Majesty's government was abandoning its crown subjects of the empire to private persons to administer them, on behalf of His Majesty.

Sir Percy's details of the process of administrating African policy was a departure from his initial African policy recommendations as contained in his Interim Report, and also as proposed by his commissioners in their memorandum of 2 October 1908. In the former, Sir Percy proposed to Crewe to administer the African in a manner that Lord Lugard administered the Northern Nigeria Protectorate, where African chiefs, under the supervision of British Resident exercise administrative and judicial responsibilities, without any role being assigned to a private person(s) to administer the Africans on behalf of His Majesty's government.

In the case of the EAP, the inclusion of a board trustees to administer subjects of the crown did not form part of his initial proposal, and it was based on the inclusion of the board of trustees that Crewe kicked against his revised African policy recommendations. In this regard, Sir Percy failed to come up with an African Policy that the CO believed could provide the desired result, after having initially approved of his policy. He failed to provide a convincing explanation as to the policy, which led to the rejection of his recommendation by the CO.

However, Sir Percy never gave up when, on 18 May 1910, he reiterated in his Main Report, that the Africans should be administered through their chiefs and elders. Crewe replied to him, agreeing to the proposal. Thereafter, Lewis Harcourt was appointed the new Secretary of State for the Colonies, On his assumption of office, he approved of Sir Percy's request, in a confidential dispatch of 7 December 1910, Harcourt approved of Sir Percy to carry out a limited measure of African policy as proposed, in his memorandum for provincial and district commissioners of 18 May 1910.[62]

With the latter, Sir Percy introduced to provincial commissioners and district officers some guidelines on the role of chiefs and elders and headmen in the administration of African reserves. The measure provided a basis of chiefs and elders to administer their people with the supervision of provincial commissioners and district commissioners. The memorandum provided some semblance of African policy, where Africans were allowed to govern their people.[63] Sir Percy believed that the latter course was necessary and failing to carry out such reform could jeopardize the African tribal authority.[64]

But one of the challenges of this limited policy measure that became a source of concern to Sir Percy was how the government could control Africans in areas outside their own reserves. In areas where African, European and Indian interacted, it would be difficult to control the Africans, more especially, the youth, who saw the European way of life as model and held their own ways and institutions in contempt. More importantly, the court could contest to his limited reform measure, as he had not requested the CO to repeal or amend the Order-in-Council, 1902, which empowered the court to administer Africa reserves.[65]

As to African youth, Sir Percy believed, as they looked up to the European ways of life, a situation that could denationalize them, as well as produce new attitudes and assumptions that were inimical to the authority of the chiefs, and could be an obstacle to the development of the African political institutions. Sir Percy added that western civilization could lead to denationalization as the Africans preferred the independence of the town, as a wage earner, to the authority of the elders in a tribal society.[66]

In this regard, Sir Percy believed that the African would have preferred to earn his wages working on the European farm rather than holding to his own reserve and living under the order of his chief. Such a view did not turn out to have been the case, as the wage workers refused to go out to work on European farms, and it caused the local authorities to compel Africans before they could go out to work for wages on the European farms, in addition to the taxation that Sir Percy imposed on all African males so as to force them out to the European farms to work for wages, so as to be able to pay taxes imposed by the government, presumably to source labor for the whites' farms.[67]

Sir Percy pointed out that the presence of Europeans in the protectorate would not undermine African policy, a concern, which could not be substantiated. If the British colonial officials could float an exclusive apartheid policy of administration within South Africa, indirect rule in Northern Nigeria, there would have been no reason for their failure to institute an indirect rule in the EAP. In the case of EAP, it would have even had a better chance of survival as both whites and the Africans lived in separate areas, a policy reminiscent of the apartheid South Africa, and which Sir Percy worked for its evolution, when he proposed that they should be established in certain areas that would be exclusive to them, as much as the highland was exclusive to the settlers.

This was a clear demonstration of land and administration policies that reflected his experience of South Africa's apartheid policy of administration. The establishment of separate settlements which Sir Percy believed was a safety valve against interracial discord does not suggest that it was meant to establish peace and stability in the country, in view of the policies he implemented or he proposed to implement on each of the three races of the country.

Therefore, his policy of separate settlement for each of the races of the protectorate under the guise of establishing peaceful settlements among the racial groups in the country, suggested that he was determined to establish a

South Africa's model of apartheid policy of administration for the protectorate. Therefore, African policy in the EAP would have had a better chance of survival, if it had been introduced as a well elaborated system, similar to that of Northern Nigeria, the presence of the white-settlers notwithstanding.

In a desperate attempt to save his African policy, he revised his African policy and followed up with the CO, transmitting it in a form of a memorandum on African policy. A memorandum, dated 18 May 1910, stipulated certain uniform functions of political officers in the discharge of their functions, and the role of chiefs and elders, in the administration of their people.[68] The memorandum was a step forward, in the application of African policy, but the memorandum did not transform into a policy of government. It was a mere administrative document to guide provincial commissioners' and district officers in the discharge of their functions.

The memorandum could not be debated in the legislative council because, even if it was done, it would not have amounted to a policy document as Sir Percy failed to request for the amendments of the Order-in-Council, 1902, which authorized and empowered the High Court of the protectorate to exercise control over African reserves. Therefore, for any documents to form part of government policy on African administration, the Order-in-Council would have to be repealed or amended so as to afford for the administration of Africans by their own chiefs and elders, as recommended in Sir Percy's Interim Report and, in Ainsworth and Hobley's memorandum.

But as Sir Percy had not pressed the CO to repeal or amend the Order-in-Council, his proposed African policy was rejected. Persistent to pursue his proposed African policy, Sir Percy revised his position that he transmitted in the form of a memorandum that was supported by the CO. The support afforded Sir Percy the opportunity to introduce certain reforms in the administration of Africans, which were considerably less than what he had proposed for the African administration.

CONCLUSION

The African policy advocated by Sir Percy was that of an indirect rule, which Lord Lugard implemented in Northern Nigeria. His proposed policy was accepted by the CO that Africans be administered by chiefs and elders. As for policy of administration, initially, the CO accepted his proposed administration of Africans by their chiefs but later on, it was turned down, in view of Sir Percy's departure from the initial policy he proposed to the CO, having brought in the idea of a trustee to administer the Africans.

But the CO required detail of the process of carrying out the policy. In the detail, Sir Percy made a provision for a trustee to administer African reserves, a view which His Majesty's government believed that, it was the trustee of the African people not a private person. Churchill had in 1907 rejected the question of placing the Africans under a trustee, and as it became a policy, Crewe could not see his way in approving of Sir Percy to place Africans under the administration of private persons.

It was in consideration of the complication that might arise by placing the African under a trustee, and more importantly, it had been ruled out by Churchill before the Commons that government was the trustee of Africans that his proposed policy failed. His memoranda of strengthening the African and working through their institution, in African areas, a reform he made in May 1910, did not turn out to be a policy of government. It was left to individual idiosyncrasy and personal originality of each provincial or district officer.

More importantly, the measure was inadequate to provide effective and efficient policy of African administration within the reserves, and further complicated by the presence of other races, with whom the Africans interacted outside the reserves. Therefore, in all the proposed policy recommendations on African administration, Sir Percy had not been successful in implementing any one of them, therefore, it was a failed attempted introduction of the indirect rule, similar to the Lugard Northern Nigeria's policy of administration. A policy that Sir Percy revered, but which he failed to successfully provide details based on his initial proposal so as to convince Crewe, to move on, and instead, introduced new elements into the proposal that caused Crewe to reject the proposal outright.

The interaction of the Africans with other races, outside their reserves, could only complicate the application of African policy, whenever there was a dispute between African and any of the two races, as different laws governed them, and the question of which law would be applied in the event of dispute outside the reserve came forth. Therefore, in all the proposed policy recommendations on African administration, Sir Percy had not been successful in implementing any one of them. It was a failed attempted introduction of indirect rule, similar to the Lugard's Northern Nigeria's policy of administration.

Another failure for Sir Percy's policy of African administration was demonstrated by his inability to safeguard African land through the initiation of a land policy that would safeguard African reserves. As there was no policy, African reserves were left vulnerable to big syndicates and interest groups. Sir Percy had earlier on pointed out that they might grab African land if safeguards were not in place. But he never put safeguards in place as examples of syndicates and interest groups attempting to grab African land marked his governorship. In all Sir Percy's proposed recommendations for African administration, he had not been successful in implementing any one of them. From his failed attempt to introduce indirect rule, to his backing of the provincial commissioners in their quarrel with the court, to his inability to protect African land. Sir Percy's policy of African administration was one of promise, as reflected in his Interim Report, rather than actual performance in the form of implementation of his policy ideas. This reflects on his subsequent policy of economic development of the colony for the eventual solvency of the colony's economic predicaments.

NOTES

1. Mungeam, *British Rule in Kenya*, 213–14.
2. Ibid.
3. Lord Lugard, *Dual Mandate in British Tropical Africa* (London: Anchor Books, 1965), 94–6.
4. Mungeam, *British Rule in Kenya,* 213.
5. Ibid.
6. Lugard, *Dual Mandate in British Tropical Africa*, 95.
7. Mungeam, *British Rule in Kenya*, 211.
8. Memorandum by John Ainsworth and C. W. Hobley, confidential, 2 October 1908, enclosure in Sir Percy to Crewe, confidential, 13 November 1909, CO 533/63.
9. Sir Percy to Crewe, Interim Report, confidential, 13 November 1909, CO 533/63.
10. Ibid.
11. Lugard, *Dual Mandate in British Tropical Africa,* 198.
12. Sir Percy to Crewe, Interim Report, confidential, 13 November 1909, CO 533/63.
13. Ibid.
14. Ibid.
15. Ibid.
16. Ibid.
17. Ibid.
18. Ibid.
19. Ibid.
20. Ibid.
21. Ibid.
22. Ibid.
23. Ibid.
24. Ibid.
25. Ibid.
26. Memorandum by Ainsworth and Hobley, 2 October 1908, CO 533/63.
27. Sir Percy to Crewe, Interim Report, confidential, 13 November 1909, CO 533/63; Memorandum by Ainsworth and Hobley, 2 October 1908, all in CO 533/63.

28. Memorandum by Hamilton to Sir Percy, 1 December 1908, enclosure in Sir Percy to Crewe, confidential, 13 November 1909, CO 533/63.

29. Sir Percy to Crewe, Interim Report, confidential, 13 November 1909, CO 533/63.

30. Ibid.

31. Minute by Butler to Read, 14 December 1909, on Sir Percy to Crewe, Interim Report, confidential, 13 November 1909, CO 533/63.

32. Ibid.; Memorandum by Ainsworth and Hobley, 2 October 1908; Memorandum by Hamilton to Sir Percy, 1 December 1908, all in CO 533/63.

33. Ibid.

34. Minute by Butler to Read, 14 December 1909, on Sir Percy to Crewe, Interim Report, confidential, 13 November 1909; CO 533/63.

35. Ibid.

36. Ibid.

37. Ibid.

38. Ibid.

39. Ibid.

40. Ibid.

41. Ibid.

42. Ibid.

43. Crewe to Sir Percy, telegram, 7 January 1910, CO 533/63.

44. Ibid.

45. Sir Percy to Crewe, Interim Report, confidential, 13 November 1909, CO 533/63.

46. Ibid.

47. Sir Percy to Crewe, secret, 6 May 1910, CO 533/73.

48. Ibid.

49. Ibid.

50. Ibid.

51. Lord Cranwoth, *Kenya Chronicles* (London: Macmillan and Co., Ltd., 1939), 63.

52 Sir Percy to Crewe, Interim Report, confidential, confidential, 13 November 1909, CO 533/63.

53. Crewe to Sir Percy, telegram, 12 May 1910, CO 533/73.

54. Crewe to Sir Percy, confidential, 31 May 1910, CO 533/73.

55. Ibid; Sir Percy to Crewe, secret, 6 May 1910, CO 533/73; Mungeam, *British Rule in Kenya*, 223.

56. Crewe to Sir Percy, confidential, 31 May 1910, CO 533/73.

57. Ibid.

58. Sir Percy to Crewe, secret, 6 May 1910, CO 533/73.

59. Crewe to Sir Percy, confidential, 31 May 1910, CO 533/73.

60. Lugard, *Dual Mandate in British Tropical Africa*, 198–207.

61. Crewe to Sir Percy, confidential, 31 May 1910, CO 533/73; Mungeam, *British Rule in Kenya*, 223.

62. Harcourt to Sir Percy, confidential, 7 December 1910, CO 533/73.

63. Sir Percy to Harcourt, Further Report Upon the East Africa Protectorate, confidential, 18 March 1912, CO 533/102.

64. Mungeam, *British Rule in Kenya*, 227.

65. Memorandum by Hamilton, 1 December 1908, enclosure in Sir Percy to Crewe, confidential, 13 November 1909, CO 533/63.

66. Memorandum by Ainsworth and Hobley, 2 October 1908, enclosure in Sir Percy to Crewe, confidential, 13 November 1909, CO 533/63.

67. Ogot, "Kenya Under the British," 254.

68. Harcourt to Sir Percy, confidential, 7 December 1910, CO 533/73; Sir Percy to Harcourt, Further Report, Upon the East Africa Protectorate, confidential, 18 March 1912, CO 533/102.

Chapter 6

Economic Development Policy

In economic development policy, Sir Percy, as he did with the issues of land administration policy, faced difficult challenges and lack of success similar to that of his predecessors in addressing this very critical issue. Here, as in those issues as well, Sir Percy rushed to undertake a study of economy and transport development and submitted detailed proposals to the CO. Just as in these issues, Sir Percy's rush to tackle economic and transport development led to proposals that were less than complete and produced an outcome that was hardly successful. Sir Percy's economic development policy was premised on low railway rates for a coastward-bound shipment, with a view to induce farmers to produce more for exports. The policy was introduced with the view that European settlers could be induced to produce for export for economic solvency of the protectorate, as well for the farmers to earn a little from the reduced railway rates. While Sir Percy was governor, the colony witnessed economic prosperity, as it could balance its budget by 1912. The colony succeeded in pulling itself out of its economic predicament, as it did away with the annual grant-in-aid from the British Treasury. The economic prosperity of the colony was presumed by A. H. M Kirk-Greene's "Canada's proconsul," to have been achieved as a result of Sir Percy's policy of induced agricultural production by means of a reduced railway rate on a coast-bound shipment. In fact, his economic policies of low railway rates on coastward bound shipments from European farmers had not helped in accelerating the colony's economic development to a considerable degree, when Sir Percy left the colony in 1912. Sir Percy's favoritism and backing for European settler export production over that of African peasants came at a particularly critical juncture in Kenya's colonial history. It highlights one of the most fundamental contradictions identified by Lonsdale and Berman that characterized the early years of the EAP. It was that associated with accumulation and control.

Sir Percy supported accumulation by European settler farmers rather than African peasants facilitated by merchant capital.[1] Sir Percy was aware that peasant production for export provided the means for balancing the protectorate's budget by 1912 and that the products of settler farms and plantations was "minuscule," but he either misunderstood the EAP's economic situation or he chose to disregard it in his simplistic view that European settler agriculture would provide the future basis for the colony's prosperity. Sir Percy's failure was therefore not just a personal shortcoming of an administrator "caught between the policy objectives of economy and morality but that of ignoring this most basic of contradictions of early colonial Kenya's political economy.[2]

Sir Percy's reasoning for the reduction was to induce settler farmers to produce more for export, as the rates, which Sir Percy claimed was their difficulty in marketing, must be reduced. He pointed out that once more exports could be secured, the colony could collect duties from exports and imports, which could enable the colony to achieve economic solvency. Therefore, following the reduction of rates, it becomes necessary to examine the agricultural production of the country and the exports and revenue with a view to ascertaining if it was the production of the European farmers that brought home the revenue desired that effectively helped the colony do away with its dependence on grants-in-aid from the British Treasury.

By the time Sir Percy assumed the administration of the East Africa Protectorate, he was recognized as a leading expert in the British Empire on the subject of building and operation of railways. The EAP provided an opportunity for Sir Percy to utilize his experience and expertise for the economic development of the EAP. The building and development of railways began with the construction of the Uganda Railway that was started in 1896 and completed in 1901. The railway ran from the coast to Lake Victoria, and it had been an expensive enterprise for the British Treasury. While the single rail linked the interior with the coast, many parts of the protectorate with economic potential lay far away from the main line. There was thus need for construction of additional adjunct railways that might help to facilitate the transport of agricultural products from remote locations to the coast for onward shipment to European markets. Sir Percy quickly recognized this and sought to carry through the construction of adjunct railway lines, so as to facilitate his proposed economic development policy of reduced railway freight with a view to induce farmers to produce so that the railway could realize the money invested in its construction. Also, it was expected that as a result of the reduction of railway rates, farmers would make savings and earn a living on such savings.

Therefore, the construction of railway for the shipment of these farm produce as well as encouraging European production for the economic development of the EAP, where receipts from shipment of farm produce would help the EAP to be financially self supporting, became the cornerstone of his economic policy for the development of the EAP. Nevertheless, the economic policy he advocated had not produced the desired result by the end of his administration, as it was African agricultural production that paved the way for the economic solvency of the country rather than receipts from shipments of the European produce. As to the building of the adjunct railways, they had not proved to be very promising as he had proposed, and by the time he left the protectorate, much of the economic and infrastructure development the country needed had not been achieved. Development problems in economics and transportation continued to pester the colony. Therefore, this chapter seeks to assess what was the economic position on his assumption of government, what were the exports of the colony, and the total government revenue receipts on export and on poll and hut taxes between 1908 and 1913 that were instrumental in accelerating the economic prosperity of the colony.

SIR PERCY'S ECONOMIC DEVELOPMENT POLICY

Hitherto, the policy of the EAP emphasized the need to maintain law and order while commercial activities were left to private enterprise.[3] But Sir Percy believed that it was necessary for the government to get involved in stimulating economic development in order to be self-sufficient.[4] It should be noted that Sir Percy assumed government when the annual expenditure of the protectorate as at 1908–09, stood at £703,102 while its annual receipts were £485,000.[5] Despite the British Treasury's annual grant-in-aid of £138,000; the colony could not balance its annual budget.[6] Sir Percy quickly recognized it was the high cost of railway shipping that discouraged production, as most farmers could not afford the railway shipping rates. As a result, railway wagons moved empty coastward as no shipment could be procured.

Therefore, Sir Percy proposed the development of European agriculture for export and the reduction of coastward rates on the Uganda Railway so that the European farmers could make savings and be encouraged to produce.[7] Sir Percy wasted little time in presenting these development ideas to the CO, which had the authority to make final decisions as to general policy within the dependent empire. However, Sir Percy presented his ideas and policies piecemeal rather than as part of a well-developed and comprehensive plan.

Sir Percy made the first intimation of his economic plans for the EAP in November of 1909. He told the CO that the development of European agriculture was key to his ideas to promote the protectorate's economic improvement, and one way to accomplish this was to reduce the rates on the coastward railway traffic for commodities such as maize, groundnuts, and beans. Sir Percy made this recommendation clear in a telegram of 12 November 1909.[8] Such a policy, he claimed, would not only encourage farmers to increase production, but also by increasing traffic, this would increase railway receipts.

The increased exports that would result would also increase the earnings of farmers. As things stood, Sir Percy told Crewe, the high freight rate charged by the Uganda Railway meant that most railway wagons went empty to the coast as farmers could not afford to fill them. With the colony's poor state of revenue generation, Sir Percy told Crewe that the situation was unsustainable and suggested that no matter how efficient the administrative machine of the country would be, it could not satisfy the economic want of the country, if it remained in its present condition.[9] Sir Percy sought to be given a free hand in deciding the rates, and of encouraging the European settlers to engage in agricultural production for export.[10] This constituted the governor's main argument that lowering the coastward rates would stimulate production and allow a little profit for farmers. Thus Sir Percy requested that the CO approve an immediate reduction of railway rates.

In a separate confidential dispatch of 13 November 1909, accompanying his Interim Report, Sir Percy reiterated his proposal for a reduction of rates. He told Crewe that by this reduction he desired to accentuate the economic development of the colony. The reduction of the railway rates was to be the first step in that direction.[11] In his Interim Report, Sir Percy deplored the absence of an economic development policy as the government had to depend on grants-in-aid from the British government for its annual fiscal expenditure. Sir Percy pointed out that this was contrary to the tradition in Northern Nigeria, the Transvaal and Orange River colony. According to his analysis, the revenue for the EAP was contributed by several different sectors. In 1909–10, for example, Uganda and German East Africa contributed £200,000. The white population of the EAP contributed £100,000 and the African population £200,000 while the British taxpayers' contribution that came in the form of a grant-in-aid stood at £138,000. This provided total revenue generated for the fiscal year 1909–10 at £638,000.[12]

At the CO Butler noted the prominence Sir Percy had given in the confidential dispatch to the reduction of rates as part of his economic policy. In his minute he stated: "it is pleasing to be in a position to tell him that we have already laid this proposal before the Treasury, and have supported it in the strongest possible manner."[13] Butler added, "It is evidently a question which we must fight to the bitter end in the unfortunate event of the Treasury not agreeing outright."[14] Butler earlier noted: "there is already a special rate of 1/2d. a ton per mile for maize (and other grain), the continuance of which has been sanctioned till the 31st of Dec. 1909, when the matter is to be reconsidered."[15] However, Butler minuted that Sir Percy should provide evidence that there was the need for the reduction of the railway rates, and added that "a more expeditious procedure was necessary to make his case," before the CO could be ready to transmit his request to the Treasury.[16]

At the same time, Butler concurred in Sir Percy's proposal, when he stated that Sir Percy has experienced personnel of tried ability under him to help him achieve his desired economic policy. Butler pointed out that with H. A. F. Currie, Manager of the Railways, who Butler described as an experienced officer, with years of experience of the local conditions who could be relied upon for the success of the railway development.[17] Also, Butler pointed out that there was Mr. MacDonald whose opinion in agricultural matters, according to Butler, could be relied upon.[18] More importantly, as for the railway, Butler pointed out that Sir Percy was an expert on the question of the railway; therefore, no apprehension should be entertained on such a proposal.

Butler suggested that since Sir Percy had proposed a policy that he believed would relieve the strain in both directions, and which Sir Percy guaranteed that it would not occasion any loss of revenue, Butler stated that, it would be unfair for the CO to reject his proposal and recommended further that Sir Percy's proposal should be tried, when he stated that Sir Percy should, "I think, be given a free hand in dealing with coastward rates."[19] Therefore, Butler suggested that a copy of Sir Percy's request be forwarded to the Treasury, with a note that "Lord Crewe trusts that they will agree to the proposal."[20]

But there were hesitations by Read when he stated that this was not the first time the CO had attempted to get a freer hand with regard to the Uganda Railway, but they were unsuccessful.[21] Read expressed his frustrations on how the affairs of the Uganda Railway were being managed, when he stated that "under the present system we are tied hand and foot and cannot make the smallest alteration in the rates without Treasury's approval."[22] Read added that "this excessive centralization seems to be especially pernicious in the case of an enterprise like a railway and I hope that we shall succeed in securing greater freedom" for Sir Percy.[23] Fiddes concurred with Read, and recommended for a detailed proposal on the administration of the Uganda Railway.[24] Seeley concurred in both Fiddes and Read's minutes, and minuted to Crewe that, "I entirely agree with Fiddes, no doubt you can induce the Treasury to agree." Seeley, in his comment, suggested that Crewe could induce the Treasury to reconsider its position on the administration of the Uganda Railway.[25] Crewe agreed, and stated that, "this question must be pressed on the Treasury, and I hope they will see that our attitude is reasonable."[26] Crewe also stated that "to govern a railway on the equator from here, is like conducting a war by an Aulic Council."[27]

Therefore, Crewe instructed Fiddes to draft a dispatch to the Treasury, which Fiddes sent in a confidential dispatch of 6 December 1909, to the Secretary of the Treasury, with an enclosure of Sir Percy's telegram of

12 November 1909, transmitted to the Secretary to be laid before the Lord Commissioners of the Treasury. Crewe also told the Commissioners that any periodic alterations of rate by Sir Percy would be reported from time to time and urged the Treasury to relax its tight hold over the affairs of the railway, as officials on the ground could be capable of supervising its affairs, should be given a free hand, and that the affairs of the railway should be allowed as flexible as possible.[28] But to the dismay of the CO and Sir Percy, the Treasury replied on 20 December 1909 that, "in the absence of any detailed explanation and authority, the power to fix coastward rates should not extend below the minimum of 1/2d. per ton per mile."[29] Without flexibility on the control of the Uganda Railway rates, the situation could complicate the ability of the protectorate's authorities to manage the railway and improve the economy. This was clearly seen when the Treasury refused to approve Sir Percy's request for lowering the rates to 1/3d. but instead pointed out that it had already offered a generous minimum concession of 1/2d. on raw products for exports. Crewe intimated to Sir Percy the decision of the Treasury in a telegram of 28 December 1909 that the Treasury approved the minimum railway coastward rates of 1/2d on raw products for export.[30] These measures pointed to future difficulties for Sir Percy's policy.

Sir Percy replied to Crewe in a telegram of 10 January 1910, regretting that the Lord Commissioners of the Treasury could not have adopted full terms of Crewe's letter to the Treasury of 6 December 1909.[31] Sir Percy also told Crewe that the 1/2d. minimum was not a substantial concession on raw products for export. Sir Percy added that the product he wished to base the prosperity of the colony was maize which was, as at 1909–10, at a prohibitive rate of 1/2d.[32] Sir Percy also reiterated in his telegram the desirability of being given a free hand in any alteration of the rate and was also willing to notify any proposed alteration below 1/2d.[33] Sir Percy thus rejected the Treasury's offer and asked Crewe to resubmit his request to the Lord Commissioners of the Treasury for a reconsideration of their decision on his low rates request.[34]

In the CO, Read minuted "speaking rightly the maize comes from a distance of 300–400 miles."[35] Read added that the export of maize at 1/3d. per ton per mile which Sir Percy presented and requested to secure a low rate would be resent to the Treasury, with his telegram as an enclosure. Read added that the CO's message to the Treasury should press that the governor should be given "full freedom for which we asked in our of 6 Dec. and saying we should be glad to have an answer with regard to the proposed rate for maize at the earliest opportunity as there may yet be time to bring the rate into force for this years Crop and explain that so far as we can judge, the proposed rate is an average rate of about 1/3d. per ton per mile."[36]

Fiddes in his minute expressed his concurrence with Read's comment but stated that the reduction would have only applied to maize.[37] Seeley supported the latter as he stated, the Treasury should be reminded that the governor has "special experience of railway working."[38] Crewe agreed with Seeley's minute and instructed Fiddes to draft a letter to the Lord Commissioners of the Treasury.[39] Therefore, a dispatch, dated 17 January 1910 with an enclosure of Sir Percy's request in his telegram of 10 January 1910, was addressed to the Secretary of the Treasury, requesting the Lord Commissioners of the Treasury to reconsider their decision in respect of maize only.[40] The Commissioners, who had the last word on the management of the finances of the Uganda Railway, refused to approve Sir Percy's request for a reconsideration of the rate.[41]

Sir Percy's proposal and the position of the Treasury on the reduction of the rate were one of the initial difficulties occasioned by Sir Percy's proposed desire for a speedy acceleration of the economic development of the protectorate. The Treasury's attitude right from the start suggested that it would not be easy for Sir Percy to have his way despite the approval of the CO of his proposed economic development of the colony. But it was left for Sir Percy to devise other means to secure the consent of the Treasury.

In reaction to the Treasury's rejection of his application and in an effort to press the Treasury to agree, be addressed a private letter of 14 June 1910 to Seeley, intimating to him his disappointment with the Lord Commissioners of the Treasury for rejecting his application. Sir Percy told Seeley that all his requests were denied by the CO, and even the railway rates reduction that were approved by the CO were defeated by the Treasury.[42] Seeley replied to Sir Percy, in a telegram of 9 July 1910, intimating to him that he would look into the question of the rates.[43] Thereafter, Seeley transmitted Sir Percy's requests and grievances to Crewe, in a private letter of 1 August 1910 for further consideration.[44]

In the CO, Read minuted that "we must try to get Sir P. Girouard into a more cheerful frame of mind."[45] Read added, "I have remembered the point in his letter when he says that the lower rates have been defeated by the Treasury, I assumed that he is referring to the rates other than those on maize and beans."[46] Read commented further that he had the understanding that Sir Percy wanted to lower rates on such commodities which he wanted to start export trade with.[47] In the case of the other articles, Read stated, "Sir Percy was anxious to be given permission to reduce rates, if necessary to 1/2d. per ton per mile, but the Treasury fenced the concessions by so many safeguards" that made it practically difficult to move them lower than Sir Percy had anticipated.[48] Read added, "So long as the Treasury retain their antiquated ideas about these matters," he could not think any progress could be made.[49] Read added that they have sent "official letter to the Treasury" over the issue but no progress had been made, unless Crewe or Seeley could approach the Treasury, privately.[50]

Upon such approach, and subsequent meeting between Fiddes, Read, and Cranworth of the Treasury, Sir Percy secured the approval of the Treasury on the lower rates for coastward shipments on the Uganda Railway.[51] Thereafter, in a further reply to Sir Percy, in a confidential letter of 31 July 1910, Seeley stated that the issue of the rates had been revisited, and he should expect the Lord Commissioners approval soon.[52]

The success of Sir Percy's economic development policy depended on low rates as an inducement for farmers to produce more and he recommended for the railway rate of 1/3d. on a coastward bound shipment of products for export. But the Treasury refused and retained its 1/2d. per ton per mile which they considered as a generous concession on products for export. The Treasury had the final word on the Uganda Railway, having invested an enormous sum of money for its construction. Therefore, if Sir Percy would be given a free hand on the railway, such approval would have to be granted by the Lord Commissioners of the Treasury. The commissioners refused to grant such a free hand to Sir Percy, considering that the railway rate was reduced to the lowest barest minimum, recently. The reduction in railway rates had been Sir Percy's policy of moving the economy forward.

It could be recalled that Sir Percy had insisted on a low rates, when he was the railway commissioner of the Transvaal colony. But Milner refused, believing that the reduction would be inimical to the colony, pointing out that Sir Percy had already imposed low rates, which made it difficult for the colony to balance its annual budget. Therefore, he refused any reduction of the rates; pointing out that the railway had to pay and the profit from the railway would be invested elsewhere for the development of the colony. In fact it was the disagreement over the railway rates that led to the resignation of Sir Percy as commissioner of the Transvaal railways.

Therefore, the question of low rates would not help move the colony forward, rather it would stagnate further investment, as it would take a long time before the railway could pay, and to invest the profit from the railway in other areas for the development of the colony. Therefore, even though the Treasury consented to the idea, it did not lead to the economic development of the colony, in view of the insignificant number of the European famers who were afforded low rates on the Uganda Railway.

In essence Sir Percy failed to learn a lesson from his attempted effort to lower the rates on the Transvaal railways, when he was the railway director in that colony. Even though, the reduction had been considered, that did not improve or encourage the European agricultural production for export. It turned out to be an ineffective policy instrument for the economic development of the country. In this regard, Sir Percy did not appraise the condition critically or his policy had not proved to be a gateway to the economic success that suggested that he had not been informed of the nature of the economy in that country to warrant his proposed economic policy.

Another aspect of Sir Percy's economic development policy involved the construction of branch or adjunct railways. Sir Percy believed that improved transport infrastructure would enhance the EAP's prosperity, but here, as with his proposed reduction of railway rates, the policy he advocated failed to deliver the promised results. This will be illustrated by examining Sir Percy's advocacy for and administration of the Nairobi-Fort Hall-Thika railway project and the Magadi Railway.

NAIROBI-FORT HALL-THIKA RAILWAY

A railway linking Nairobi to Fort Hall, later altered to connect the capital of the protectorate only with Thika, the site of several European settler estates, was the first to be taken up by Sir Percy. It was to provide a feeder line that would join the main Uganda Railway at Nairobi. Such a line to connect Nairobi with Thika and Fort Hall had been proposed to the CO in 1906, and the then parliamentary undersecretary of State, Winston Churchill, enthusiastically endorsed it.[53] Sir Percy soon came to the view that it was necessary to revisit the question of building adjunct railways so as to provide the desired transportation to support his economic development policy.[54] Such railways would provide the means for shipping commodities from productive agricultural centers of the colony as well as increasing the colony's receipts from the working of the line.[55] Churchill's visit to the protectorate in 1907 further reinforced the interest in railway development, both in the EAP and in London. Churchill was impressed with the cultivation in the Embu area to the northeast of Nairobi and indicated that the CO could consider application for railway extension to the productive areas.[56]

Later that year, a reconnaissance survey was sponsored by the East Africa and Uganda Corporation. Captain A. G. Stevenson carried out the survey for a railway from Nairobi through Thika and Fort Hall to Embu. Stevenson's report suggested that the railway of around 99 miles would be relatively easy to construct and would be economically viable.[57] However, the corporation did not follow up the survey with action to undertake construction of a rail line. It was Sir Percy who revisited the idea of a railway from Nairobi to Thika and Fort Hall. Soon after his arrival, he visited various areas lying some distance from Nairobi where European settlers had started farming. The settlers around Thika who were developing sisal and coffee estates impressed him, but he was also struck by the fact that their farming was hindered by the absence of a reliable transport. As noted in the previous chapter, Sir Percy hoped to facilitate European export production as the mainstay of the protectorate's economy and he believed that if the European farmers could be induced to produce more export crops it would improve the economy of the EAP.[58]

Therefore, Sir Percy told Crewe, in telegram of 1 April 1910, that the desire to build the railway was not primarily motivated by the need for economic development. Rather he emphasized that the need for the railway was dictated by the unfolding ecological and environmental problems of the area under consideration for the rail link.[59]

The road between Nairobi and Thika had been closed due to the outbreak of the cattle disease, East Coast Fever, and the government had quarantined the Nairobi and Fort Hall areas for a period of two or three years. It was out of such circumstances that Sir Percy sought a means to ease these transportation difficulties by revisiting the question of the construction of a Nairobi to Thika railway.[60] At this point, Sir Percy had provided little more than a justification for the line. He gave no detailed information as to the possible costs of construction, nor did he provide detailed estimates as to the type and amount of traffic that might be anticipated if the railway was built. The CO and the Treasury would not be likely to approve such a scheme without information such as estimated costs of construction and possible traffic on the proposed route. But when Sir Percy followed up in a telegram of 9 April 1910, he stated that he could not provide an exact estimate of imaginary traffic; however, he was confident there would be more production in the region that would be served by the rail line in the following year as European farmers were bringing more land under cultivation in view of the anticipated reduction of railway rates. Production during the current year had been hampered by drought, he added, but there was no doubt in the governor's mind that the proposed line would cover the cost of its construction.[61] Sir Percy added that the area under discussion could produce two harvests a year, especially maize and beans, but not much had been produced by African farmers because of the high cost of shipping. With modern transport available in the form of a railway or tramway, large quantities of produce would be raised, according to Sir Percy, as the large numbers of Kikuyu living near the line would raise large quantities of maize and beans.[62]

However, the CO was not impressed with this explanation. Officials there wanted more precise details as to the cost of construction and assurance that the imperial investment in the line would be realized. This meant that some specific information as to costs of construction and the expected traffic were necessary before the CO could take any action in recommending this scheme to the Treasury. Crewe made these points in a telegram to Sir Percy on 27 April 1910. The telegram emphasized also that the CO wanted specific details so as not to be faced, when the current emergency situation was over, by a demand that the proposed line could only be made to pay by a further extension.[63]

More than a month after Sir Percy first raised the issue of the rail line, he finally responded with more detail. Yet he still hesitated in giving precise estimates as to the cost of construction and the prospect for traffic in the post emergency period. His estimates of the latter were general, but he noted that both European and African producers in the region would likely harvest between 200 and 400 tons of produce. Sir Percy also told Crewe that there were an increased number of settlers taking up farms around Thika and that there was potential for increased production among Kikuyu peasants. However, he could not give details to "annual expenditure and receipts. . . ." He stated that the cost of construction would nevertheless be recovered.[64] As to the estimate of cost of construction of what he now termed a tramway, Sir Percy gave a rough figure of £2,000 per mile. Further, Sir Percy told Crewe that he was prepared to raise capital charges from specific savings. The construction would thus serve as an object lesson in the construction and development of lines in the EAP so that its success would prove that the construction of such a line was the proper way to promote economic development.[65] Sir Percy also reminded Crewe that Churchill had travelled through the region and would surely support the railway scheme. Thus the governor urged for swift action in favor of the proposed line as he also promised to obtain £20,000 locally if the Treasury could provide £40,000.[66]

The CO now had more details of Sir Percy's railway/ tramway scheme, but officials were not filled with enthusiasm for the governor's plan. It had taken some time to obtain more details of the scheme, but uncertainty remained. Butler undertook a detailed examination of the issue, and his minute indicated a lack of confidence in Sir Percy as well as uncertainty that the CO could trust him as the man on the spot.[67] These were significant issues as this would not be the last time that the CO would suspect that Sir Percy was not telling the whole story, or providing sufficient details, in support of a course of action he enthusiastically proposed.

To start with, Butler was not convinced by Sir Percy's estimates of the costs of construction. Butler noted the lack of convincing data that the capital for the construction could be met from savings made on expenditure approved for the 1910–11 financial year.[68] Butler was also doubtful that the £20,000 Sir Percy promised to raise would be forthcoming. He stated: "this is a clear case of £20,000 in the bush."[69] He also worried about the lack of detail as to how the money raised for construction would actually be spent when he minuted that "the whole question is surrounded by considerable doubt."[70] Despite these doubts, Butler was still willing, in May of 1910, to trust the judgment of the man on the spot. The governor's strong assurance "that it will be all right in the end" seemed to Butler to mean that the CO should forward the scheme to the Treasury for their approval despite his concern that it was "taking a big step in the dark" in their reliance on "the judgment of the personality of the Governor."[71] Since Sir Percy indicated that the proposal was a vital one, Butler ruled out rejecting his proposed railway/tramway line even though he minuted: "I cannot say that I personally feel very uncomfortable in being forced to that conclusion."[72] He recognized the possibility that Sir Percy might be misleading the CO and that the Treasury might in any case reject his plan, but he proposed to go ahead and submit the scheme to the Treasury with a request of approval of the funds requested.[73]

Seeley also advocated despite doubts that the Treasury would approve. It was the "man on the spot" argument that proved influential in Seeley's decision. He noted that he did not subscribe to that belief in every situation in the colonies, but Sir Percy's presumed knowledge of local conditions and expert knowledge in the field of transport caused Seeley to trust the man on spot who knew more about "such matters than most men."[74] Crewe also subscribed to this ideal when he minuted that Sir Percy had "special capabilities" for judging the position with regard to transport. However, he added an interesting observation that will be important to remember in assessing this issue as well as Sir Percy's administration more generally. Crewe noted that a man in such a responsible position as governor "ought to be given a chance." He added, Sir Percy might make it or make mistakes.[75] On the strength of these opinions, the CO addressed a dispatch to the Treasury seeking approval for Sir Percy's proposed railway/tramway. The CO included all correspondence on the subject with the dispatch and justified the request by the need to rely on the judgment of the governor.[76] The latter statement suggests that the CO was not comfortable with certain aspects of the scheme, such as the fact that the scheme would immediately pay for itself, but Crewe felt he had no option than to accept Sir Percy's proposal. In the dispatch to the Treasury, the CO requested a loan of £40,000 be advanced to Sir Percy for the construction of twenty miles of tramway. The construction of the remaining 10 miles would depend on Sir Percy realizing the savings of £20,000 he had promised.[77]

However, the Treasury refused to approve the request. The Treasury replied on 6 June that they could not sanction the construction of the proposed line, and instead they recommended either an improved system of motor transport or a monorail.[78] Both these alternatives were presumed to be less expensive than the proposal from Sir Percy. Crewe transmitted the Treasury's decision to Sir Percy in a telegram of 10 June 1910 together with a request for his comments.[79]

SIR PERCY'S TRAMWAY

With the rejection of his proposal, Sir Percy now had not only to comment on the Treasury suggestion of motor traffic or monorail, but he needed to come up with some means of overcoming the skepticism of the CO and the Treasury. He now took up advocacy for a tramway as an easier undertaking than a railway he had proposed; he just changed the name but not the proposed project. It was merely a means to try to get around the refusal of the Treasury.

Sir Percy replied to Crewe's transmission of the Treasury decision in a telegram of 16 June 1910. He first made clear the impossibility of using road transport instead of a rail line by claiming that "efficient system of motor traffic" would require larger expenditure than could be justified for that class of transport.[80] As to the idea of a monorail, Sir Percy stated that an experiment in Kampala was successful, and it could be suitable for the EAP. Thus Sir Percy recommended the construction of a monorail. Considering the topography of the country, this was the type of rail line that would work better in the EAP.[81] But just two days later, Sir Percy had a change of mind. He sent another telegram to Crewe on 18 June 1910 in which he sought to clarify his position. It was a substantial clarification as he now told Crewe that he was not recommending a monorail for the EAP; rather he was suggesting that reference might be made to consulting engineers. But he went further in stating a preference for the construction of a tramway that could use the old rolling stock of the Uganda Railway, as the best solution to the transport problem.[82]

In addition, Sir Percy indicated a preference for a tramway because of the topography of the country could not afford either motor or monorail traffic with relative ease. He further justified his support for a tramway by stating again that if the tramway was approved, he could find £20,000 from local sources to support the construction.[83] From the contents of the two telegrams, it was clear that Sir Percy's telegram of 18 June 1910 was a retraction of one of his recommendations that the CO should consider a monorail for the EAP. He now advocated the building of a tramway to relieve the serious transport situation. He once again claimed that such a line would assist in the development of the large agricultural district inhabited by Kikuyu, where a million Africans, as well as some European settlers, were working to develop agricultural commodities for sale.[84]

The ball was now in the CO's court. In an attempt to clarify the situation and reach consensus on the revised proposal of Sir Percy, a conference took place between Read and Butler of the CO and Mr. Cawston of the Treasury. As a result of the conference the CO and the Treasury ruled out the monorail idea, but they decided before considering the tramway scheme that further information should be sought from Sir Percy. Thus a telegram of 28 June 1910 was addressed to the governor, demanding to know the actual cost of "Fort Hall motor transport, if the road were made suitable."[85] The telegram also asked for the cost to the government if the colonial state had to provide vehicles to haul the goods and passengers by road.[86]

Sir Percy replied in a telegram of 3 July 1910 that it would cost £54,000 to make the Fort Hall road suitable for motor traffic. This was clearly not a cheap alternative. Sir Percy added that available motor vehicles could carry very little, and it would be necessary for such carriers to charge high rates.[87] On the strength of Sir Percy's telegram, the CO sent a letter to the Treasury, pointing out it was useless to seek a remedy to the transport issue by any other scheme than a tramway. Crewe also reiterated that Sir Percy was confident that a tramway represented a cheaper alternative.[88] These arguments did little as the Treasury refused to accept Sir Percy's proposal. The Treasury replied to Sir Percy on 5 September 1910, pointing out that the information furnished with regard to the proposal was insufficient for the Lord Commissioners of the Treasury to approve the construction of the line. The Treasury agreed to approve the scheme only if they could be availed with a full explanation, including details of the estimates of costs of construction and equipment together with a report on the nature of the traffic likely to be forthcoming.[89]

This continued lack of approval for a scheme that Sir Percy's expertise should have facilitated raises interesting and important issues with regard to his administration. Even after prolonged correspondence, the CO and the Treasury were unwilling to give way to the wishes of the man on the spot. Crewe might hope that Sir Percy be allowed to make it or make mistakes, but the Treasury was not willing to do so without precise and detailed information. Sir Percy's changes of mind as to monorail, tramway or railway were another factor that did not count very heavily in his favor. In fact this episode points to future problems for Sir Percy. His seeming unwillingness or inability to provide all the details desired in London were troubling. He wanted to be given a free hand, as the man on the spot, to solve a transportation problem regarding which he was an expert. But he had not acted in ways that gained the confidence of the CO. He had yet to achieve success some five months after he initiated his proposal for the railway/tramway. The suspicion his actions aroused among his superiors and with the Treasury were indeed characteristics of a less than stellar administrator.

Nevertheless, Sir Percy kept plugging away in support of the line from Nairobi to Thika and Fort Hall. For example, he sent a confidential dispatch to the CO on 1 November 1910 in which he provided estimates for a railway line thirty-one miles long which would cost £60,000.[90] Sir Percy now estimated that the actual traffic would amount to 70,000 or 80,000 tons annually; mainly maize and beans, and that passengers and casual goods traffic should also be expected on this route.[91] These new estimates did not end the correspondence of the adjunct railway. The CO made a further request for more precise information as to potential receipts as well as estimates for the annual cost of working and maintenance.[92] While in London in December, Sir Percy provided revised estimates on all these matters.[93]

Even upon the receipt of new estimates of the cost of construction and profit on the traffic that would be carried, there remained doubts in the CO, and approval for the project dragged on. Butler, for example, was concerned that Sir Percy had not appraised the question of costs and prospects of a tramway adequately.[94] Despite misgivings, the CO continued to back Sir Percy's proposal. In a dispatch of 10 February 1911 Crewe included the tramway proposal as one of three schemes to be funded by a loan of 250,000 from the Treasury.[95] Thus the tramway was approved during 1911 with this funding. When constructed to Thika, it was a railway built by the protectorate's public works department.[96]

From the foregoing discussion, it is clear that the information on the scheme provided by Sir Percy was not useful in consideration of its merits by the CO and the Treasury, in spite of the fact that it was presumed there that Sir Percy, having considerable knowledge and experience of railways, would develop the infrastructure of the colony. His performance with regard to projecting the cost of construction and effectively advocating for the approval of his scheme raised question as to Sir Percy's competence in coming up with vital information. This caused a long delay in approval and suggests that he was not a great developer and administrator who could collect relevant information as well as gauge conditions to provide useful information that would enhance the development of the railway and the colony as a whole.

It was very clear that the CO and the Treasury did not approve the project initially because they were not satisfied with Sir Percy's explanation as to the scheme. Rather they approved the scheme after a prolonged hesitation, doubt and caution that Sir Percy might not be providing the right information. In this instance, they eventually took risk to approve it, believing that he might be right in his proposition rather than that he would be mistaken. Later in 1911, however, another secretary of state found out to his dismay that Sir Percy's poorly developed recommendations and concealed motives could lead to great embarrassment and threaten the reputation of Britain as a colonial power.

The CO took the risk in approving the project not because they were satisfied with Sir Percy's explanation, but because he was the man on the spot, as Seeley had pointed out earlier. The CO caved in to Sir Percy in the end despite the uncomfortable feelings because they wanted to give him the benefit of the doubt. Yet this formed an unhappy precedent for future troubles that spelled the end for Sir Percy as a colonial administrator.

MAGADI RAILWAY

Sir Percy's part in the building of the railway to Lake Magadi, on the other hand, presents a different example of his role as a railway expert, developer of infrastructure, and facilitator of colonial economic development. The Magadi

Soda Company proposed the construction of the railway. It intended to ship soda ash from Lake Magadi to the coast via the Uganda Railway. The line also became known as the Magadi-Konza railway that joined the Uganda Railway at mile 267.

The working of the soda deposits was expected to produce wealth for the colony, and a railway was required to move the soda ash to the world market. Sir Percy came into the affair of the railway on the ground that the company's activities would benefit the economic development of the colony. Sir Percy thus did not initiate the idea of the railway line. However, he wasted little time in supporting the company's endeavor and facilitated the granting of concessions to the company. He advocated for government support for the railway's construction and purchase of rolling stock. He facilitated this funding in his approaches to the CO, and he was also instrumental in obtaining land for the company at Kilindini in Mombasa.

Finally, he was prepared to overlook the terms of the 1904 agreement between the Maasai and the British government so as to enable the company to obtain land for housing staff near Lake Magadi as well for the water supply for the soda plant and its workers.

Sir Percy was keen to promote economic development through European enterprise, as noted earlier in this chapter. In 1909, for example, he advocated that the British government should sponsor an order for new rolling stock for the Magadi railway before construction had started or the company now holding the concession, Messrs. Samuel & Co., had even exercised their option for the lease and the right to construct a railway.[97] At the CO, Butler was hesitant to support Sir Percy's recommendation as he felt it was difficult to ask the Treasury to provide the rolling stock before "we know whether the soda is going to be worked."[98] He felt sure the Treasury would feel the company was trying to rush them.[99] Early in his governorship, just as late, Sir Percy had no hesitation in rushing to demand action from the CO without contemplating the consequences of hasty action.

The question of constructing a pier at Kilindini for the company also saw Sir Percy move quickly to use state resources for the benefit of the company. Samuel & Co. approached the CO prior to Sir Percy's assumption of government to demand that larger facilities were needed at Mombasa if their export of soda ash was to be successful. The company was especially concerned that their operations would be seriously hampered if they could not have adequate storage space for soda ash cargoes since it might within the same fortnight be compelled to ship full cargoes to Britain, Europe, "ports in the East," and to America. Thus Samuel & Co. took the view that they should have a storage facility for 50,000 tons of soda at Kilindini. The company pressured the CO to state its position on what it viewed as a critical matter.[100]

Soon after Sir Percy took charge in Nairobi, the issue came before him for action. The CO asked him if there was available land at Kilindini for purchase by the colonial state. Crewe observed that the land at around Kilindini harbor will probably become extremely valuable, and it would be unwise not to wait for any better opportunity to present itself for buying land which might eventually be required for important harbor works at Kilindini.[101] Sir Percy took the request seriously and in a telegram of 19 November 1909, he reported that there were "70 acres of land in the possession of an Indian which blocked the development of Kilindini."[102] Sir Percy told Crewe that he planned to purchase the said land at a cost of £4,000 and to debit the railway capital account.[103] Sir Percy claimed that the purchase should be carried out now as he expected that the land would reach a very high price soon. The CO staff agreed with Sir Percy's recommended course of action and moved quickly to obtain funds from the Treasury so that plans for construction of a deep-water pier could begin as soon as possible.[104] As noted earlier in the chapter, funding for the completion of wharfs and storage buildings for the company's use was provided by the protectorate.

Here again, Sir Percy's action was more those of facilitation rather than an initiator of infrastructure that was to benefit the colony as well as the company. In doing so, his action has come in for criticism as using state resources too freely to promote the economic interest of one company and single industry rather than the entire colony and other users of the railway. The port facilities constructed by the government proved to be very lucrative and, some might argue, an unfair concession for the company, and Sir Percy started the process.[105]

Sir Percy also initiated another controversial and, strictly speaking, illegal action on behalf of the company developing the soda ash resource at Lake Magadi. The company felt that the climate at Lake Magadi was too hot for Europeans to reside there and requested to be allowed to lease land at Ngong to build houses for European staff. The land lay within that reserved for the Maasai under the terms of the 1904 treaty. Sir Percy was prepared to ignore the treaty and its clear guarantee that it was to remain in Maasai possession and could not be allowed to Europeans as he agreed to a lease for the Magadi Soda Company.[106] This, of course, would not be the last time that Sir Percy was to ignore the terms of the 1904 treaty with the Maasai, and, as was the case with his action in 1911, Sir Percy's participation left a lot to be desired and created problems for the CO and the British government for years to come.

Matters discussed so far suggest that Sir Percy's economic understanding of the best means to promote economic development were not impressive and the results inadequate. This came also in question in a particularly important issue that had a huge impact on Kenya's future. This was in his failure to carefully study the prevailing economic situation in the EAP as he sought to recommend the type of productive system the protectorate's economic development should follow. Sir Percy knew that the development of an export economy for the country was a vital key to economic solvency. In seeking to overcome the significant contradiction noted at the start of this chapter, Sir Percy failed to note and take advantage of the clear statistical information as to the sale and export of commodities produced in the EAP. Ainsworth demonstrated that peasant production could provide exports. Sir Percy could have used state resources to back both peasant and settler production as a means of dealing with the contradictions that he inherited.[107] Yet he did neither.

ECONOMIC ACTIVITIES

Sir Percy proposed the development of an export economy for the country for the eventual solvency of its economic predicament. He based his proposition on the export of European agricultural products, which he supported by concessions on import and export duties. On the other hand, he did not support African production, believing that it was the European production that could turn the tide of the economy. Sir Percy was confident that the introduction and cultivation of European agricultural commodities for export would produce what could support the country's needs, and surplus products could be exported for the country to earn the desired duties. Therefore, Sir Percy was open to supporting the settlers' agricultural production for the eventual solvency of the country's economic predicament.

One of the misapprehensions of policy that Sir Percy brought to bear on his agricultural development policy was separate agricultural development. In this regard, Sir Percy considered that it was the settlers' production that could lead to the economic prosperity of the country. He had not considered any positive contribution from other races; the Indians and the Africans. All his support on agricultural development was geared toward supporting the settlers' production to the detriment of the Indians and the Africans who were also active in agricultural cultivation and trade. In this, Sir Percy failed to note and take advantage of the future impact of his economic development policy.

In his drive to afford a priority for settler-cultivation, Sir Percy refused to listen to any contradictory advice. He did not believe that it would take years before settler production in the highlands could contribute to agricultural development. As to the preposition advocated by John Ainsworth that production in the Nyanza basin would have to support the white highlands, the area where the Europeans lived and had their farms, Sir Percy disagreed.

Referring to this issue in his Main Report, completed in 1910, Sir Percy told Crewe, without mentioning Ainsworth by name, that as they had attracted the white population into the protectorate, they were morally bound to support them "in proving this beautiful and attractive region."[108]

Sir Percy was wrong in his assessment, as it was the coast and the Nyanza basin that paved the way for the economic prosperity of the protectorate, especially in agricultural production, rather than his presumption that the white highlands would provide the economic development the colony needed. It was African production in the Nyanza basin that provided the bulk of the produce exported that helped the protectorate to earn revenue and do away with the grants-in-aid from the British government, beginning from the 1912–13 fiscal year.[109]

The latter development suggested that Sir Percy had not appraised the condition of the country sufficiently to inform his proposed European agricultural development for export trade on the highlands only, disregarding other areas for development. It also suggested that Sir Percy was not abreast with the conditions to recommend a better alternative, or conducive areas, where the government could invest so as to afford the country the desired economic prosperity. His vision of transforming a peasant economic production to an agricultural production where, industry, wage labor and mechanized agriculture would have been the norm failed as he limited his policy to a few Europeans whose production could barely support subsistence let alone consider production for export.

He aimed for an economy oriented toward the production of desired metropolitan agricultural products for its industries. Such a policy would provide receipts for the Uganda railway by means of shipment of goods, and export duty receipts for the country. Therefore, Sir Percy considered the presence of European settlers would best help develop the colony through export trade. But the task was beyond the numerical strength of the Europeans whose production in 1912, amounted to 20,000 bags of maize being exported to the European market.[110]

The prosperity of the colony viz-viz other crown colonies, on the west coast of Africa and in the South Africa, might have informed his decision to develop export trade. By this measure, Sir Percy hoped that the colony could generate the desired revenue to fund its administration and do away with the annual grants-in-aid from the British Treasury.[111] The question of development of agriculture for exports and the generation of the desired receipts for the colony's economic prosperity, was not only a priority to Sir Percy, but also to the CO and the British Treasury which had to support the country with grants-in-aid.[112] It was the colony's dependence on grants-in-aid, which prompted Sir Percy's economic development policy so that the country could be self-supporting.[113]

But as Sir Percy was determined to raise the country to a new economic height, he introduced the reduction of railway rates as an incentive that could spur farmers to produce for export from which the government could levy duties on both exports and imports with a view to funding the government fiscal expenditure.[114] But the extent to which his policy could achieve the latter goal remained a distant possibility, having failed to objectively appraise whether or not his proposed policy could provide the desired outcome.

It was very clear that in 1909, the agricultural exports of the colony were not enough to support its financial needs. The African production for export in 1909 stood at 75 percent and in 1910, it decreased to 74 percent, while in 1911, 1912, and 1913, the percentages were 61, 66, and 68 percent of the total exports respectively. On the other hand, the European production for export in 1909 and 1910, were 1 and 3 percent of the total. While in 1911, 1912, and 1913, they were 7, 8, and 12 percent, respectively.[115] Based on these economic statistics, it is clear that during Sir Percy's term of office the protectorate's exports came mostly from African production. But it was also on record that the economic success of the country was not because of Sir Percy's economic policy, but it owed its success to the African farmers, receipts from poll and hut taxes, and duties from export of goods originating from neighboring colonies, as well as the changing economic logic of the time that produced demands of commodities that were chiefly found or exported from the East Africa rather than the handiwork of Sir Percy.[116] It could be seen from the colony's agricultural output that the policy that turned the tide of the economy lacked support from Sir Percy. This could be seen from the economic activities of the colony that it was the African peasant production, especially from Nyanza, that accelerated the economic development of the country rather than Sir Percy's economic development policy. Sir Percy's economic development policy was designed for the European settlers, who were numerically too small to effect any change. The major export commodities that Sir Percy hoped to be the bulk of the colony's exports, once the European settler-economy developed, would be wheat, coffee, and sisal, among other things. As he was determined to develop the settler economy, he afforded them all the support and encouragement they needed to produce.[117]

Sir Percy's proposed economic development strategy would only be possible when farms were made accessible to prospective settlers who could invest in agriculture. But in view of the lack of a land policy that could provide access to farms with relative ease and also provide safeguards against land accumulation and dummying, the proposed economic development by means of European agricultural cultivation could not have a chance of success, as there was no adequate legislation on the land alienation and allocation to afford prospective farmers easy access to farmland.[118] In addition to the latter, there was the issue of competing land title claims on the coast,

African land policy, and Arab land tenure system governed by Islamic law.[119] All these conditions became a difficulty for Sir Percy's government in coming up with a uniform land policy that could provide easy access to farmland for European settlers so that cultivation could commence with a view to accentuating exports production of the colony.[120] This was in addition to the delay and uncertainty that occasioned the execution of his proposed estimates for the project.

However, the African production, which lacked the support from the government, eventually turned the economic tide of the protectorate, rather than the settler production.[121] African exports of favored agricultural products to neighboring countries earned both the peasants and the colony incomes for further investment.[122] Therefore, the increasing economic prosperity of the colony during Sir Percy's tour of duty was, to a large extent, occasioned by the change in the global socioeconomic and political logic of the time, rather than the performance of Sir Percy's reduction of coastward rates and the subsequent agricultural products being exported.[123] In this regard, Sir Percy's shortsighted vision of economic development, by limited production by a few, failed to afford the country the desired result. This suggested that Sir Percy had not made sound assessment of the colony's economic problems so as to be in a position to provide remedies.

The CO presumed that Sir Percy could fix the economic problems of the country, in view of his past record of performance, especially in the development of railways in the Sudan, Northern Nigeria, and the Transvaal. But that did not happen, and, instead, he failed to effect the economic development he proposed on his assumption of the government.[124] Therefore, to be judged as a fine administrator, Sir Percy's performance should have been above board as for the development of agricultural production for export.[125] He should have drawn from his experience of Northern Nigeria where the African peasants produced the bulk of groundnuts exported out of the country. Northern Nigeria, unlike the EAP, was not a settler colony, where color set the preference in the application of policy. But economic production for exports, designed to earn receipts from duties, should have been extended to whatever group that was judged to have the capability of production for exports rather than limiting state support to the very few. This was surely a missed opportunity for Kenya's future economic development. Sir Percy had the ear of the CO at the start of his term, and he could have moved Kenya's economy away from dependence of European producers, but he chose to ignore economic facts and base his policies on racist conceptions of political economy.

A final example of Sir Percy's inadequate development record may be gained by a close study of the EAP's economic statistics for the period of his governorship. The detail that follow on the progress of the economy, year by year, offers insight into the gradual but sustained economic growth in exports as well as in revenue. These statistics, as well as the information provided from government reports pertaining to these subjects, provide the final means of evaluating Sir Percy's governorship in terms of economic development policy as well as in revenue.

EXPORTS AND REVENUE

Expansion in value of export and the detail on the progression of the economy, year by year, offer insight into the gradual but sustained economic growth in exports as well as in revenue. The expansion in value of exports and in the protectorate's revenue marked the years of Sir Percy's governorship. However, an examination of the export and revenue statistics shows that in certain areas the growth had little connection to, or was not impacted by, the introduction of Sir Percy's economic development policy. Statistics for the financial years 1908–09 through 1912–13 clearly illustrated this point. For 1908–09, the year before Sir Percy assumed leadership of the colonial state, revenue amounted to £485,668 with the imperial grant-in-aid at £138,000. Among the main heads under revenue were customs duties, the hut tax paid by African households, and revenue generated by the railway.[126] For 1909–10, revenue increased to £503,040 while for 1910–11 a further increase to £609,586 was recorded. Railway earnings, increased customs revenue, and expanded collection of hut and poll tax provided the bulk of the increase.[127] For 1911–12, Sir Percy's last year in charge, revenue reached £729,078. Of this, hut and poll tax reached its highest ever figure, £146,215, a clear indication of an ever greater African contribution to revenue and a reflection of growing production and sale of commodities for export. For 1912–13, revenue increased by 30 percent and reached an all-time high of £952,525. For the first time since the establishment of the EAP, no grant-in-aid was received from the British government.[128]

The improved revenue situation owed much to increases in value of the protectorate's exports during these years. This was reflected in increasing revenue from custom duties, hut and poll tax receipts, and railway income. For 1908–09, exports totaled £436,313 in value, during the following year these rose to £590,057. These figures included exports from Uganda, German East Africa and the Belgium Congo. The value of the protectorate's exports alone was £190,668 for 1909–10. For 1910–11, exports value expanded dramatically to £276,489. For the year ending 31 March 1912, the value of exports rose to £333,670. As mentioned earlier in the chapter, the bulk of this expanded export production came from African peasants, especially those in Nyanza Province. The accompanying table, which shows the origin of the protectorate's exports from African and European producers, demonstrates the point. During 1911–12, for example, grains produced by Africans increased by 90 percent in value and reached a peak £108,568, surpassing hides and skins as the protectorate's leading exports by value.[129] Exports of sim sim and maize, largely from Nyanza led to increases.[130] For example, over 8,000 tons of maize was exported from Nyanza Province. The province was now the railway's best customer, and it also contributed most to the protectorate's hut and poll tax receipts. During 1911–12, for example, £57,676 was collected

Table 6.1 Shows the Protectorates Products Produced by Each of the Races of the Protectorate and Its Exports Thereon

Category	*1908*	*1909*	*1910*	*1911*	*1912*	*1913*
African						
Hide and Skin	26	40	40	33	23	37
Maize	—	1	5	—	—	—
Beans and Peas	1	3	4	3	5	5
Sim sim	—	16	13	15	14	20
Oil seeds linseed, cotton, castor, sim sim	—	1	—	2	1	—
Other grains (millet, rice)	—	—	—	—	1	—
Cotton	6	7	5	2	13	1
Groundnut	1	—	1	1	2	2
Gee	5	2	3	3	3	1
Potatoes	6	5	3	2	4	2
Total percentage	45	75	74	61	66	68
European Settler						
Coffee	—	1	1	3	2	5
Sisal	—	—	—	—	1	2
Other Fiber	—	—	—	—	1	2
Plantation Rubber	—	—	—	1	1	1
Wool	2	—	2	3	3	2
Total Percentage	2	1	3	7	8	12
Miscellaneous						
Coconuts/Copra	29	14	15	11	4	7
Gum copal	1	1	1	1	—	1
Bee wax	19	5	6	5	3	2
Wild Animal Skins	3	3	1	1	1	1
Wild Rubber	—	—	—	5	2	1
Mangrove bark	1	1	—	—	—	—
Total percentage	53	24	23	23	10	12
Mix	—	—	—	—	—	—
Maize	—	—	—	9	16	8
Percentage total	—	—	—	9	16	8

* This denotes export of product was under half of one percent.

** This denotes that export after 1910 came from African and European farmers as well, but no recorded export had been made.

Source: Maxon, *Struggle for Kenya*, 32.

in Nyanza, almost 40 percent of the total collected for the year.[131] The export from Nyanza African farmers owed the success to the efforts of Ainsworth who ensured Africans were allowed to work on their farms and that seeds were distributed to them, rather than being coerced to work for wages on the European farms and estates.[132]

From the above table it could be understood that substantial increase in agricultural exports came from the African peasants. In 1908, the African Peasant production stood at 45 percent, but by 1909 to 1913, African peasant generated more than half of the export of the commodities. The commodities that feature prominently in the exports were maize, cotton, beans, peas and sim sim.[133]

CONCLUSION

Sir Percy's proposed policy had been approved when the CO accepted his request and the Treasury approved lowering the rate, but not without a lengthy correspondence and frustration on the part of Sir Percy, in view of the Treasury's hold on the affairs of the Uganda railway. It also had to cause the intervention of Seeley before the CO could press on the Treasury to consider the question of the rate in favor of Sir Percy's recommendations. But the lowering of the rates did not ameliorate the economic condition of the Europeans, as it had not encouraged production substantially.

Where it did, the output of the farmers was hampered by chronic droughts, especially in 1910–11 harvests. The question of lowering rates as a policy of development had not to a large extent achieved the desired result. As for the agricultural production, there were considerable improvements in production, but it could not make any significant impact on the country, as the Europeans were too small to effect the economic development of the entire colony. In view of the limited numerical strength of the Europeans, and government assistance in providing seeds, land allotments were not easy to come by, making it difficult for the European farmers to achieve their desired production, their numerical strength notwithstanding.

It was true that during Sir Percy's administration the country achieved its economic height, when it was able to do away with a grant-in-aid from the British government. But it was also clear that it was not the economic policies of Sir Percy that led to the economic development of the country to the extent that it was self-supporting; rather the development was achieved because of the change in socioeconomic and political logic of the time. The latter came about by underconsumption in Kenya, the African agricultural production from the Nyanza basin which produced enough for consumption and export of goods desired in neighboring countries, led to the economic progress of the country rather than the European agriculture he had supported.

Revenue derived from exports of other colonies being transported on the Uganda Railway and shipped through Mombasa to neighboring countries was also the key to success. This suggested that Sir Percy had not fully appraised or grasped the colony's potentials for development before transmitting his proposed economic policy. His reliance on a small number of European settlers alone for the economic development of the colony was not well informed as exports of African goods needed in neighboring colonies plays a significant role in accentuating the economic success of the colony. Therefore the lack of success in his economic agenda was born out of his lack of a comprehension of the socioeconomic condition of both the EAP and the neighboring countries. The failure in this regard could not have been expected of Sir Percy, having been presumed to be an outstanding administrator. It was very clear that his preferential treatment of the European over the remaining races, especially on the economic development of the colony, played a significant role in his failure to come up with an enduring economic policy for the development of the colony. It was also the same reason that saw to his failure to fix the economy up to the time he left the colony.

But such economic policy, at the same time, required efficient infrastructure to operate successfully, and it was in view of such need that the question of construction of adjunct railway lines to facilitate shipments of goods that came forth. Therefore, Sir Percy recommended the construction of the abandoned Nairobi-Thika, Magadi railways as adjunct of the Uganda Railway. The question of railway construction and development was associated with Sir Percy was known to have been an expert in both civilian and military railway construction and administration, as in some others during his time in the EAP, his performance was mixed. In this direction, he was successful in obtaining approval for the Nairobi to Thika railway, but the approval was delayed due to his failure to provide the desired information and data that could be presented to the Treasury. Moreover, his method of dealing with the issue, which included imprecise and incomplete replies to requests for costs and potential traffic, and concealing his true intentions from his superiors, were not characteristic of an outstanding colonial administrator. This was not the only time he was able to achieve his desired policy goal after a long and frustrating correspondence with the CO.

For the Magadi line, Sir Percy could take even less credit. It was highly likely, for example, that the railway would have been built without his direct involvement. He did act to facilitate the soda company's interest and potential profit at the expense of the well being of the colony as a whole. He acted decisively to obtain the land for piers and storage facilities at Kilindini and to provide land on which the company could build houses for European staff, but his actions caused later difficulties and has been criticized as unfair to the Maasai of Ngong and other port users. This was therefore a mixed legacy marked more by promise than performance.

NOTES

1. Lonsdale and Berman, "Coping with the Contradictions," 491.

2. Ibid, 492.

3. Bruce Berman, *Control and Crisis in Colonial Kenya: The Dialectic of Domination* (Athens: Ohio University Press, 1990), 75–77; Maxon, *Struggle for Kenya*, 19–20.

4. Sir Percy to Crewe, telegram, 12 November 1909, CO 533/63.

5. *East Africa Protectorate Report for 1908–1909*, 7–8.

6. Ibid.; Mungeam, *British Rule in Kenya*, 220.

7. Sir Percy to Crewe, telegram, 12 November 1909, CO 533/63; Mungeam, *British Rule in Kenya*, 210.

8. Ibid.

9. Ibid.

10. Ibid.

11. Sir Percy to Crewe, confidential, 13 November 1909, CO 533/63.

12. Sir Percy to Crewe, Interim Report, confidential, 13 November 1909, CO 533/63.

13. Minute by Butler to Read, 14 December 1909, on Sir Percy to Crewe, Interim Report, confidential, 13 November 1909, CO 533/63.

14. Ibid.

15. Ibid.

16. Ibid.

17. Ibid.

18. Ibid.

19. Ibid.

20. Ibid.

21. Minute by Read to Fiddes, 17 December 1909, on Sir Percy to Crewe, Interim Report, confidential, 13 November 1909, CO 533/63.

22. Ibid.

23. Ibid.

24. Minute by Fiddes to Crewe, 19 December 1909, on Sir Percy to Crewe, Interim Report, confidential, 13 November 1909, CO 533/63.

25. Minute by Seeley to Crewe, 1 January 1910, on Sir Percy to Crewe, Interim Report, confidential, 13 November 1909, CO 533/63.

26. Minute by Crewe to Fiddes, 22 November 1909, on Sir Percy to Crewe, telegram, 12 November 1909, CO 533/63.

27. Ibid.

28. Crewe to Secretary of the Treasury, confidential, 6 December 1909, CO 533/63.

29. Secretary of the Treasury to Crewe, confidential, 20 December 1909, CO 533/63.

30. Crewe to Sir Percy, telegram, 28 December 1909, CO 533/70.

31. Sir Percy to Crewe, telegram, 10 January 1910, CO 533/71.

32. Ibid.

33. Ibid.

34. Ibid.

35. Minute by Read to Fiddes, 14 January 1910, on Sir Percy to Crewe, telegram, 10 January 1910, CO 533/71.

36. Ibid.

37. Minute by Fiddes to Crewe, 14 January 1910, on Sir Percy to Crewe, telegram, 10 January 1910, CO 533/71.

38. Minute by Seeley to Crewe, 15 January 1910, on Sir Percy to Crewe, telegram, 10 January 1910, CO 533/71.

39. Minute by Crewe to Fiddes, 15 January 1910, on Sir Percy to Crewe, confidential, 10 January 1910, CO 533/71.

40. Crewe to the Secretary of the Treasury, confidential, 17 January 1910, CO 533/71.

41. Secretary of the Treasury to Crewe, confidential, 5 February 1910, CO 533/71.

42. Sir Percy to Seeley, confidential, 14 June 1910, CO 533/74.

43. Seeley to Sir Percy, telegram, 9 July 1910, CO 533/74.

44. Seeley to Crewe, confidential, 1 August 1910, enclosure of Sir Percy to Seeley, private, 14 June 1910, CO 533/74.

45. Minute by Read to Fiddes, 21 July 1910, on Sir Percy to Seeley, private, 14 June 1910, CO 533/74.

46. Ibid.

47. Ibid.

48. Ibid.

49. Ibid.

50. Ibid.

51. Minutes by Read to Fiddes, 14 July 1910, Fiddes to Read, 14 January 1910, and Seeley to Crewe, 12 July 1910, all in CO 533/71.

52. Seeley to Sir Percy, confidential, 31 July 1910, CO 533/74.

53. John Mwaruvie, "The Political Economy of Railway Development in Kenya," in *Studies in the Economic History of Kenya* ed. Maurice N. Amutabi (Lewiston, NY: Edwin Mellen Press, 2009), 38.

54. Charles Miller, *Lunatic Express* (Nairobi: Westland Sundries, 1971), 567–8.

55. *East Africa Protectorate Report for 1909–1910*, 24.

56. Winston Churchill, *My African Journey* (London: The Holland Press, 1908), 19.

57. Mwaruvie, "Political Economy of Railway Development in Kenya," 38–9.

58. Ibid., 39–40.

59. Sir Percy to Crewe, telegram, 1 April 1910, CO 533/73.

60. Ibid.

61. Sir Percy to Crewe, telegram, 9 April 1910, CO 53373.

62. Ibid.

63. Crewe to Sir Percy, telegram, 27 April 1910, CO 533/73.

64. Sir Percy to Crewe, telegram, 5 May 1910, CO 533/73.

65. Ibid.

66. Ibid.
67. Minute by Butler to Read, 7 May 1910, on Sir Percy to Crewe, telegram, 5 May 1910, CO 533/73.
68. Ibid.
69. Ibid.
70. Ibid.
71. Ibid.
72. Ibid.
73. Ibid.
74. Minute by Seeley to Crewe, 8 May 1910, on Sir Percy to Crewe, telegram, 5 May 1910, CO 533/73.
75. Minute by Crewe to Fiddes, 8 May 1910, on Sir Percy to Crewe, telegram, 5 May 1910, CO 533/73.
76. Fiddes to Secretary of the Treasury, 19 May 1910, CO 533/73.
77. Ibid.
78. Secretary of the Treasury to Crewe, 6 June 1910, CO 533/73.
79. Crewe to Sir Percy, telegram 10 June 1910, CO 533/73.
80. Sir Percy to Crewe, telegram, 16 June 1910, CO 533/74.
81. Ibid.
82. Sir Percy to Crewe, telegram, 18 June 1910, CO 533/74.
83. Ibid.
84. Ibid.
85. Crewe to Sir Percy, telegram, 28 June 1910, CO 533/74.
86. Ibid.
87. Sir Percy to Crewe, telegram, 3 July 1910, CO 533/74.
88. Crewe to Secretary Treasury, 3 August 1910, CO 533/74.
89. Secretary of the Treasury to Crewe, 5 September 1910, CO 533/75.
90. Sir Percy to Harcourt, telegram, 1 November 1910, CO 533/73.
91. Sir Percy to Crewe, confidential, 21 December 1910, CO 53378; Berman & Lonsdale, *Unhappy Valley*, 88.
92. Crewe to Sir Percy, confidential, 15 December 1910, CO 533/78.
93. Sir Percy to Crewe, confidential, 21 December 1910, CO 5333/78; Minute by Butler to Read, 10 January 1911, on Sir Percy to Crewe, confidential, 21 December 1910, CO 533/78.
94. Ibid.
95. Crewe to Secretary of the Treasury 10 February 1911, CO 533/102.
96. Mwaruvie, "Political Economy of Railway Development in Kenya," 42–3.
97. Sir Percy to Crewe, telegram, 8 October 1909, CO 533/63.
98. Minute by Butler to Read, 11 October 1909, on Sir Percy to Crewe, telegram, 8 October 1909, CO 533/63.
99. Ibid.
100. Samuel & Co. to undersecretary of state, confidential, 3 February 1909, CO 533/63.
101. Crewe to Sir Percy, confidential, 8 October 1909, CO 533/63.
102. Sir Percy to Crewe, telegram, 19 November 1909, CO 533/63.
103. Ibid.

104. Crewe to Secretary of the Treasury, confidential, 24 November 1909, CO 533/63.

105. Mwaruvie, "Political Economy of Railway Development in Kenya," 42–3.

106. Ibid., 44–5.

107. Lonsdale and Berman, "Coping with the Contradictions," 491–93.

108. Sir Percy to Crewe, Main Report, confidential, 26 May 1910, CO 533/74.

109. Great Britain, *East Africa Protectorate Report for 1912–1913* (London: HMSO, 1914), 4; Maxon, *Struggle for Kenya*, 31.

110. Great Britain, *East Africa Protectorate Report for 1911–12* (London: HMSO, 1913) 9.

111. Sir Percy to Crewe, telegram, 12 November 1909; Sir Percy to Crewe, Interim Report, 13 November 1909, confidential, all in CO 533/63.

112. Ibid.

113. Ibid.

114. Ibid.

115. Maxon, *Struggle for Kenya,* 31.

116. *East Africa Protectorate Report for 1911–1912*, 7–11.

117. Sir Percy to Crewe, telegram, 7 January 1910, CO 533/71.

118. J. A. L. Montgomery to Sir Percy, Report of the Department of Lands, East Africa Protectorate, confidential, 9 March 1910, CO 533/73.

119. Ibid.

120. Ibid.

121. Maxon, *Struggle for Kenya*, 31; *East Africa Protectorate Report for 1912–13*, 7–9.

122. Ibid.

123. Ibid.

124. Ibid.

125. Ibid.

126 *East Africa Protectorate Report for 1909–1909*, 4.

127 Great Britain, *East Africa Protectorate Report for 1910–1911* (London: HMSO, 1912), 4.

128. *East Africa Protectorate Report for 1912–1913*, 4.

129. *East Africa Protectorate Report for 1912–1913,* 4–5.

130. *East Africa Protectorate Report for 1911–1912*, 4–5.

131. Ibid.

132. Ibid.

133. Maxon, *Struggle for Kenya*, 32.

Chapter 7

Land Policy

At the time Sir Percy assumed the governorship of the protectorate, one of the most critical issues that faced him was the land question. The CO was particularly concerned with the amendment of existing legislation governing the grants of land to European settlers, the conditions governing such grants, the development of a system that would open land to potential European cultivators, and the protection of African land rights among many land issues. The CO had been disappointed in the lack of success in dealing with these matters that characterized the governorship of Sir Percy's predecessor, Sir James Hayes Sadler.

The amendment of the Crown Lands Ordinance of 1902, engaged Sadler in a correspondence with Crewe over Elgin's recommendations, which Sadler declined to include in the amendment of April 1909. Crewe deferred assent on the ordinance as it did not reflect Elgin's recommendations, and upon Sir Percy's assumption of government, Crewe asked him to consider Elgin's recommendations with a view to including them in the amendment of the ordinance. The CO hoped that Sir Percy would be able to deal effectively with the land question, including the passage of a new ordinance with specific clauses that the CO believed would effectively check land speculation, which was seen as a major problem and a threat to the protectorate's future development.

Sir Percy proved unequal to the task set for him when he took over the governorship of the EAP. Not only did he fail to implement the type of legislation desired by the CO, but under his governorship land speculation continued as Sir Percy was unwilling and unable to enforce existing regulations relating to grants of land and conditions of tenure. This failure was primarily caused by Sir Percy's favoritism and support for the protectorate's European settlers. Here as in other important issues, such as the Maasai move, he followed policies aimed at winning favor of the settlers, rather than those that would have enhanced the general well being of the protectorate and its entire population.

As the land question has long been viewed by historians of the EAP as being one of the most fundamental in determining the course of its development, Sir Percy's actions not only can be viewed as a failure in the short term. In the longer term, his actions, and lack of action, helped to entrench European privilege economically and politically, to the detriment of Kenya's future. In the sphere of administration of grants of land, based on the existing condition, Sir Percy had not performed to the satisfaction of the CO. He had proposed to develop the economy, and in doing so, the land question became a significant asset in achieving his policy recommendations.

Successive governments had done little in opening the land for the settlers to cultivate, and Sir Percy proposed that as he wanted to develop the economic potential of the protectorate, which he viewed in the development of large scale farming and industry, land must be open to prospective farmers, so that the protectorate would earn the desired funds to be self supporting. The CO believed that there must be regulations to safeguard grants of land. Measures should be designed not only to regulate land dealings, but also for the government to share increased land value to improve the future welfare of the colony.

But Sir Percy refused to budge and applied only a few policy measures; these were freehold and fixed rents, believing that it would provide government with the desired safeguards, but in the end his policy produced bitter consequences for the government and the settlers, as immigrants could not secure grants, in view of speculation. In view of the latter, Sir Percy could not be considered to have introduced an effective policy of dispensing lands. In view of the outcome of his policy, neither could Sir Percy be considered as the best administration of land policy, as there were extraordinary land dealings that produced speculation and dummying. Against the background of irregularity in the administration of regulation in grants of lands, the administration of land policy designed to provide land to settlers had not been as successful as Sir Percy proposed. He had proposed to develop the economy, and in doing so, the land question became central.

But the grants of land in the protectorate compounded his proposed economic development as it had been characterized by lack of a uniform legislation, which failed to satisfy farmers, and had been a factor in accentuating the difficulty of accessing grants of land to prospective farmers. The latter condition was accentuated further when Sir Percy refused to allow enabling legislation that could have mitigated the difficult position in land grants in the protectorate. Against the background of irregularity in the administration of legislation in grants of lands, the administration of land policy designed to provide land to settlers had not been successful as Sir Percy proposed.

Land grants had been marred by irregularity, especially in speculation and dummies, as Sir Percy refused to enforce revision of rents, and insisted that land tax must be dropped. Harcourt agreed not because it was the right course of action for him to follow but he wanted to move on. The latter position of Sir Percy must have been informed by his belief that land should be opened up to big business to develop the country. Therefore, the dispensation of land was characterized by irregularities that could be noticed in grants of land, which showed flagrant violations that he failed to stop.

This formed the basis of his weakness, not only in coming up with effective policy, but also of enforcement of policy that would have sanitized land dealings. The latter produced speculations and dummying, which Sir Percy failed to combat. The Colonial Office thus lost control of affairs, especially in land dealings, and had to defer to Sir Percy's successor all questions on land policy.

LAND LEGISLATION

Since 1905, when the CO took over the administration of the EAP from the Foreign Office, it had been preoccupied with framing legislation that could make land accessible to settlers. The colony relied on the Crown Lands Ordinance, 1902, in dispensing Crown lands to settlers entering the country. The ordinance could not effectively provide the desired safeguards in land dealings. Therefore, the CO sought to amend the ordinance by means of legislation. The search for an enduring land policy, by which land could be administered, remained the main objective of the CO in the EAP.[1]

Therefore, the CO sought to make land accessible for European settlement as well as establish certain safeguards against excessive accumulation and speculation.[2] The CO sought by means of legislation to establish some government control over land dealings and ensure that farmers developed their land holding in accordance with the working regulations of land administration. The Secretary of State for the Colonies, Lord Elgin, put forward these objectives in a confidential dispatch of 19 March 1908 to the Governor of the EAP, Sadler, for consideration. Elgin proposed land be granted on 99-year leases with a revision of rentals after 33 years, at 5 percent of the unimproved value of the landholding, the introduction of land tax, and anti-dummying measures.[3]

Elgin's proposed regulations could not be introduced as settlers objected to these regulations, particularly the reevaluation of rentals and introduction of land tax on the introduction of the land bill in the Legislative Council, in 1909. Settlers demanded an extended term of leases, as the terms of the bill would limit their profit from agriculture and land speculation.[4] When the bill was passed, the reevaluation was altered to fixed rentals, the land tax was dropped, and the provision of development conditions that should be met, before a landholder could transfer the property as an anti-dummying measure, was also dropped.[5] The CO rejected the bill as it desired these provisions so as to secure a share in the increased value of the land, as well as to safeguard land against excessive accumulation and speculation. The settlers' objection jeopardized the original bill, and the CO retained these regulations pending a time, when the ordinance would be amended.

Sir Percy, upon his assumption of government, found the protectorate engaged in correspondence with the CO about how best they could amend the Crown Lands Ordinance of 1902, which had been amended in April 1909, a few months before his arrival.[6] But Crewe deferred assent on the ordinance, as relevant regulations laid down by his predecessor, Lord Elgin, were not included in the amendment of the ordinance.[7] Crewe was categorical that the government adheres to the view that "means must be sought of securing to the government a share in the increased value of the land."[8] In order to meet this task, the CO was committed to legislation that would regulate the conduct of land dealings, as well as provide the government through laid down regulations as proposed by Elgin; a share in the increased land value.[9] Sadler was asked, in a confidential dispatch of 7 January 1909, to include in the amendment of the ordinance and in all future grants of land, a revision of rents after the 33rd and 66th years on a 99-year lease, surtax, and 3–5 years development conditions which must be met, before land could be transferred to another person.[10] Elgin's regulations sought to curb larger accumulation of land in the hands of individuals by the enforcement of these regulations "so far as it is possible to do so."[11] The CO maintained that the provision of the bill stood as recommended by Elgin, until there was the need of amendments of any particular provision arising from the debate in the Legislative Council of the protectorate. Even then, it was the details of the provision that may be altered not the particular measures enunciated by Elgin.

The CO believed that the alterations made in 1909 were not considered in detail, and therefore, Crewe, upon Sir Percy's assumption of government, asked him, in a confidential dispatch of the 16 September 1909, to consider Elgin's regulations in a further amendment of the April 1909 ordinance.[12] Sir Percy replied to Crewe, in a confidential dispatch of 30 September 1909, requesting more time to meet the inhabitants of the country and also to acquaint himself with the local conditions of the protectorate, before he could report his observation on the April 1909 ordinance.[13] Also, Sir Percy told Crewe, "If government is to strictly adhere to the policy of sharing in incremental values in keeping down the accumulations of land - the latter a very difficult matter."[14]

Therefore consideration of the amendment of the April 1909 ordinance was deferred until a time when Sir Percy would have the opportunity of meeting the inhabitants of the colony, and also of acquainting himself with the local situation, so that he would have an opportunity of considering the "matter on the spot."[15] On receipt of Sir Percy's dispatch, the CO was optimistic that Sir Percy would include Elgin's regulations in the amendment of the ordinance. Butler, in his minute on Sir Percy's confidential dispatch of 30 September 1909, stated "the views expressed in a section of the dispatch were in accordance with the views expressed by Sir P. Girouard in his dealing with the land question in Northern Nigeria. It is probable, therefore, that he is not in any way suggesting that we should depart from those principles, but is seeking a firm declaration of policy which will support him in dealing with local opinion."[16] But Parliamentary Undersecretary of State Seeley stated that a dispatch should be transmitted immediately, stating that they should not ignore the revision of rent clauses in the amendment of the ordinance.[17] Seeley's minute was in reference to Elgin's revision of rents provision that he strongly believed should not be ignored.

However, in another round of minutes on Sir Percy's dispatch, Butler stated that even Sir Percy's dispatch of 30 September 1909 left the door opened for further consideration and amendment of the ordinance, as he expressed his desire to study the Ordinance and to make his recommendations.[18] Also, in a further comment, Seeley argued that the issue as stated in their dispatch of 7 January 1909 should be brought up.[19] Seeley was making reference to Elgin's regulations transmitted to Sadler for inclusion, which the governor refused to include, and should therefore be brought up for Sir Percy's consideration.

The CO was hopeful that Sir Percy would consider these regulations in the amendment of April 1909, and apprehension as to whether or not these regulations would form part of a further amendment of April 1909 ordinance was laid to rest in the short run. Crewe, while waiting on Sir Percy's comment, reverted to conditions of grants of land as contained in Elgin's regulations of 19 March 1908, and also as provided in the CO's notice of introduction of the regulations of 7 May 1908.

The CO expressed their strict adherence to the principles enunciated in Elgin's dispatch of 19 March 1908, believing that it would provide the desired safeguards, and stood firm in support of such regulations. Again, while Sir Percy was working on his Interim Report Upon the EAP, he referred to the land question, when he reiterated his earlier question to Crewe, "If government is to strictly adhere to the policy of sharing in incremental values in keeping down the accumulations of land- the latter a very difficult matter."[20] From the latter reiterated statement, it would be difficult to suggest that Sir Percy would be willing to consider a legislation that would allow the government to have a share in the increased value of land.

However, Sir Percy put the amendment of the land ordinance on hold for six months. Thereafter, he reported to Crewe, in a confidential dispatch of 17 February 1910, that he had come to the conclusion that the best possible course of action to be taken was the adoption of the ordinance passed by the protectorate Legislative Council in April 1909.[21] Sir Percy also told Crewe that the colonists were reasoning on false premises in their opposition and that the proposals would undoubtedly prove of lasting benefit to the community.[22] However, Sir Percy suggested to Crewe that he would nevertheless prefer to sacrifice the measure, as there were strong feelings against such measures in the protectorate.[23] Sir Percy also told Crewe that he was in total support of the omission of the graduated land tax provision from the ordinance and defended his position by corroborating the view of the land committee that moderate grants of farms would prevent speculation and dummying, as long as development conditions were met.[24] Again, Sir Percy supported the amendment further when he told Crewe, "I can see no great objections to reasonable accumulations in the hands of reputable capitalists."[25] Sir Percy argued further that there was a "very strong feeling… in the country entirely adverse to any revision of rentals within the period of a 99 years lease."[26] Sir Percy contended that the protectorate was likely to be self-governing before 33 years, when the first revision of rents was expected; therefore, "it should be left to the good sense of the future population to deal with these incremental values and that we are today sufficiently protecting the rights of future generation by retaining practically the whole of the land as leasehold."[27]

As to excessive accumulation of large areas of land, Sir Percy also told Crewe in February that it did not matter how much land a farmer held as long as he could effect development on his land. He therefore pointed out that it was within the interest of a capitalist to take possession of a large area of land, and it was also unnecessary to introduce a land tax and anti-dummying regulations.[28] Sir Percy accepted the 1909 ordinance in its entirety as it supported the interest of the settlers, which would afford them the opportunity of grabbing land without any measures that would limit them in doing so. He wanted to allow the settlers do as they wished, especially as exemplified by Delamere's land grab by means of dummying, when he was subdividing his Njoro estates presumably for dummying purposes.[29]

The CO's officials were unhappy with Sir Percy's position on the amendment, as he supported the position of his predecessor against Elgin's regulations that the CO wished to form part of any future amendment. The CO viewed Elgin's regulations as the best measures that would provide the needed safeguards against land speculation and dummying. The CO not only refused to budge, but were also exasperated with his reply. Butler, in his minute, stated that Sir Percy was "prepared to throw over, in deference to the wishes of the White Settlers, the conditions imposed by the Secretary of State."[30]

As Sir Percy supported the April 1909 ordinance, he clearly departed from the land policy enunciated by Elgin, and his own view of safeguarding land and opening up land to immigrants and cultivators who could invest and develop the country. The latter, Sir Percy had clearly enunciated in his Interim Report Upon the EAP of 13 November 1909.[31] Therefore, Sir Percy adopted the settler's desire on land policy by relegating his own proposed policy and the government's regulations of safeguarding the land to the interest of the settlers by supporting his predecessor's view. His support of Sadler's view was informed by his desire to shield the settlers from legislation that would not only regulate their land dealings, but would also require the settler to pay land taxes and a revision of rents for the future welfare of the country. Sir Percy supported the settlers against the British government, but the CO refused to accept his recommendations.

The divergence of opinion between Crewe and Sir Percy on the position of the amendment of April 1909 ordinance became the first source of discord between Sir Percy and the CO. The officials of the CO wanted to include the revision of rentals after every 33 years on a 99-year lease, surtax, and transfer of land after development conditions were met, as contained in Lord Elgin's confidential dispatch of 19 March 1908, in all future grants.[32] Sir Percy's rejection of the regulations might have heightened Crewe's reservation, arising not only from Sir Percy's rejection of the regulations, but also from his perusal of both bi-annual returns of grants of land for 1 January to 31 June, and 1 July to 31 December 1909, respectively. In the latter two, Crewe learnt that Sir Percy had not been applying Elgin's regulations on all new grants of land. Elgin's regulations, it was believed, would, in the end, form the working regulations for all grants of land in the protectorate, and therefore must be included in all grants, pending the time when they will form part of a new land ordinance.[33] In view of Crewe's observation, he addressed a confidential dispatch of 10 May 1910 to Sir Percy, enquiring whether revisions of rents were being included in all new grants of land.[34] Crewe's enquiry might have been in connection with grants of land concessions in which he noticed from the returns of grants of land that it was unlikely that revision of rents was applied to certain grants, especially a grant to Heatley of an additional 5,000 acre concession.

The question of irregularity in Heatley's grant came up when the acting Governor, Jackson, addressed a confidential dispatch of 15 August 1909, to Crewe, with enclosed returns of grants of land for 1 January to 31 June 1909, for Crewe's consideration. Following Crewe's perusal of the returns of grants of land, Crewe, in a confidential dispatch of 30 October 1909, asked Jackson, in the absence of Sir Percy, to furnish further information in respect of returns of grants of land ending 31 June 1909.

In the returns, Crewe observed that Heatley's grant was reflected in section 2. 1 and repeated in section 2.2 as provided in the returns of grants of land ending 31 June 1909.[35] Crewe asked Jackson of areas granted to both Gale's and Heatley's concessions, and conditions applied in the grant of an additional 5,000-acre concession to Heatley.[36] Jackson replied to Crewe, in a confidential dispatch of 15 January 1910, that the area granted to Heatley was in section 2.1 of the returns, and, it was not the one in section 2.2 of the returns of grants of land. However, Jackson told Crewe that the two areas granted to both Gale and Heatley were identical.[37] As for conditions on which these grants were made, Jackson also told Crewe that a freehold rate of two Rupees per acre was inserted in error and that the actual rate charged was Rs. 1 per acre for freehold and half anna per acre per annum for leasehold.[38] Also, Jackson stated that the deeds of Gale's grant were only registered on 20 May 1909 and appeared therefore in the returns of grants ending 31 June 1909.[39] Jackson also told Crewe that, in concurrence with his dispatch of 30 October 1909 instructing the governor to grant an additional 5,000 acres to Heatley, he has instructed to affect the grant accordingly.[40]

But the fact of the matter in this additional grant to Heatley was that the revision of rentals as laid down in Elgin's regulation was not included in Heatley's grant. Heatley's concession of an additional 5,000 acres appeared in the returns January to June 1910. Heatley's concession was given on a freehold; no revision of rental after 33rd and 66th years on 99-year lease was applied. In view of Crewe's perusal of bi-annual returns of grants of land for 1 January to 31 June, and 1 July to 31 December 1910, Crewe doubted whether laid down regulations as provided by Elgin were being complied with. His doubts were confirmed that Heatley's grant was made on a freehold condition, which brought to the open that revision of rents had not been applied on Heatley's grant.[41]

Sir Percy's refusal to enforce the revision of rents provision of the regulation was not on Heatley's grant alone, as Harcourt discovered similar violation in grants that contravened the regulations. The latter grant was not made in compliance with the regulations and the CO had no means of compelling an unwilling Sir Percy to enforce the revision of rents provision in all grants, a provision desired most by the CO. Even though Sir Percy was quick in defending his action that it was not too late to include revision, its inclusion could spark a protest from the European settlers.[42] He also believed that the colonists would have self-government before the first revision of 33 years. Therefore, future decision as to the revision should be left for the colonists to decide, once they were independent.[43]

As Sir Percy succeeded in dropping these land regulatory measures, the revision of rents and land tax provisions in grants of land, he had deprived the government a share in the increased value of land after the 33rd and 66th years on 99-year leases. The provision dealing with the revision of rents was held with utmost importance in the CO, as it was believed that the provision would not only safeguard against dummying, but would also afford the government, through the revision of rents after every 33 years, a share in the increased value of the land.

But Sir Percy refused, and the CO had to fold their hands to see Sir Percy doing what he wished. The administration of grants of land without the application of land tax and the refusal to apply revision of rents meant that grants were vulnerable to fraudulent practices. This was further accentuated by lack of supervision and enforcement of penalties, in a case where defaulters were caught. Under the conditions that Sir Percy retained, grants of land were characterized by irregularities that caused the CO to enquire from time to time of the conditions on which grants of land were made. In the latter, there was an absence of a clear intimation in the returns of land as to the application of revision of rents regulation in the grants, as well as the price of first and subsequent revisions to be applied.[44] The provision was part of the regulations stipulated in the notice of introduction of Elgin's regulations of 19 March 1908.[45] It was also in compliance with the notice of introduction of the regulations, which Crewe transmitted to Sadler in his confidential dispatch of 7 May 1908, with an enclosure of Elgin's regulation of 19 March 1908.[46]

Thereafter, the protectorate's Commissioner of Lands, Colonel J. A. L. Montgomery, had issued a circular notice of introduction of the regulations in the protectorate, on 1 June 1908.[47] But Sir Percy refrained to apply the regulations and had never replied to Crewe as to why he refrained from introducing the said regulations, leaving Crewe in the dark as to whether or not revision of rents was being applied in all new grants of land. Crewe availed himself of information that a revision of rents provision of the regulations was not being applied in all new grants as he directed. But Crewe would have to hear from Sir Percy, as the man on spot, whether or not the regulation was being applied. But as Sir Percy declined to reply, Crewe continued to approve grants based on Sir Percy's recommendations. Certainly not without caution and doubts that Sir Percy might not have been applying revision of rents in all new grants of land.

Crewe was able to get to the bottom of the issue from the report of the sitting of the East Africa Department's Land Committee, CO, on 21 June 1910. The Committee, in reporting one of their sitting, in a confidential dispatch of 21 June 1910, told Crewe that during the meeting of the committee, it noted from a statement made by the EAP's late Commissioner of Lands, Montgomery, that Sir Percy refrained from including the revision of rents after 33rd and 66th years on 99-year leases, in all new grants, since the issuance of the regulation of 7 May 1908.[48]

The CO was unhappy with Sir Percy's noncompliance with the regulations, and his action provoked anger in the CO when Butler, in his minute on the report, stated, "it was very thoughtless of the people in the Protectorate to refrain from enforcing this rule without any formal notification and without telling us that they had done so."[49] Butler added, "we have imagined all along that new grants since the regulations were issued included this very important condition."[50] Butler recalled, "this belief has not been without its influence in considering applications for additional grants of land (e.g. Mr. Heatley's concessions), and has also made us perhaps underrate the consequences of delay in dealing with the new Lands Ordinance."[51] Butler added that "Naturally the urgency of arriving at a decision on that Ordinance was not felt so keenly when it was believed that requirements laid down by Lord Elgin, which are embodied in the regulation referred to were being complied with."[52] Therefore, Butler transmitted another draft copy of the regulations, which Montgomery issued in the protectorate and transmitted a copy to the CO as notification of introduction of the regulations in the protectorate.[53]

Therefore, Crewe, relying on the committee's report and a minute by Butler, addressed a confidential dispatch of 6 July 1910 to Sir Percy, deploring his action for noncompliance with the revision of rentals provision of the regulations. Crewe, in a hearty expression of anger, told Sir Percy; "I understand from Colonel Montgomery, late Commissioner of Lands, that No. 2 of the regulations for the grant of lands, dated the 7th of May 1908, has not been applied in the case of new grants made since that date."[54] Crewe also stated that the regulations provided for the revision of rent at the end of the 33rd and 66th years of a 99-year lease, which was, he stated, "of course, a condition of the greatest importance." He added: I should be glad to know whether it is the fact that this condition has not been included in new licenses or leases granted since the 7th May of 1908, and, if not, why, for what reason the operation of the regulation has been suspended."[55] Also, Crewe told Sir Percy "this is the first intimation which has reached me that this regulation was not being applied. Enquiries as to conditions on which land is granted have been applied with the regulations of the 7th of May 1908 in the belief that all these regulations were operative."[56] Crewe added, "I may also observe that the belief that the revision of rent formed one of the conditions on which new grants of land were being made has not been without its influence on myself in considering applications for the grant of additional areas, and in the consideration of the Land Ordinance."[57]

Exasperated, Crewe believed that Sir Percy disguised the fact of the matter to him, when refraining from inclusion of the said provision in all grants. Crewe felt that Sir Percy deceived him, when he refused to disclose the true position of grants. Crewe believed that all provisions of the land regulations were being enforced which made him not push for the immediate amendment of the ordinance, believing that, at last, it would be Elgin's regulations that would prevail in any further amendment of the April 1909 ordinance.

After some delay, Sir Percy replied to Crewe, in a confidential dispatch of 15 August 1910, defending his action that it wasn't too late to include the rental re-evaluation provision into the new leases, in addition to other conditions.[58] But Sir Percy warned that the inclusion of such a provision could spark dissatisfaction and opposition in the protectorate and undo the good the government had done.[59] Sir Percy argued that the inclusion of the revision of rentals would discourage prospective immigrants into the country. Sir Percy also argued that the provisions of the revision of rents held no significance, as the country would be independent before the first 33 years revision.[60] Therefore, the question of future land dealings should be reserved for the future populations of the country to decide upon. Sir Percy also pointed out that in June 1906 even Sadler did not apply the provision of the revision of rents in granting a 547 square miles lease on the coast to Upland Syndicate of East Africa, on a fixed rental.[61]

But Crewe was not satisfied with Sir Percy's explanation, as well as his handling of the land dealings in the protectorate. He received the reply for what it was worth, and he continued to raise more observations and questions arising from his perusal of returns of grants of land, and in his consideration of applications for grants of land.

A sound administrator of government policy would not respond to Crewe in the way Sir Percy did. More importantly, as a custodian of government policy, Sir Percy failed to nurture and sustain the implementation of government regulations for opening up land for prospective immigrants and for the development of the protectorate economy, which he strongly advocated in his telegram of 12 November 1909 to Crewe and reiterated the same position, in his confidential dispatch of 13 November 1909 to Crewe.[62] Sir Percy's action in this regard could hardly be considered of an administrator who could defend government policy of greatest importance, in view of the CO's determination not only in safeguarding lands against speculation and dummying, but also for the government to have a share in the increased value of land. In the latter requirements of the government, Sir Percy had not effectively carried out any of them, having refrained to do so, and had never informed the CO of his refusal to enforce the said regulations.

The implications of his action on the administration of government policy were below the expectations of the CO for the discharge of his responsibilities. In fact, his action was detrimental to the government policy of land administration, a gross failing on his competence in the execution of government policy, which clearly exposed his bias and advocacy of settlers' interest at the expense of government. This was a failing of Sir Percy, as the CO was confident that he could effectively carry out the task entrusted to him, but they were disappointed with his performance, as he had failed to do so. His action was informed by his desire to defend the cause of the settlers against legislation that would demand them to contribute to the welfare of the protectorate. His action in considering that the country would be independent before the 33-year first revision was uncalled for, as it did not form part of His Majesty's government policy in that protectorate. Therefore, Sir Percy's view that the country would be independent before the 33 years, when the first revision of rents would be due, was subversion not only from His Majesty's government policy, but also of the policy of administration he had enunciated for the protectorate in his Interim Report, as to the land question.[63] Therefore, Sir Percy's departure from a laid down policy of administration in respect of the land question, which he also considered a cardinal issue in the economic development of the protectorate, did not amount to a sound administration of policy from a person considered as an outstanding British colonial administrator and proconsul.[64]

In another blow to Sir Percy's administration, Crewe, determined to address the festering land question, refused to concede to Sir Percy's wishes of retaining the provision of the land ordinance without the inclusion of Elgin's regulations. Therefore, Crewe referred the land bill to a committee for further recommendation with a view of including Elgin's regulations in a further amendment of the Land Ordinance of April 29 1910. This was necessary as Crewe disagreed with all Sir Percy's explanations as to the suitability or otherwise of applying Elgin's recommendations.

The body at the CO that was given the task of deliberating on the desirability of including Elgin's recommendations, in the amendment of the land ordinance, was a Sub-Committee of the Land Concessions Committee, chaired by Colonel John Barton Seeley.[65] Other members of the committee were drawn from the CO, such as W. D. Ellis, H. F. Batterbee, Sir H. J. Read, Bertram Cox, legal assistant, and the late Commissioner of Lands, East Africa Protectorate, Colonel J. A. L. Montgomery who testified on the settlers' view.[66]

The committee, in the course of its proceedings, heard and collected evidence especially in the form of a memorandum from Mr. Pemba Reeves, an expert on New Zealand's land question and development. Reeves, in a memorandum of 4 May 1910, recommended that the government should control transfer of lands and be strict in grants of the remaining 4,000 square miles of land.[67] Reeves recommended further that land grants must be regulated to ensure that big businesses were not allowed to take over control of the remaining land and that free transfer of land should be allowed for the future, after development conditions were met.[68]

But such transfer must be subject to adequate white occupation of the land, which must be insisted upon as a condition of transfer in the case of the remaining land.[69] Reeves's testimony was important to the Seeley-led committee in its resolution of the land question as it formed part of the recommendations they transmitted to Crewe. Seeley, in his recommendations in a confidential dispatch of 13 July 1910, told Crewe to adhere to his decision as to the provision in the law of penalties against dummying, in which individuals and syndicates caught with multiple grants of land in their possession, for the purpose of holding what was reasonably unacceptable by the regulations, such grants be revoked and farms forfeited to the government.[70]

Seeley drew Crewe's attention to a possible development of a strong feeling of resentment among settlers in the protectorate once his recommendations were implemented. But he also recommended to Crewe, that such resentment could be addressed, if they could request the Treasury to set aside a certain definite sum of money each year for the improvement of communications.[71] Also, Seeley suggested that such a project would mitigate the feeling of resentment among the white settlers, and would also stimulate further immigration into the protectorate.[72] Seeley added that the proposed improvement policy, if adhered to, would "justify government's claims for share of the land's increased value, which it could hardly help to create by its own action."[73] In concluding his recommendations, Seeley wrote that such improvements would be to the advantage of all the races of the protectorate.[74] Seeley pointed out that whilst recommending the desirability of doing something to improve communications in the protectorate, he also recommended that a letter should be addressed to Sir Percy, intimating to him the resolutions and inviting him to London so as to produce a joint report.

After the submission of the report to Crewe, it was passed through the normal CO's administrative channel for consideration. Thereafter, Crewe, in a confidential dispatch of 19 July 1910, told Sir Percy that the committee had reported, and he should travel home, with a view to producing a joint report with the committee.[75] However, the resolution of the committee did not resonate with Sir Percy, when he replied in a confidential dispatch of 10 September 1910, objecting to the recommendations of the committee.[76] Sir Percy left for London, on 14 November 1910 for discussion of the land regulations with Harcourt, and returned to Mombasa, on 21 February 1911.

G. H. Mungeam's *British Rule in Kenya* noted that Sir Percy met Lewis Harcourt, on the committee's resolution, in December 1910.[77] Crewe had been transferred as Secretary of State for the India, while Harcourt was appointed Secretary of State for the Colonies, in November.[78] Sir Percy argued before Harcourt in favor of the settlers, but Harcourt refused to budge, and maintained the CO's position on the amendment of the ordinance.

Also, Harcourt rejected the ordinance of April 1909.[79] Harcourt followed up the discussion with Sir Percy, in a confidential dispatch of 3 February 1911, that he had represented the settlers view with much force and ability.[80] However, Harcourt reiterated the CO's position on the revision of rents when he told Sir Percy that the government must have a share of the increased value of land after every 33 years.[81] Also, Harcourt told Sir Percy that he "wished to retain the provision against land accumulation lest the ideal of a large white population in the white highlands should be seriously prejudiced," Harcourt added, his responsibility was for the future welfare of the protectorate.[82]

Harcourt, whilst being clearly categorical of his position on the land question, had at the same time considered Sir Percy's objection on the committee's resolution. He told Sir Percy, in that same dispatch of 3 February 1911, to redraft the bill, including all the deleted provisions, and to submit it for his consideration.[83] Sir Percy left London for the East Africa Protectorate, on 26 February 1911, but he could not report on the revision of the ordinance to Harcourt until four months later.

In the interim, he maintained his stand against enforcements of revision of rents and his insistence that land tax be dropped on new and prior grants not registered as of 28 February 1911. With Harcourt consenting to the request, a land grant was made under fixed rents and freehold conditions. Fixed rents and freehold conditions of grants caused irregularities in land grants, and prompted the CO to enquire from time to time, of conditions under which, land was being allotted. These conditions, and the consequence of dropping the land tax on all grants, brought grants under fixed rentals and freeholds conditions, which voided all safeguards desired in land dealings.[84] With such a method of grants, there was now a distant possibility of coming up with a land bill any time sooner as Sir Percy reported to Harcourt, on 3 May 1911, that he had not been able to redraft a good land bill.[85] Sir Percy asked Harcourt if the legal adviser of the CO could be asked to redraft the bill in consultations with the protectorate's Crown Advocate, R. M. Combe, and the Treasurer who were on leave in England.[86]

The CO was irked with his letter. Butler, in his minute, suggested that if the law was drafted in the CO, it will be assumed that "this law which is apparently obnoxious to the majority of the white population…has been dictated from home not only in general policy but also in detail."[87] Harcourt was angered by the dispatch and minuted "Oh yes! We shall reply effectively to these tactics. If his legal advisers are so inefficient they had better look out for private practice at home…. I may have to tell him that if I suspect him of such action…he wd. be at once recalled."[88] The CO were clearly not happy with Sir Percy's action as he disappointed Harcourt who gave him the opportunity of coming up with a new land bill, but he failed to do so. Sir Percy could not allow amendment of the ordinance of April 1909, and did not come up with a revised bill as Harcourt expected him to do so. As there was no progress made on the revision of the bill and with the application of fixed rental and freehold conditions of grants, it was impossible to believe that Sir Percy had administered land in a manner that would provide the desired safeguards. It also suggested that he had not proffered any solution to the problems of land dealings, and instead, compounded it. Despite Sir Percy's refusal to revise the bill, Harcourt was hopeful that the land bill, if revised, would provide the desired safeguards, and therefore, he asked two officials of the protectorate, Combe and the Treasurer who were on leave in London, to revise the bill and in case of any difficulty to consult the CO's legal adviser.[89]

Combe was also told to use the New Zealand Income Tax Assessment Act of 1908, to settle the knotty question of land taxation, which had been unsettled, and had been part of the problems hindering the passage of the bill.[90] Combe concluded his revision of the bill in September 1911, and the bill was referred to the standing Land Committee, East Africa Department, CO, for further deliberations and resolution. Even then, the section dealing with the land tax had not been properly settled.[91] The Land Committee reported in November 1911 on the assumption that it was desired to adhere to the principles laid down in Elgin's dispatch of 19 March 1908.[92] Elgin's regulations had always been a reference point for any review of the land bill as the CO was not comfortable with the fixed rentals and freehold conditions of grants that Sir Percy had been applying on all grants.

ADMINISTRATION OF GRANTS OF LANDS

Irregularities in grants of land had been taking place before Sir Percy assumed the government of the protectorate, but they were minimal. A simple clarification could sometimes resolve the misunderstanding or expose the level of irregular grants being made. But upon Sir Percy's assumption of government, grants of land were characterized by irregularities that produced speculation and dummying. Harcourt discovered irregular land dealings in Sir Percy's returns of 1 January to 31 June 1911, which caused him to address a confidential dispatch of 28 October 1911, demanding further clarification on such returns. Harcourt asked Sir Percy to furnish further information as to conditions of grants of land and the number of persons holding grants who were complying with the terms of their grants.[93] Sir Percy replied to Harcourt, in a confidential dispatch of 14 February 1912, with enclosures by the Land Officer R. B. Wright. In Sir Percy's dispatch, he told Harcourt that, as to conditions of grants of land, he was made to believe that they were in concurrence with the general policy laid down in respect of land administration, which was the policy of His Majesty's government that "one of the principles to be maintained in the land laws was the prevention of 'undue accumulation of properties' in the hands of individuals."[94] Therefore, Sir Percy told Harcourt that in furtherance of the said policy, he was instructed not to grant an area exceeding 150,000 acres, and all land transfers that would increase someone's area beyond that must be referred to him (Harcourt) for approval.[95]

In spite of Sir Percy's knowledge of the limits on the acres allowed for him to grant, he refused to comply with such limits and went out of his way to allow the Sintu Avenue Syndicate to acquire 320,000 acres of land. In that case, he defended his action in making larger grants to syndicates when he told Harcourt of his belief that companies with genuine interest of developing their land, especially on the coastal areas of the protectorate, should be allotted sufficient land for their development. He specifically pointed to a case where he granted larger areas of land to a group of individuals who were running an estate as partners. Such action was in contravention of the regulations as he was expected to seek approval from Harcourt before he could approve of the grants of such acreage to the syndicate, which were beyond what was allowed for him to approve.[96]

However, Sir Percy told Harcourt, in his dispatch, that upon his assumption of government, he discovered that a large area of crown land in the highlands had been surveyed into farmlands, and on a particular day, applications for grants and occupation of such land were entertained. As to conditions of grants, applicants must show proof of means of a certain amount, occupation of a grant within 6 months from the date of grant by the leasee or a European agent, and fulfillment of certain development conditions. Also, the leasee must prove, in this case, evidence that he has effected some development on his land, and the lease being procurable after 3–5 years, when development conditions were met.[97] But Sir Percy had not been supervising grants of land to ensure landholders complied with these conditions of grants. Some settlers took advantage of government failing in that direction to speculate or dummy their grants.[98] Sir Percy defended his action by criticizing the varied requirements set out in the regulations described above. He stated that one of the problems with this method of making grants was the danger of a real hardship being imposed upon bona fide farmers who arrived in the protectorate to take up land. They might find it difficult to obtain a grant though there was uninhabited land available that could be thrown open for allotments.[99] These allotments could not be possible until the land was surveyed. In this situation, new arrivals in the country found it difficult to secure farms from government grants and had to resort to purchasing from speculators, or from government auction of lands in the settled areas, which was a very rare occurrence.[100]

Sir Percy could have fixed the latter problem associated with the method of grant, but despite available land and an increased number of surveyors that had entered into the country in 1911, Sir Percy could not open up land for surveying and allotment to meet the demands of applicants for farmland.[101] The land in the settled areas was disposed by auction as Sir Percy had pointed out, but even then, Sir Percy's auction was not directed to meet the needs of immigrant settlers who were committed to making EAP their home. His auction of township land, for example, was to meet the very best interest of syndicates. This was clearly demonstrated in 1911 when he auctioned ten township plots in an ambiguous circumstance to a syndicate, in contravention of the rule.[102] The action caused the CO to warn him against future occurrence of similar grants.[103] Therefore, the latter problems that Sir Percy raised had not been without its influence in mitigating the prospect of immigration into the country, and of making farms available to settlers for agricultural development.[104] But Sir Percy never opened up land for allotment to meet the needs of immigrants entering the colony, and such action was a drawback on the prospect of immigration which, it was hoped, would accentuate the development of the colony.

As for the number of persons holding land and complying with their obligations of developing their land, Sir Percy added that there were over 3 million acres of land which had been alienated in 460 names, placing the average holding at 7,000 acres; but Sir Percy opined that it was near impossible to calculate accurately, in view of the nature of grants of land he had described in the preceding paragraphs.[105] But he was optimistic that 7,000 acres were more than enough for a grant, when he stated, "Originally speaking, a farm of 3,000 to 5,000 acres is sufficient for any single individuals who are running an estate as partners."[106] Therefore, Sir Percy urged Harcourt; in his February dispatch, that in his own opinion that should be stopped.[107] He specifically pointed to a case where he granted larger areas of land to a group of individuals who were running an estate as partners. However, Sir Percy suggested, "in the district 2,000 to 4,000 acres would suffice for a plantation destined for the production of tropical products, and a similar grant of 3,000 to 5,000 acres would appear to be sufficient for a crown grant in the highlands."[108]

Certainly, Sir Percy's proposition about the acreage suitable for individual and/or syndicate were quite sufficient, but Sir Percy failed to ensure that such acreage was accepted by the CO and committed in legislation. It was only in February 1912 that he recommended such acreages as suitable holdings for different categories of farmers, but then it was too late for him to secure the CO consent on his recommendations, since he soon resigned. Again, despite his recommendations on size of acreage, he allowed the Sintu Avenue Syndicate to acquire ten township plots, which were supposed to have been, presumably, disposed of by means of auction.[109] These reform recommendations should have been made to the CO in 1909, when Sir Percy assumed government, but he had not presented the problem of land regulations to the CO for consideration. His decision to drop the regulations were also against the advice of Wright who insisted that the regulations should be retained so as to sanitize the condition of grants, but Sir Percy refused to budge.

RETURNS OF GRANTS OF LANDS

A summary of grants being made and the number of applications for grants were necessary for Harcourt's understanding of Sir Percy's administration of land. Return of grants, as provided by Wright, detailed applications and grants being made and pending applications for grants. This came about following Harcourt's confidential dispatch of 28 October 1911, demanding clarification, on the general conditions of grants, and sanction to stop dispensing land under certain conditions.[110] But before he could stop Sir Percy, Harcourt was in receipt of additional information about his request for the number of people holding land in the protectorate, through returns of grants. Sir Percy replied to Harcourt on the question of the number of persons holding grants, in his dispatch of 14 February 1912 with enclosure of returns of land grants by Wright, dated 14 February 1912.[111] The latter dispatch, disclosed how deplorable the protectorate's land grant and that not much had been done by Sir Percy's administration to rectify the prevailing land speculation. Other than his failure to solve the pressing problem of speculation and dummying, he failed to open up land for prospective European settlers, thus inhibiting the immigration of new famers interested in taking up land. Harcourt specifically requested clarification on the general conditions of grants, including the number of applications for grants and a summary of grants made, in October 1911, and he was prepared to order the governor to stop dispensing land under certain conditions.[112]

In Wright's returns, he advised Sir Percy against dropping the land tax and applying fixed rental conditions, as they would worsen the condition of land grants in the colony. Wright, in his returns of grants of land for 1 July to 31 December 1911, indicated in both his covering dispatch, and the returns of grants of land that at the time of dropping the land tax, there were 202 standing applications for 381 farms, which would have to be granted under fixed rentals, in view of dropping the land tax regulation, as a condition of grants of land.[113] However, Wright told him, in his covering dispatch, that the dropping of the land tax provision would cause the 202 farms to revert to fixed rents, and advised Sir Percy against dropping the regulations. Sir Percy refused to heed the advice and insisted to Harcourt that the regulations should be dropped. The effect of his action in dropping land tax brought 300 farms in Uasin Gishu, West Kenya, Sotik, Kinangop, Gilgil, and the first part of Londiani grants under fixed rents.[114]

In the latter areas, farms had been granted but were not registered by the time of Sir Percy's arrival in the country. At best, if the land tax and revision of rents had been allowed as conditions of grants, what Sir Percy should have done under the land regulations of penalties for violators, was to register those farms, and enforce land tax and revision of rents on those grants. In the alternative, he could revoke the licenses and forfeit to the government those farms. But neither of the two penalties was enforced, and, instead, he reported to Harcourt his observation as to such extraordinary grants being made before his assumption of government, in his confidential dispatch of 14 February 1912 and further additional information in another confidential dispatch of 21 February 1912, all detailing applications for land and grants administration.[115]

In Wright's enclosed dispatch for the return of grants of land of 1 July to 31 December 1911, was a table showing three-year grants of land: 1909, 1910, and 1911.[116] Wright reported that as at 31 June 1911, there were 387 applications pending for grants in a July–December 1911 grants period. Also, Wright reported that there were 184 new applications registered as at 31 June 1911, making a total of 571 applications for grants in the July–December 1911 grants.[117] Wright also stated that in the July-December 1911 grants, there were 214 registered completed deeds compared with 158 registered deeds in the January–June 1911 period. However, out of these applications, there were 24 applications cancelled or withdrawn. With such cancellations, the remaining total number of applications stood at 328, against the earlier applications of 387 that were supposed to have been allotted, in the January–June 1911 grants.[118] Therefore, Wright categorized all the applications that were at various stages of allotment under different headings, with the applicable number of applications pending action in that category. For example, there were "pending return or draft deeds" (9), "pending engrossment" (10), pending return of counter part deeds or money" (32), "pending registration" (89), or a total of 140 out of the 328, which were at a final stages of completion, thus leaving 138 applications for further consideration, and leaving 20, considered normal and satisfactory under other head.[119]

However, a majority of applications pending return had been included in the January–June 1911 returns, when Campbell was acting for Wright, and a large number of the applications, especially those on the coast, where "complications in respect of native claims and titles defeat immediate settlement, are likely to keep this item high for some time."[120] However, Wright pointed out that the cause of the large number of pending applications, as stated by Mr. Campbell, was the question of the removal of the Maasai. Wright pointed out that the cause of the large number of pending applications was beyond the control of the land office, as it had to do with the removal of the Maasai, and the allocation of their land to applicants. Also, Wright stated that it was necessary to give a detailed account of the grants which, without "this explanation, might reasonably be the subject, if not of criticism, of question with regard to "pending survey."[121] Despite the detail provided by Wright, the performance of the colony in opening up land to prospective immigrant was not commensurate with demands.

In fact, Wright appeared to have been surprised that the number of grants under the latter head was not larger than expected, as conditions of survey had improved, as licensed surveyors had moved into the country, and assisted the Department of Lands. Thus improvement in the survey of land would continue to ease the problem of pending applications under this head. But in spite of the improved condition of survey, Sir Percy had not been able to open up land for survey with a view to allot farms to prospective immigrants. Lack of opening up farms had hampered immigration and agricultural development as farmers were waiting to get farms but no land was open for the surveyors despite their presence in the country.

Sir Percy's reluctance to open up land for prospective immigration had not been without its influence in mitigating the flow of immigration into the colony. It frustrated European settlers desire to move into the country as farms were not easy to secure. This development could not have been said to be in the best interest of development or administration, if the desired development program were to be judged successful or if Sir Percy was to be judged as a successful administrator who could be said to have accentuated the successful administration and development of the country.

IRREGULARITY IN GRANTS OF LANDS

From the preceding returns of grants, moreover, Harcourt also discovered some irregular land dealings that caused him to address a confidential dispatch to Sir Percy, demanding further clarification. Harcourt addressed the confidential dispatch on 8 April 1912 to Sir Percy stating that he discovered that the Sintu Avenue Syndicate was granted leases of 10 township plots at rupees 15 per annum for each plot. Harcourt also told Sir Percy: "I presumed that the plots were sold in auction in the usual manner, and, if so, I shall be glad to be informed of the sum paid in each case for the right to lease."[122] Harcourt added, "in the case of township plots the auction price at which the right to lease was sold should have been included in the returns as well as the rental payable in respect of the plot."[123] Harcourt added that this was necessary in order that "Returns may furnish a complete record of the consideration received by government for all crown lands alienated."[124]

Harcourt also advised Sir Percy to impose a limit on large blocks in townships, presumably for speculation purposes. Harcourt also asked Sir Percy to send him his observations as to the best means of addressing the concerns he raised. Harcourt also observed that in the Naivasha Province, Messrs. Newland and McCall had been granted 1,000 acres of agricultural land freehold. In this instance, however, Harcourt reminded Sir Percy that the right to purchase freeholds was one of the conditions stated in the original leases, and, in such a situation, it should have been stated in the returns of land that the "freehold was granted under the terms of the original lease."[125] In spite of efforts to affect safeguards in land dealings, this was an example of Sir Percy's failure to furnish full information of dispensing land to the CO.

In this regard, Harcourt was concerned that land dealings in the protectorate were being carried out in an unusual manner. Harcourt observed that there were irregularities in documenting land dealings, which was a cause of concern, as Sir Percy failed to fully furnish the CO with details of the procedure being followed in dispensing lands. More importantly, Harcourt learnt from the returns of grants that laid down regulations were being compromised in dispensing crown lands. The latter case was not the only case where evidence of irregular grants arising from his administration of grants of land could be established.

There were many of them, and one of such grants not only exposed irregular land dealings, but also exposed Sir Percy's disposition toward allowing the settlers to grab land at the expense of the government. This could be seen from W. G. Sewell's land transaction, which Sir Percy reported to Harcourt in a confidential dispatch of 22 February 1912, with an enclosure of Sewall's land transactions. He stated he needed Harcourt's guidance as to the best way to handle Sewall's land transactions.[126]

In Sir Percy's submission on Sewall's application, he told Harcourt that Sewall was allowed to acquire 17,773 acres. Sewall had also asked to be allowed to acquire by transfer a farm of 640 acres at Mazeras, and Sir Percy concluded "I should be glad to know whether the fact that his other holdings are all in the highlands would be considered to justify a small additional grant at the coast."[127] Therefore, Sir Percy told Harcourt that he needed the CO's advice on how to document Sewall's land transactions.[128]

The CO wondered as to why Sir Percy should send such a transaction for their advice. However, Batterbee minuted that Sir Percy should be referred to the laid down regulations for his compliance on the said subject rather than refer to Harcourt for guidance.[129] Read, Butler, and Fiddes concurred with Batterbee's comments. But nothing was heard until the protectorate's acting governor, C. C. Bowring's, confidential dispatch of 4 March 1912 raised the case once more. In his dispatch was an enclosure of Sewall's letter, addressed to Sir Percy and dated 27 February 1912. Bowring told Harcourt that Sewall requested that his proposal should be favorably considered. Bowring reiterated that what Sewall stated in the letter appeared to be correct, except if he parted with his Kinangop farm, and with the acquisition which Sewall wished to make, he would still have an area of 17,134 acres, even if he parted with the Kinangop farm, and his possessions would not violate government regulations.[130] In support of Sewall's application, Bowring praised Sewall as having the largest wheat farm.[131] However, Bowring added that of great importance was the undisputable fact that Sewall had effected considerable development of his land.[132] Sewall stated in his letter to Sir Percy of 27 February 1912, enclosed in Bowring's dispatch to Harcourt of 4 March 1912, that he was granted a single grant of 4,466 acres from crown lands and that he bought the remainder of his land.[133] As to his 4,466-acre farm, Sewall stated that he had fulfilled all conditions on the above farm at Kinangop and had concluded arrangements to sell his farm to a sheep farming syndicate, when permitted by law, on 2 August 1912. Sewall also told Sir Percy that he had a larger area of 1,500 acres under cultivation on his farm at Njoro than anyone's farm in the protectorate. As to his Kinangop farm, Sewall stated that it was of utmost value to him as the grass on his Njoro farm had little or no nourishment in it, and he must have a place to rest his 600 head of oxen; which number he required to work his farm. The farm, he added, was near his Njoro farm. However, Sewell told Sir Percy that if he could not be permitted to buy the farm he would have no option other than renting grazing which would be an unnecessary hardship on him. As to the homestead at Mazeras that he wished to transfer to his name, he had done all the development on the farm of one and two years rubber trees and having 500 acres ready to plant which he would plant that year. Sewell allayed apprehension of the authorities when he told Bowring that, if the transfer were allowed he would have 15,000 acres, which was still less than the limit allowed, as the farm at Kinangop was 4,468 acres.[134] Therefore, Sewell added that he had done a lot more work than anyone on his wheat farm, and that his purchase of additional acres would not exceed the limits allowed by the government.[135] Batterbee, in his minute, expressed his reservations as to these transactions, when he said that he would allow Sewall to acquire the 3,281 acres.

But it was understandable from this case that Sewall wanted more land not because he never had enough for his needs, but because he desired to make a profit out of these land purchases. One of his farms was disposed of to a sheep faming syndicate, but he stated that he would certainly not want to encourage speculation.[136] However, Batterbee recommended that while he would not have objection to Sewall acquiring the 640 acres at Mazeras as recommended by Sir Percy, but he objected to the other in view of the fact that the rest were in the highlands.[137] Read stated in his minute, "I think that we might let him have the 640 acres on the coast…but I would not do more than this."[138] Anderson doubted the entire transactions, when he minuted, "Is there any truth in his statement as to the grazing on his Njoro farm? and is he stock farming?"[139] In response, the East Africa Department of the CO minuted, "East Africa dept. has no infn. on these points. Mr. Stordy, Chief Vet. Officer is on leave and might know."[140]

Therefore a decision on Sewall's land transactions was deferred and a request for more information on Sewall's transaction was sought from the protectorate's Chief Veterinary Officer, R. J. Stordy. In a reply to the enquiry, Stordy's letter, dated 9 April 1912 addressed to Batterbee, was received in the CO. Stordy told Batterbee, "Yes, I know Sewall quite well. He is a wheat farmer; at least he is an active member of the Wheat Growers Association."[141] As for Sewall's pending application, Stordy added, "His request seems to me unreasonable. If Sewall is prepared to sell such portion of his present holding as makes it worth the while of a sheep farming Syndicate to purchase, then surely he is parting with more of his farm than would prove sufficient for the resting of his work oxen, for no Syndicate would propose to purchase a paltry 3,000 acres on which to run sheep."[142] In addition, Stordy wrote that Sewall did not need 600 oxen to work his holding. Stordy disagreed with Sewall's application despite Sir Percy and Bowring's recommendations that the application be granted. Stordy supported his objections to Sewall's application when he observed that:

> There must be many hundreds of oxen working the extensive farms in the Njoro district; but I cannot remember having heard the grazing completely condemned, nor can I believe that on a 13,000 acre Njoro holding no nourishing grazing can be found. It is astounding the number of far-fetched arguments that are raised over and over again by the East Africa land grabbers. Personally, I have always been opposed to extensive holdings, and as the area suitable for white colonization is, comparatively speaking, a small one, and as we are always being told by experts and the settlers themselves of the marvelous fertility of the soil and the carrying power of the pasture–lands, then I say extensive holdings, while very desirable from the capitalist's point of view, are not essential for the furtherance of the Protectorate, but are detrimental to its best interests.[143]

Thereafter, Batterbee recalled the previous correspondence on Sewall's land transaction. He stated, "in view of what Mr. Stordy says, I do not think that he had attached much importance to Sewall's statement as to grazing.[144] Anderson, Butler, Read, Fiddes expressed their concurrence with Batterbee's minute.[145] Harcourt, in his minute, made a reference to a minute by Read, and stated, "as proposed as Mr. Read's minute of March 29 at once."[146] Harcourt's minute was an instruction that Read's minute of 29 March 1912 in respect of this subject should form the reply to both Sir Percy and Bowring's confidential dispatches, with an enclosure of Sewall's letter to Bowring. Read, in his minute of 29 March 1910, as shown above, refused the application for a grant of 3,281 acres as it was in the highlands, but recommended that Sewall should be allowed to acquire the 640 acres he applied for at Mazeras, on the coast.

Thereafter, Harcourt replied to Sir Percy, in a confidential dispatch of 17 April 1912, "in view of the extent of Mr. W. G. Sewall's present holdings of land, I am unable to approve of his being permitted to purchase two additional areas of 328 acres."[147] Harcourt also pointed out that "having regard, however to the fact that his Sewall's [sic] other holdings are in the highlands, I will raise no objection to his being allowed to acquire a farm of 640 acres at Mazeras."[148] The CO was able to get to the bottom of such an extraordinary transaction and confirmed not only their doubts as to transparency, worthiness or otherwise of the transaction, but also their cautious reservations and doubts as to Sir Percy's knowledge of the protectorate to inform the proposed policy reforms he had wanted to carry through.

The question of transparency in Sir Percy's dealing with the CO had been disclosed, but such action of the CO of passing behind Sir Percy to seek information from his subordinates had been the dynamics of the CO when, on his assumption of the administration of the protectorate, Sir Percy warned the CO that, if they sought information from his subordinates on any issue under consideration, he would resign. He made reference to his predecessor's predicament in a similar situation when the CO by passed him to seek information from his subordinates. In fact Sir Percy was right in his criticism of the CO as it not only embarrassed Sadler and subsequently led to his transfer to the Windward Islands. Also, there was a similar case involving the former commissioner of the protectorate, Sir Charles Eliot, over the grant of land to a syndicate, which the then Secretary of State for the Foreign Office, Lord Lansdowne, claimed that the grant interfered with the Maasai nominal grazing reserve, an issue which led to his premature resignation, in 1904. His apprehension was allayed by Fiddes who asked him to treat the staff with respect taking into consideration their pioneering administrative role in the early days of the protectorate, and if he did as Fiddes advised such action would never have happened.

Fiddes's counsel notwithstanding, the CO, with the knowledge of Fiddes, went out of the way to seek information from his subordinate staff, Stordy. The CO's suspicion of Sir Percy's sinister action in dispensing land had been brought to the open when they got to the bottom of such extraordinary practice. They sought and obtained information behind his back that Sewall's grant did not comply with the regulations and therefore denied the application. The CO found that the allocation to Sewall, which Sir Percy supported, would be used for speculation. Therefore, the application and their enquiry disclosed how Sir Percy disregarded the land regulations in dispensing crown land which does not in any way suggest that he had dispensed the land in a manner consistent with the regulations. His failing in this aspect was very clear and it could not be considered to have been an excellent job to be expected from an outstanding administration, as the grant would have compromised the land regulations.

This correspondence indicated that Sir Percy, instead of treating the Sewall case as laid down in the land regulations under the 1902 ordinance, or the 1909 proposed land bill amendment, or at least to enforce upon Sewall the auction regulations, declined to do so. Sir Percy was fully aware that Sewall's land transactions became complicated for him to resolve in view of Sewall's purchase of large acreage, which might be used for speculation.[149] Sir Percy referred the transaction to Harcourt so as to exonerate himself from blame, having known that the transaction was extra-ordinary in spite of the fact that it did not violate government regulations but it suggested that the grant might be used for speculations.

Instead of Sir Percy refusing Sewall's applications, he supported it and forwarded to Harcourt for consideration. From Sewall's holdings, it was clear that Sir Percy was unwilling to stop settlers from land speculation, a violation that made it difficult for prospective farmers to secure farms. If Sir Percy could support an application with a potential for speculation, it would be difficult for any suitable land regulation to be applied in the colony, and that would not in any way be considered to have been in the very best interest of the colony and neither does it constitute an effective and successful administration of crown land. Such irregularity does not portray Sir Percy in the very best category of administrators, if considered from his initial recommendations on the evolution of a land policy for the colony. At the time of presenting this recommendation in February 1912, Sir Percy had less than three months to resign. Therefore, his recommendations were too late and of no effect. Even if his proposal was approved, he could not have effectively implemented the regulations, as they were not of significant difference from the existing regulations that he refrained to apply. Again, the ineffectiveness or lack of enforcement of the existing legislation was partly responsible for the prevalence of speculation and dummies, and still Sir Percy would have been indifferent to the administration of the legislation. Therefore, the condition of land administration would have been the same, his recommendations notwithstanding. In the highlands, Sir Percy suggested that it would be good for individual farming rather than farming by a big syndicate. Therefore, he recommended personal occupation, a land board to screen applicants for grants of land, no second grant from the crown land to a person already holding a crown grant, discontinuing grants by means of power of attorney and for persons who have never visited the country.[150] However, Sir Percy pointed out in his dispatch that the whole system was thoroughly bad and it should be discontinued, and that it was the conditions of grants that produced land speculation and dummying.

On receipt of Sir Percy's dispatch in the CO, Batterbee, in his minute, expressed his concurrence with Sir Percy's proposal when he noted that Sir Percy had made a strong case that all applications should be made by personal presence and personal occupation upon grants of land, and by insisting on such conditions, only bona fide farmers could access to farm land. Batterbee pointed out that the governor, by the applications of these measures, if approved, would prevent land accumulation.[151]

However, Batterbee observed that the governor was concerned with the deplorable state of affairs in land dealings, and wanted to put a stop to it, by affecting regulatory measures to prevent dummying and grants of land by means of power of attorney, which could only be "prevented by stringent measures if a farmer of the governors proposal" was to have access to land.[152] Batterbee stated that he saw no reason why it should not be true that such measures should be applied for the benefit of the farmer.[153] However, Batterbee also stated that the "Secretary of State certainly has no desire to stand in the way of anything, which would prevent the accumulation of land in the hands of individuals."[154]

With regard to Sir Percy's proposal that no second grants of crown land should be made to the same person, Batterbee observed that there was an objection on the question of the number of acres to be allotted as crown grants were 2,500 acres and extended to 5,000 acres. But Sir Percy should be asked how he proposed to do that in view of the differences between his recommendations and the existing limits on grants of crown land. In this case both latter two options were viewed as complicating with each other, therefore, a means must be sought for a proper land dispensation.

On the question of regulating land allotment by an advisory board, Batterbee recommended that the responsibility should be given to the Land Board. But Batterbee observed that the Land Board might be not be effective as it would only recommend, but not decide.[155] However, Batterbee was in full concurrence with Sir Percy's recommendations when, in concluding his minute, he pointed out flaws in the existing method of dispensing crown land that "the present method of allotment has nothing to recommend it, and the sooner it is abolished the better."[156] It suggests the need for a procedure to recommend prospective applicants for a grant of land, as there was no such procedure in place. The procedure would minimize the fraudulent application for a grant of land.

As to Read, he expressed his general agreement with Sir Percy's recommendations and Batterbee's minute when he recalled his visit to the protectorate and commented that the protectorate's Director of Agriculture who had an "extensive knowledge of the country and the settlers and who had several years previous experience of colonial service in S. Africa, urged upon me when I was in the protectorate the necessity for an advisory board, which could bring candidate before it and see whether they were likely to make good settlers, could examine into their financial position (at present money is sometimes lent for a day or two to enable an applicant to show that he has the means of developing his property and as soon as he has got his grant, is lent to someone else for a similar purpose)."[157] This suggested that the land board if adopted as a means of land grant would not solve the problem of land speculation and dummying in the colony.

However, as to the proposed regulations, Read expressed his full concurrence as to the 99-year leases and the reservation of the right to impose a land tax, whether progressive on all land leased by the crown or only on undeveloped lands, would regulate land dealings in the protectorate. Read was optimistic that they could find a solution to the land question that would not only be acceptable to the settlers, but would also safeguard the government interest.[158]

But Anderson disagreed with Sir Percy's recommendation, and the minutes of Batterbee and Read on the desirability of the land board as a means of screening applicants for grants of land. He minuted, "I must say that the idea of a land board to pass settlers does not commend itself to me. They would of course only allot to their friends, and after all what is the advantage of controlling the original allotment unless we insist also on complete control of transfers, and so render land unmarketable unless the transfer or transferee are in the good graces of the board."[159]

Anderson also challenged the local authorities for failing to observe conditions on land grants as well as to effect inspection to ensure compliance with the laid down conditions. Anderson opined that there was the need to affect a systematic procedure for inspecting farms; so as to ensure that laid down conditions in the land regulations were being carried out. Also, Anderson added that the land board would be a tool for grabbing the crown land by a few individuals when he stated, "these patent advices of Ld. Delamere & Co. for keeping East Africa select, and the management of the Crown Estates in their own hands, will only lead to further & worse trouble. I do not see why the merchant or the small shopkeeper should not be allowed to add farming to his business, if he is so disposed."[160] In fact Anderson was concerned that Lord Delamere would have access to more than what was reasonably acceptable by the government, if there was no effective legislation to regulate the conduct of land dealing. But from all indications, Sir Percy was an unwilling partner in coming up with the required safeguards, as he has been reluctant in allowing effective legislation to be applied in land dealings.

Therefore, his attitude would have paved the way for Lord Delamere and others to acquire what was reasonably unacceptable acreage to the detriment of government policy.[161] This action could in no way be attributed to a good administrator under whatever circumstance. Anderson pointed out that the cause of the whole trouble was that they were giving something for nothing and stated, "the individual who gets it, very often only wants it to sell & reap the advantage of his luck in getting an allotment."[162]

In his analysis, Anderson was very critical of Sir Percy when he pointed out that if Sir Percy could auction some farms, why couldn't he use the auction method universally, and, "couple it with stringent conditions of personal occupation, and more stringent development conditions, which should be enforced strictly by forfeiture for non-compliance, without compensation."[163] Anderson also stated that as government would have all farms surveyed before allotment was made, there would be no difficulties in carrying out "periodical auctions as surveys are completed, and the terms of occupation should be made clearly known and strictly enforced."[164]

In concluding his minute, Anderson condemned the proposed idea of a land board whose "proceedings would be a target for Members of the Parliament, especially Mr. Ramsay MacDonald or Mr. MacCallum Scott," and contended that, if his recommendations were accepted, "there will be less of this evil."[165] Lord Emmott[166] disagreed with Anderson, and expressed his general concurrence with Sir Percy's recommendations, when he said, "Sir J. Anderson's minute presupposed that the Land Board is an unsuitable body for making recommendations as to applicants for farms. The composition of this board was (and so far as I know is) four officials and three unofficial representing different districts. I see no reason on the face of it why such a Board should indulge in log-rolling."[167] Therefore, Emmott expressed his willingness to defer to Sir Percy's proposal, when he stated, "On the whole I shd. be inclined to adopt the Govrs proposal & give them a fair trial."[168]

However, Emmott added that he favored the Land Board, as "even if we run the risk of occasional unsuitable man being selected by a Land Board we shall also (provided the board is properly manned and does its duty) obtain a far better choice on the whole. On the other hand, I agree that we ought to keep a tight hand on transfers. This is more easily done under a more elastic system than under a plan of universal auction."[169] After discussion between Anderson and Harcourt the latter asked Anderson to arrange the modalities of how Harcourt's decision could be implemented. Anderson, in his minute to Fiddes, stated that as for the East African lands, S of S has decided for the present to drop the idea of taxing land already alienated and to confine further discussion to the question of the terms and conditions upon which lands still in hand should be leased. "Will you say who will be selected to go into this matter with Sir P. Girouard?"[170] Fiddes stated, "we can't do better than leave it to those who have discussed it hitherto i. e. Mr. Read, Mr. Risley, with the assistance of Mr. Butler and Mr. Batterbee."[171]

Therefore, Harcourt, while agreeing to defer to the Governor's proposal, also expressed his willingness to allow the committee members to revisit the question, taking into consideration Sir Percy's recommendations. Initially, the committee decided to settle the land tax question before they engaged in further deliberation of the recommendations, when they sought and obtained recommendations from the protectorate's Land Ranger, Arthur C. Tannahill, who was on leave in London at the time. However, there was hope that a land bill for the administration of land policy could have been realized as the bill had been revised.

But before action could be taken on the report, Sir Percy arrived London, in March 1912, for his leave, and had the opportunity of discussing with Harcourt the question of dropping the land tax provision from the revised bill.[172] Sir Percy told Harcourt, in a confidential dispatch of 4 March 1912, to drop the land tax provision from the bill.[173] Harcourt consented to the request and asked the committee to reconsider the matter with some modification of the principles of land tax.[174] With the dropping of the land tax regulation and the addition to Sir Percy's refusal to enforce the revision of rents regulation on all grants, grants of land were marred with irregularities, which characterized Sir Percy's administration of land policy. It was true that before his arrival to the protectorate, there were irregularities in grants of land, but during his tour of duty, it reached a new level never seen before.

It was this situation that the CO were avoiding by insisting on applying Elgin's regulations, but as Sir Percy refrained from doing so, they had no option other than to watch the man on the spot do as he wished. As the revision of rental provision was abandoned, all grants of land would be made on freehold or fixed rents, by implication Sir Percy forced his way in granting land under fixed rental. Also, he had not been applying the revision of rents, which the CO insisted upon, but he refrained to do so. But the dispensing of land was attended with irregularity, as the dropping of the land tax opened up land to increased speculation and dummying never seen before, which caused Sir Percy to recommend remedial measures to combat the practice.

Therefore, Sir Percy recommended certain remedial measures for Harcourt's approval, in his confidential dispatch of 14 February 1912, believing that if they were enforced, speculation and dummying would have been minimized.[175] Sir Percy's proposed measures were the establishment of an advisory board to screen applicants for grants of land, discontinuation of grants by means of power of attorney, disallowing grants to persons who had never visited the country, and requesting authority from Harcourt to veto land transfer, as he found expedient.[176] But his recommendations came late and were overshadowed by the Maasai removal. Sir Percy removed them from their Laikipia land without the approval of Harcourt to do so. His action on the Maasai was motivated by his desire to grant the land to the settlers, which was further accentuated by pressure for more fertile land from the settlers. In view of his role in the latter case, Harcourt forced him to resign after a prolonged meeting in the CO, on 8 May 1912. The meeting disclosed how Sir Percy disguised information from Harcourt, on the Maasai case, and in view of the magnitude of the case before the Commons, Harcourt forced him to resign, believing that Sir Percy lied and had made him lie before the Commons. Thence, Sir Percy must go.[177] The Maasai move was also a land policy question that portrayed how Sir Percy removed the Maasai from the reserves and granted their fertile land to European farmers without the consent of the CO.[178]

These actions regarding land could hardly be attributed to a successful administrator who must keep the CO informed of all developments in the protectorate and desist from any action that would embarrass His Majesty's government. The promise of farms to farmers and the removal of the Maasai was no less an embarrassment to His Majesty's government, an action that caused the CO to ease Sir Percy out of office. The incident, clearly demonstrated that Sir Percy shirked his responsibility, failed to live up to his proposed African policy and to respect the authority of His Majesty's government. There was no less a failure than this, and nor was there a greater disservice than this, and in no way could his performance in this regard be considered outstanding.

CONCLUSION

The CO's main policy objective in the EAP was to make land accessible to the European settlers. The CO's sustained effort at the amendment of the 1902 land ordinance was confronted with objections from the settlers and reluctance from the governor to enforce Elgin's proposed land regulations. The settlers viewed the regulations as obstacles to their profit in agriculture and land as the regulations could limit the profit they could earn by speculation. The governors, especially Sir Percy, favored the settlers, and therefore, he shielded them against any land regulation that would be detrimental to their economic interest, even if the regulation was for the best interest of the government.

The administration of land regulations in dispensing crown lands had tasked both the CO and the protectorate in an uneasy way. Sir Percy was expected to not only amend the April 1909 ordinance, but also to administer Elgin's regulations in dispensing crown lands. Sadler refused to apply Elgin's regulations in the amendments of the Crown Land Ordinance, 1902, which caused Crewe to defer his assent on the new ordinance of April 1909. The CO believed that Sir Percy would be the right person to affect the amendments of the ordinance, but he not only failed to amend the April 1909 ordinance, but he rejected important provisions; revision of rents and surtax, as condition of grants, which formed important parts of Elgin's regulations.

Sir Percy's action in that direction, caused grants of land to be based on fixed rents and freehold grants, thereby opening up land to speculators and dummies. Supervision to ensure compliance with the few left over conditions of grants had not been affected, and that allowed leasees to do as they wished with their farms. The dropping of the land tax and the refusal to enforce revision of rents had destroyed the CO's efforts in search of safeguards in land dealings finally and had opened up land to increased speculation and dummying never seen before. The latter condition of land dealings finally or belatedly caused Sir Percy to recommend remedial measures to combat the practice, in 1912.

These violations were accentuated by lack of supervision to ensure whether or not leasees complied with the terms of their grants, and where violations were discovered, penalties were never enforced on violators as provided in the law of penalties on land dealings, and that allowed leasees to do as they wished. The cause of his reluctance to enforce regulations, which would have regulated the settlers' conduct in land dealings, was mainly informed by his desire to support the settlers in their quest for a better land dealings, even if, it were at the expense of the government. But his support of the settlers' interest to the detriment of government interest had cost the government both in policy and in earnings. This was characteristic of Sir Percy's administration that has been illustrated in other chapters. With land, as with the Maasai move, this proved a major weakness of Sir Percy's governorship.

NOTES

1. Maxon, *Struggle for Kenya*, 54.
2. Ibid.
3. *East Africa Protectorate Report for 1908–1909*, 9.
4. Berman, *Control and Crisis in Colonial Kenya*, 75–6.
5. Ibid.
6. Sadler to Crewe, confidential, 29 April 1909; Crewe to Sadler, confidential, 7 January 1909, CO 533/62.
7. Ibid.
8. Ibid.
9. Elgin to Sadler, confidential, 19 March 1908, CO 533/43.
10. Sadler to Crewe, confidential, 29 April 1909, CO 533/59.
11. Ibid.
12. Crewe to Sir Percy, confidential, 16 September 1909, CO 533/62.
13. Sir Percy to Crewe, confidential, 30 September 1909, CO 533/62.
14. Ibid.
15. Ibid.
16. Minute by Butler to Read, 13 October 1909, on Sir Percy to Crewe, confidential, 30 September 1909, CO 533/62.
17. Seeley to Crewe, 14 October 1909, on Ibid.
18. Minute by Butler to Read, 15 October 1909, on Ibid.
19. Minute by Seeley to Crewe, 16 October 1909, on Ibid.
20. Sir Percy to Crewe, Interim Report, confidential, 12 November 1909, CO 533/63.
21. Sir Percy to Crewe, confidential, 17 February 1910, CO 533/71.

22. Ibid.
23. Ibid.
24. Ibid.; Dummying is a means of acquiring a larger area of land that was beyond what the law could allow. For more detail see Huxley, *White Mam's Country,* 269.
25. Sir Percy to Crewe, confidential, 17 February 1910, CO 533/71.
26. Ibid.
27. Ibid.
28. Ibid.
29. Huxley, *Whiteman's Country,* 177; Sorrenson, *Origins of European Settlement in Kenya*, 120.
30. Minute by Butler to Read, 6 March 1910, on Sir Percy to Crewe, confidential, 17 February 1910, CO 533/71.
31. Sir Percy to Crewe, Interim Report, confidential, 13 November 1909, CO 533/63.
32. Elgin to Sadler, confidential, 19 March 1908, CO 533/62.
33. Crewe to Sadler, confidential, 7 January 1909, CO 533/62.
34. Crewe to Sir Percy, confidential, 10 May 1910, CO 533/74.
35. Crewe to Jackson, confidential, 30 October 1909, CO 533/62.
36. Ibid.
37. Jackson to Crewe, confidential, 15 January 1910, CO 533/71.
38. Ibid.
39. Ibid.
40. Ibid.
41. Ibid.
42. Sorrenson, *Origins of European settlement in Kenya*, 120.
43. Ibid.
44. Report of the East Africa Land Committee, confidential, 13 July 1910, enclosure in Seeley to Crewe, confidential, 13 July 1910, CO 533/82.
45. Crewe to Sadler, confidential, 19 March 1908, CO 533/62.
46. Seeley to Crewe, Report of the East Africa Land Committee, confidential, 21 June 1910, CO 533/82; Montgomery to Monson, confidential, 1 June 1908, CO 533/62.
47. Ibid.
48. Ibid.
49. Minute by Butler to Fiddes, 28 June 1910, on Ibid.
50. Ibid.
51. Ibid.
52. Ibid.
53. Ibid.
54. Crewe to Sir Percy, confidential, 6 July 1910, CO 533/82.
55. Ibid.
56. Ibid.
57. Ibid.
58. Sir Percy to Crewe, confidential, 15 August 1910, CO 533/76.
59. Ibid.

60. Ibid.

61. Ibid.; Sorrenson, *Origins of European Settlement in Kenya*, 123.

62. Sir Percy to Crewe, telegram, 12 November 1909; Sir Percy to Crewe, confidential, 13 November 1909, all in CO 533/63.

63. Sir Percy to Crewe, Interim Report, confidential, 13 November 1909, CO 533/63.

64. Kirk-Greene, "Canada in Africa," 211.

65. Seeley, between 1908 and 1912, was Under-Secretary of State for the Colonies and became Secretary of State for War in 1912. He was also a member of the Privy Council in 1909. According to the *Dictionary of National Biography* "Since his chief, Lord Crewe was in the Lords, important work fell to the under-secretary, in particular the introduction of the measure which brought the Union of South Africa."

66. Report of the East Africa Department's Land Committee, confidential, 13 July 1910, enclosure in Seeley to Crewe, confidential, 13 July 1910, CO 533/82.

67. Report of the Land Committee, confidential, 13 July 1910, CO 533/82; Sorrenson, *Origins of European Settlement in Kenya,* 121.

68. W. Pemba Reeves, memorandum, 4 May 1910, enclosure in Seeley to Crewe, Report of the Land Committee, confidential, 13 July 1910, CO 533/82.

69. Reeves, memorandum, 4 May 1910, enclosure in Seeley to Crewe, Land Committee Report, confidential, 13 July 1910, CO 533/82.

70. Seeley to Crewe, Land Committee Report, confidential, 13 July 1910, CO 533/82.

71. Ibid.

72. Ibid.

73. Ibid.

74. Ibid.

75. Crewe to Sir Percy, confidential, 19 July 1910, CO 533/82.

76. Sir Percy to Crewe, confidential, 10 September 1910, CO 533/77.

77. Mungeam, *British Rule in Kenya,* 222.

78. Ibid.

79. Bennett, *Kenya*, 32–3.

80. Ibid., 33; Sorrenson, *Origins of European Settlement in Kenya,* 121.

81. Harcourt to Sir Percy, confidential, 3 February 1911, CO 533/71; Sorrenson, *Origins of European Settlement in Kenya,* 121; Bennett, *Kenya*, 33.

82. Ibid.

83. Sorrenson, *Origins of European Settlement in Kenya,* 122.

84. Sorrenson, *Origins of European Settlement in Kenya,* 123; Memorandum by Wright to Sir Percy, 15 February 1912, enclosure in Sir Percy to Harcourt, confidential, 14 February 1912, CO 533/102.

85. Sir Percy to Harcourt, private, 3 May 1911, CO 533/87.

86. Ibid.

87. Minute by Butler to Read, 31 May 1911, on Sir Percy to Harcourt, confidential, 3 May 1911, CO 533/87.

88. Minute by Harcourt to Fiddes, 1 June 1911, on Sir Percy to Harcourt, confidential, 3 May 1911, CO 533/87.

89. Ibid.

90. Report of the Land Committee, East Africa Department, Colonial Office, confidential, 14 November 1911, CO 533/102; Sorrenson, *Origins of European Settlement in Kenya*, 122.

91. Sorrenson, *Origins of European Settlement in Kenya*, 122.

92. Report of the Land Committee, East Africa Department, Colonial Office, confidential, 14 November 1911, CO 533/102.

93. Harcourt to Sir Percy, confidential, 28 October 1911, CO 533/91.

94. Sir Percy to Harcourt, confidential, 14 February 1912, CO533/102.

95. Ibid.

96. Ibid.

97. Ibid.

98. Sorrenson, *Origins of European Settlement in Kenya*, 125.

99. Sir Percy to Harcourt, confidential, 14 February 1912, CO 533/102.

100. Ibid.

101. Ibid.

102. Harcourt to Sir Percy, confidential, 8 April 1912, CO 533/102.

103. Ibid.

104. Sir Percy to Harcourt, confidential, 14 February 1912, CO 533/102.

105. Ibid.

106. Ibid; Sorrenson, *Origins of European Settlement in Kenya,* 126.

107. Sir Percy to Harcourt, confidential, 14 February 1912, CO 533/102.

108. Ibid.

109. Harcourt to Sir Percy, confidential, 8 April 1912, CO 533/102.

110. Harcourt to Sir Percy, confidential, 28 October 1911, CO 533/91.

111. Memorandum by Wright, 14 February 1912, enclosure in Sir Percy to Harcourt, confidential, 14 February 1912, CO 533/102.

112. Harcourt to Sir Percy, confidential, 28 October 1911, CO 533/91.

113. Memorandum by Wright to Sir Percy, 14 February 1912, enclosure in Sir Percy to Harcourt, confidential, 29 February 1912, CO 533/102; Sorrenson, *Origins of European Settlement in Kenya*, 123.

114. Sorrenson, *Origins of European Settlement in Kenya*, 123.

115. Sir Percy to Harcourt, confidential, 21 February 1912, CO 533/102.

116. Memorandum by Wright to Sir Percy, 15 February 1912, enclosure in Sir Percy to Harcourt, confidential, 21 February 1912, CO 533/102.

117. Ibid.

118. Ibid.

119. Ibid.

120. Ibid.

121. Ibid.

122. Harcourt to Sir Percy, confidential, 8 April 1912, CO 533/102.

123. Ibid.

124. Ibid.

125. Ibid.

126. Sir Percy to Harcourt, confidential, 22 February 1912, CO 533/102.

127. Ibid.
128. Ibid.
129. Minute by Batterbee to Read, 28 February 1912, on Ibid.
130. Bowring to Harcourt, confidential, 4 March 1912, CO 533/103.
131. Ibid.
132. Ibid.
133. Sewall to Sir Percy, private, 27 February 1912, enclosure in Bowring to Harcourt, confidential, 4 March 1912, CO 533/103.
134. Ibid.
135. Ibid.
136. Minute by Batterbee to Read, 28 March 1912, on Ibid.
137. Ibid.
138. Minute by Read to Fiddes, 29 March 1912, on Ibid.
139. Minute by Anderson, 30 March 1912, on Ibid.
140. Minute by East Africa Department to Anderson, 1 April 1912, in Bowring to Harcourt, confidential, 4 March 1912, enclosure, Sewall to Sir Percy, private, 27 February 1912, all in CO 533/103.
141. Stordy to Batterbee, private, 9 April 1912, CO 533/103.
142. Ibid.
143. Ibid.
144. Minute by Batterbee to Anderson, 12 April 1912, CO 533/103.
145. Minutes by Anderson to Harcourt, 12 April 1912, Butler to Read, 12 April 1912, and Read to Fiddes, 12 April 1912, on Ibid.
146. Minute by Harcourt to Anderson, 13 April 1912, on Ibid.
147. Harcourt to Sir Percy, confidential, 17 April 1912, CO 533/103.
148. Ibid.
149. Stordy to Batterbee, private, 9 April 1912, CO 533/103.
150. Sir Percy to Harcourt, confidential, 14 February 1912, CO 533/102.
151. Minute by Batterbee to Read, 28 March 1912, on Sir Percy to Harcourt, confidential, 14 February 1912, CO 533/102.
152. Ibid.
153. Ibid.
154. Ibid.
155. Ibid.
156. Ibid.
157. Minute by Read to Fiddes, 28 March 1912, on Ibid.
158. Ibid.
159. Minute by Anderson, 29 March 1912, on Ibid.
160. Ibid.
161. Sorrenson, *Origins of European Settlement in Kenya*, 120.
162. Minute by Anderson, 29 March 1912, on Sir Percy to Court, confidential, 14 February 1912, CO 533/102.
163. Ibid.
164. Ibid.
165. Ibid.

166. Minute by Emmott, 29 March 1912, on Ibid. Lord Emmott was Parliamentary Undersecretary for the Colonies in 1912.

167. Ibid.

168. Ibid.

169. Ibid.

170. Anderson to Fiddes, 2 May 1912, on Ibid.

171. Minute by Fiddes to Anderson, 2 May 1912, on Ibid.

172. Sir Percy to Harcourt, confidential, 4 March 1912, CO 533/102; Sorrenson, *Origins of European Settlement in Kenya*, 127; Bennett, *Kenya*, 33.

173. Sorrenson, *Origins of European Settlement in Kenya*, 122.

174. Harcourt to Belfield, confidential, 8 November 1912, CO 533/102; Minutes by Read to Fiddes, 30 August 1912, Fiddes, 3 September 1912, Belfield to Harcourt, confidential, 30 August 1912, CO 533/ 102.

175. Sir Percy to Harcourt, confidential, 14 February 1912, CO 533/102.

176. Ibid.

177. Maxon, *Struggle for Kenya,* 41; *Sorrenson, Origins of European Settlement in Kenya*, 127; Mungeam, *British Rule in Kenya*, 268; Bennet, *Kenya*, 33.

178. Maxon, *Struggle for Kenya,* 41.

Chapter 8

Maasai Move and Land Compensation Issue

The second Maasai move from the Laikipia plateau became a huge issue for Sir Percy's administration in 1910 and 1911. The matter of compensation for European farmers who would be impacted by the move of the Maasai groups from Laikipia also marked that period. In confronting the challenges set by these related matters, Sir Percy failed conspicuously, just as in the examples provided in the previous chapter, to deal efficiently and fairly with issues involving land. The Maasai move from Laikipia and associated land compensation brought out quite clearly Sir Percy's failure to provide justice and fair play for the people he administered. As in other areas of administration, Sir Percy favored the claims and interests of European settlers over those of Africans in dealing with those issues. Beyond that, however, Sir Percy resorted to cover-ups in an attempt to disguise the true nature of his actions and their motivation. Furthermore, in forcing the Maasai on Laikipia to agree to leave that region, he broke his word to his superiors at CO and a treaty that had been agreed with the Maasai in 1904. These actions were hardly to be expected of a sound administrator, and indeed Sir Percy's handling of the Maasai move and associated land compensation proved major reasons for his removal from the governorship of the EAP.

FIRST MAASAI MOVE

Upon the declaration of the protectorate, in 1895, Hardinge became the first administrator, taking instruction from the FO. In Hardinge's consolidation of British authority, he came into contact with the Maasai, whom he and his successors found very useful in their war of occupation. Since the local colonial authorities contact with the Maasai, in 1895, relationship between the two had been friendly. The Maasai had at certain critical periods taken allied with the British that "revive and recreated a dying Maasai society," when the Maasai were confronted with internecine conflict that threatened to exterminate them.[1] On the part of the local colonial authorities, they considered the Maasai as interpreters and competent guides. The British local colonial authorities opined that among all the peoples on the railway line to Uganda, it was only the Maasai who could leave "material and supplies untouched."[2] When the Maasai were told that they would be removed for Laikipia, they did not resist moving, probably because they were friendly with the colonial authorities. In fact there were occasions when the British local authorities used the Maasai as mercenaries in suppressing opposition to their authority. The Maasai elder, Ole Gilisho, led some of these warriors and suppressed rebellion against the colonial authority. Despite friendly relationship between the two, the colonial authorities were unaware that the Maasai had no one leader. The colonial authorities appointed a leader by elevating the Maasai prophet, Olonana, as the Maasai exalted ruler. In addition, he and Ole Gilisho were made officials of government and paid salaries.[3] On the transfer of Hadinge, another career diplomat, Sir Charles Eliot, replaced him.[4]

Eliot assumed government of the protectorate with a title of commissioner of the protectorate. Following his arrival to the protectorate, he contemplated the removal of the Maasai from their original settlement in the Rift Valley to a different place. On Eliot's resignation, his successor, Stewart declared that the Maasai must be removed to Laikipia. This was the first of two moves associated with the Maasai in the history of the EAP. The first move was from the Rift Valley to Laikipia, in 1904. This was the first Maasai move, in which, Sir Donald Stewart entered into agreement with the Maasai elders, that some of the Maasai would vacate their original settlement in the Rift Valley for Laikipia. On the other hand, the settlers would inhabit the Rift Valley along the railway line. The Maasai moved to Laikipia in 1905 but some of the Maasai settled to the south of Laikipia or in the southern Maasai reserve.

Sir James Hayes Sadler, who did not engage himself with the Maasai question, succeeded Stewart, and upon his (Sadler) transfer and before Sir Percy's assumption of government of the EAP, the Public Works Department of the protectorate, contemplated removing the Maasai from Laikipia to the extended southern Maasai reserve. The head of Public Works Department, McGregor Ross, instructed two of its staffers to report on the desirability or otherwise of the Maasai habitation of the extended southern Maasai reserve.[5] The two-man committee reported that the southern Maasai reserve was suitable to pastoral nomadic community rather than an agricultural community.[6] The report formed the basis on which the local authorities sought to remove the Maasai for the second time. The latter effort by the Public Works Department was a hint not to be disregarded on the proposed second Maasai move, prior to Sir Percy's assumption of government. In September 1909, Sir Percy assumed the government of the protectorate, and in his Interim Report, further reinforced the desirability of preserving African reserves, as noted earlier.[7]

THE LAND COMPENSATION

The proposed Maasai move and grant of Laikipia to the European farmers on the Maasai move, did not work out as the protectorate's authorities had envisaged. The government proposed exchange was a futile enterprise. In the proposed land compensations in Laikipia for the European farmers leaving the Guaso Nyiro region, the European farmers would be removed from Guaso Nyiro to a fertile Laikipia. While the Maasai who had been living in Laikipia would be removed to the extended southern Maasai reserve. There was compensation for the removal of the farmers but there was no compensation for the removal of the Maasai. Even then, the compensation for the removal of the farmers caused discontentment among the farmers and presented the administration in a very unenviable position among the settlers. It also caused some of the settlers to leave the protectorate out of frustration, compensation being paid to them for the depreciation of their stock notwithstanding.

The farmers contended that the proposed compensation was not enough for them to relinquish their farms, and additional compensation of fifty percent of the size of each farmer's farm was added to them. The farmers agreed with compensations for their farms, but they demanded monetary, in addition to land, compensation being made over to them. The government acquiesced, but on the commencement of the move, the move collapsed. When the move collapsed, the farmers sought shelter in a nearby European settlers farms, pending government decision.

The government decision was not forthcoming. Some of the farmers returned to Guaso Nyiro, some of them refused to take the offer of compensation made to them, while a few of the settlers moved back to South Africa out of frustration. The failed removal of the Guaso Nyiro settlers discouraged prospective immigrants into the protectorate and presented the unfair dealings of Sir Percy's administration in granting compensations to the white farmers while refusing to consider the Maasai for the same compensation. The failed moves of the farmers were no less important in undermining the administration desire to encouraged immigration into the protectorate and could not be considered an effective administration, having jeopardized lives of the races of the protectorates by removing them at the time of a poor season, and also discouraging prospective immigration into the protectorate, at the time, when immigrants into the colony were being sought.

As described earlier, there was an attempt to move the Maasai out of Laikipia prior to Sir Percy's assumption of government. The Land Officer of the protectorate, R. B. Wright's, circular of 3 June 1909 told the European farmers in the Guaso Nyiro region and those living on the edge of Sotik country that the government wanted their farms for the Laikipia Maasai.[8] Wright asked the farmers whether they would be willing to relinquish their farms for the Maasai, and to receive compensation equal to their Guaso Nyiro farms on Laikipia, and half as much in another area open for allotment, especially Uasin Gishu and Sotik.[9]

Wright asked the farmers that if government were successful in the removal of the Maasai, whether they would agree to relinquish their farms on the said terms of compensation.[10] Wright asked further that if they would not accept the said terms, on what terms of compensation would they be willing to relinquish their Guaso Nyiro farms to take up other farms on Laikipia.[11] Even though the said letter was non-committal, but it was a hint, not to be disregarded, on the intent of the government to remove the Maasai from Laikipia.

The first hint suggesting that Sir Percy could not stand up to his proposed safeguards of African reserves was allowing Wright to continue with his process of compensation, which he initiated at least four months before Sir Percy assumed the government of the protectorate. Upon Sir Percy's assumption of government, he allowed Wright to issue other letters in 1910, which clearly suggested that Sir Percy was not only aware of the planned removal of the Maasai prior to his arrival into the country, but he supported it and subsequently took over the initiatives to remove the Maasai. Prior to Sir Percy consenting to Wright to continue the issuance of letters to the Guaso Nyiro European farmers, one of the late claimants of Laikipia, Delamere, having accepted compensation for his Laikipia farm in another district of his choice, also turned to Wright and pressured him to reconsider his Laikipia claims.[12]

Thereafter, Wright intimated to Montgomery of Delamere's renewed Laikipia claims. The basis of Delamere's Laikipia claims was that, prior to the 1904 Maasai agreement, there were farms allotted to 26 European farmers in Laikipia, and when it was agreed that the Maasai would be relocated to Laikipia from their original settlement in the Rift Valley, those farmers were compensated in another district.[13] Among those farmers were Delamere and Galbraith Cole who declined to take the offers of compensation being made to them by the government. Instead, they selected farms in a different district, and asked the government to approve of their choice as their compensations for their Laikipia farms.[14] The government approved of their choices; therefore, Laikipia became opened for the Maasai to move in. But despite compensations made to Delamere and Cole, the duo never acquiesced to the settlements of their Laikipia claims, when they applied to Wright, to reconsider their Laikipia claims in late 1908.[15] Delamere demanded that his

Laikipia claims stand and should be reconsidered.[16] Wright, in a memorandum of 15 April 1910, told the Commissioner of Lands, Colonel J. A. L. Montgomery, of Delamere's renewed Laikipia claims.[17] Montgomery, in a minute on Wright's memorandum, recognized Delamere and Cole's claims over Laikipia.[18]

In order to reply to Wright, Montgomery consulted with Sir Percy, and thereafter addressed a memorandum of 7 April 1910 to Sir Percy, proposing a land allocation procedure to the 26 late Laikipia claimants. Delamere and Cole topped the list of the claimants. Again, in the proposed grants of farms to the late claimants in Laikipia, Delamere and Cole were given the opportunity of first choice of farms, before any of the claimants could choose, plus half as much land, as their compensations.[19] Wright supported additional grants of half as much of their compensations, when he stated that Delamere was given the extra land because he "perhaps did certain developments on his farm."[20] Also, Wright stated that Delamere was said to have helped the government by inducing the farmers to accept the Laikipia offer. As to Cole's additional grants, Wright stated that Cole was in occupation of his farm and had affected some developments, when he agreed to accept the Laikipia offer in 1904 and therefore deserved additional compensation. Contrary to Wright's position, the Assistant Land Officer, L. M. Dundas, objected, stating in a minute that Delamere and Cole were offered half as much because, at the request of the government in 1904, they agreed to relinquish their Laikipia farms for the first Maasai move.[21]

As to developments said to have been affected by Delamere and Cole, Dundas stated that he could not ascertain any developments said to have been made by them, on their farms, that would afford them additional compensation of half as much being made over their Laikipia compensations.[22] As to the remaining farmers, they were never afforded half as much as their compensations. However, Dundas stated there was nothing in their records to show that they were promised half as much of their compensations.[23]

The remaining late Laikipia claimants, also at the request of the government, relinquished their Laikipia farms for the Maasai move, Wright and Dundas's claims notwithstanding. But they were denied an additional half as much as their compensations, which were afforded to Delamere and Cole.[24] The preferential treatment accorded to Delamere and Cole over the remaining late Laikipia claimants did not suggest that the compensation was carried out in a manner consistent with the type of compensation Wright had proposed to the farmers, in his letters of 3 June 1909 and 18 April 1910.

There was an inconsistency in the proposed compensations, in which a preferential offer was made to the two influential settlers by grants of half as much compensation. Sir Percy, in his intimation to Crewe on the question of Laikipia Maasai, disguised the inconsistency and told Crewe, in his telegram of 30 April 1910, that Delamere, who was partial to the Maasai, gave up his Laikipia farm in 1904 for the Maasai and encouraged other settlers to give up their land for the Maasai.[25] Prior to such intimation, Sir Percy had already instructed Wright to intimate to the settlers further developments on the proposed move, in which Wright, in a letter of 18 April 1910 to the settlers, conveyed a definite offer of compensation to farmers of, an equal proportion of their farms, on Laikipia and its vicinity, plus half as much, in another district; Uasin Gishu or Sotik.[26]

The letter was not only suggestive but compelling evidence of the promise of farms being made to the farmers. It also suggested that there was an impending government decision for the removal of the Maasai from Laikipia to the extended southern Maasai reserve. It also suggested that Sir Percy was drifting away from his policy of preserving the African reserves against interest groups who might grab African land within the African reserves for their own interest.[27] Therefore, Sir Percy's actions were contrary to the established administrative procedure, as the CO would expect an intimation of his proposed removal of Maasai, which Crewe would have to approve, before he could entertain the removal of the Maasai. But Sir Percy refused to tell Crewe of developments described in this section in respect of the proposed move.

The European farmers who were promised farms whenever the Maasai were removed, also had their own ordeal, as the Maasai move failed. They could not move, despite government's vacating order. These European farmers had their own share of the ordeal of the Maasai move, as they were offered Laikipia, and were told to move, as the Maasai leave. But their move also collapsed, as the Maasai could not move. The farmers demanded an addition of monetary compensation for the loss, delay and inconvenience occasioned to them by government's action. The later action was necessitated by Lord Delamere's insistence on his claims over a farmland in Laikipia. But whatever claims Delamere might have had, it should not have reversed a policy Sir Percy proposed to safeguard, especially the safeguard of African reserves, he had enunciated in his Interim Report.

Sir Percy's action on land compensation caused suffering for both the farmers and the Maasai, and undermined immigration of prospective settlers. Unfairness in compensation between the farmers and the Maasai showed his favoritism to the settlers over the Maasai. The European demands about their compensations were met by the local authorities, but as for the Maasai, no offer of compensation was made to them, despite, suffering, depreciation of stock, death of stock and loss of human lives among the aged Maasai on the commencement of the failed move.

In the long run, Sir Percy upheld the interest of the white community, over the preservation of the Maasai native reserve, when he removed the Maasai from Laikipia to the southern reserve against their wishes. Sir Percy not only failed to preserve the African reserve, a policy he advocated for, but also interfered with the reserve. The manner in which the compensation was carried out caused doubt if an administrator of outstanding capability could compromise government-approved policy, so as to safeguard the interest of a settler-community. With these clearly stated shortcomings, Sir Percy's administration of compensation did not amount to an effective administration of land compensation. It was a display of favoritism to the European settlers without due regard to the Maasai who should have been compensated. His policy of compensation was a failure and it brought his presumed competence as a fair and effective administrator into disrepute.

SIR PERCY AND THE PLANNED MAASAI MOVE

Despite this declared support for safeguarding African reserves, Sir Percy soon discovered that there was an effort to remove the Maasai from Laikipia to the extended southern Maasai reserve. Despite his recommendation for the preservation of African reserves against syndicates and interested individuals and groups, he failed to stop the proposed removal of the Maasai. Sir Percy allowed the Land Officer, Wright, and the Commissioner of Lands, Lieutenant Colonel Montgomery, to continue with the process of removing the Maasai. Even when the land office was issuing letters to the European farmers with hints that they would be removed to Laikipia while the Maasai would move to the extended southern Maasai reserve. Prior to Sir Percy's assumption of government, there was a correspondence with the European farmers, living in the Guaso Nyiro region hinting at the intention to remove the Maasai from Laikipia to southern Maasai reserve so that they could inhabit the same southern reserve with the other Maasai.[28]

Other than the removal of the Maasai to the southern reserve, there was also a move by the Maasai to attend their traditional annual ceremony in the same southern reserve. This move was not the removal of the Maasai from Laikipia; rather it was their move to the south to attend their annual circumcision ceremonies. It was reported in the Blue Book that the ceremonies were said to have commenced without the official sanction of the Maasai chief religious figure that the British recognized as chief, Olonana.[29]

According to the Maasai tradition, his sanction was needed to declare the ceremony opened. But Olonana withheld sanction on the ground that the Loita Maasai were not permitted to attend the occasion with their cattle. The restriction on the Loita cattle was a cause for concern for Olonana who, as the Blue Book notes, appealed to Sir Percy to permit them to hold the ceremony in Ngong, in view of restrictions imposed on the Loita Maasai.[30] It was also reported in the Blue Book that Sir Percy consented to this request so that the Loita Maasai could participate with their cattle in the ceremony.[31] Thereafter, Olonana instructed, in January 1910, that the Loita Maasai and Kinangop warriors should move to Ngong for the ceremony.[32] The Blue Book also notes that, in view of the restrictions imposed on the Loita Maasai, Olonana also appealed to Sir Percy that unless his authority was recognized and his instruction obeyed, he feared a disruption between the two sections of the Maasai tribes.[33]

Thereafter, the Blue Book notes that Sir Percy acknowledged Olonana's concern, and on 2 February 1910 Sir Percy convened a meeting in Nairobi, with all the Maasai leadership present. During the meeting, the Blue Book notes that Olonana made a passionate appeal to Sir Percy over the circumstances leading to the change in the Maasai affairs, since the last ceremony, when Olonana pointed out to Sir Percy that the restrictions, whereby free intercommunications between the two sections of the tribe was leading to disunity and could compromise his authority.[34]

Therefore, the Blue Book notes that Olonana appealed to Sir Percy that, "it was his most earnest wish that the northern Masai should move from Laikipia to inhabit the southern reserve."[35] However, the Blue Book notes that Sir Percy told Olonana that the removal of the Maasai out of Laikipia could not be approved without consulting other Maasai leaders; Ole Masikonde and Ole Gilisho.[36] Contrary to the views expressed in the Blue Book, Olonana never appealed to Sir Percy that the Maasai wished move out of Laikipia, and neither did Sir Percy tell Olonana that other Maasai leaders had to be consulted before a decision could be made.[37]

It should be noted that from an account of a physician serving in the protectorate, Dr. Norman Leys, Olonana did not ask Sir Percy that the Maasai wanted to move out of Laikipia.[38] However, Leys noted that the restriction of free intercommunication that the government imposed between the northern and the southern Maasai was making movements to and from difficult for such nomadic pastoralists.[39] Leys also noted that the restrictions were sufficient for the Maasai to move out of Laikipia, even before they could be asked to move out, but even then, the Maasai had not sought permission to move out of Laikipia.[40] The restrictions, Leys added, were due to government's failure to beacon the cattle route, which it promised to do, and had made it difficult for the Maasai to wander with the livestock.[41]

Leys's opinion was in concurrence with the views that Sir Percy told Crewe, in his telegram of 6 May 1910, that it was the failure of the government to beacon the cattle route it had promised to beacon that caused restrictions on intercommunication between the northern and the southern Maasai.[42] But at the same time, Sir Percy disguised the fact to Hopwood, in a private letter, when he told him, that Olonana begged him to allow the Laikipia Maasai move to the south to unite with these kinsmen.[43] Sir Percy also told

Hopwood that Olonana complained to him that his authority over his people was becoming tenuous, as movement between the northern and the southern Maasai was restricted, which made it difficult for Olonana to exercise effective control over the southern Maasai. Uniting the tribes in one place would strengthen Olonana's authority.[44]

However, Sir Percy suggested that their move, if affected, would be in the best interest of the tribe, and that everybody in the country believed that as long as the Maasai remain in Laikipia, the country could hardly be developed.[45] But restrictions imposed on the Maasai movements with their livestock due to the government's failure to beacon the cattle route, so that the Maasai cattle could not stray into the European farms was making movements between the northern and the southern Maasai sub-tribes increasingly difficult, and Olonana's authority over the southern Maasai was becoming increasingly tenuous. With such difficulty, the Maasai did not need to be told to move, they would choose to do so, if they were given the option. But even then, they did not choose to move out of Laikipia to the extended southern Maasai reserve.[46]

But Sir Percy, out of pressure for Laikipia land from the white farmers, and his desire to allot Laikipia land to those farmers, disguised the fact to the CO, when he told Crewe, in a telegram of 7 March 1910, that the Maasai wished to move out of Laikipia to Ngong, in the south, stating that the Maasai wished to move out of Laikipia to join their kinsmen, in the southern reserve, and that they were the first to suggest that they wished to move.[47] On receipt of Sir Percy's telegram, in the CO, another letter with its last page missing, dated 3 February 1910, and addressed to Professor Gilbert Murray, written by Dr. Norman Leys, was also received.[48]

In the letter, Leys dismissed Sir Percy's claims that the Maasai wished to move when he stated, "great wrong would be done to the Masai."[49] Leys added that settler pressure for fertile farmland was the chief cause of the government desire to move the Maasai, and not the Maasai wish.[50] Therefore, Leys asked Murray, "if the government was going to break its promise to the Masai?"[51] The promise that Leys referred to, was that the government, in the 1904 treaty it entered into with the Maasai, promised that the Maasai would inhabit Laikipia as long as they exist as a race.[52]

In the CO, Fiddes, in his comments on the two documents, stated "either the letter was false, in which case the writer should be dismissed, or it was true, which made the governor's position impossible."[53] But Fiddes supported Sir Percy's position, stating that they were "bound to believe him."[54] Fiddes added that the matter should be investigated, and warned that, "great circumspection is necessary in dealing with this matter, which might easily give rise to a tornado in the House of Commons."[55] Moreover, Fiddes made reference to the 1904 treaty between Stewart and the Maasai, and observed that, "nothing could be more solemn and binding in form," than a treaty of 1904.[56] Also, Fiddes suggested further that, "If the Masai wished to move, a treaty equally solemn and binding as that of the 1904 must be procured."[57] Therefore, Fiddes recommended that Sir Percy should be told to suspend the proposed move, and to await further directives by dispatch.[58] Seeley and Crewe expressed their concurrence with Fiddes, as they never commented further, other than endorsing their initials on the documents. Therefore, Crewe instructed for a telegraphic reply to Sir Percy that he should suspend the move, pending further directives by dispatch.[59]

As the CO was drafting a full reply, Sir Percy refused to wait for Crewe's dispatch, and informed Crewe that the move had already commenced.[60] In fact, Crewe and other officials in the CO were stunned, and no one could believe that Sir Percy could direct the removal of the Maasai without Crewe's approval.[61] The CO officials were exasperated with Sir Percy's action, when Butler, in his minute stated, that it was amazing that Sir Percy should have "forgotten his duty so as to lend himself to an irrevocable step without first obtaining the approval of the Secretary of State.[62] Fiddes's frustration could be clearly inferred from his minute, when he stated that the whole issue had a very ugly look.[63] Crewe became concerned that Sir Percy's action might cause the Commons to demand an explanation on the move, when he sated, "this might easily become a very awkward question."[64] Therefore, Crewe addressed a telegram of 21 April 1910, directing Sir Percy to suspend the move, allow the Maasai to return to Laikipia, and to await further instructions by dispatch.[65] Sir Percy told Crewe, in a telegram of 22 April May 1910, that the move has been suspended, and the Maasai were told to return to Laikipia.[66]

The action was the worst-case scenario of an administrator carrying out responsibilities that were not sanctioned by the home government had he preferred to await instructions from the CO on whether they would consent to the move or not. Such action did not portray Sir Percy as a successful administrator as he had not been consistent and open to the CO as to the true position of his action other than disguising the facts of the matter.

The preliminary arrangements of the Maasai move, especially Wright's letters to the farmers with intimations of modes of compensation the government would offer to the farmers, should the government be successful in removing the Maasai, and the eventual removal of the Maasai, were shrouded in secrecy. The CO was never informed of any proposed movements and no approval was sought for such movements or for the promise of farms being made to the late Laikipia claimants. Sir Percy's action amounted to disregard for the established working norms, where he was expected to inform the Secretary of State for the Colonies of all government activities in the protectorate.

In addition, for a successful administration of a protectorate, and for a governor to be successful, he must ensure harmonious working relations with the CO and keep them informed of all activities of government, and refer issues that required Crewe's attention to him, for his consideration and approval, before Sir Percy could execute any action.[67] But Sir Percy refused to do so, and transmitted intimations of his action, when the Maasai move collapsed.[68] This was not how a governor could be a successful administrator, when he failed to provide a clear intimation of his actions and failed to seek approval before taking action, which provoked anger and hostility against him in the CO. For a successful administrator, he must cultivate good relations with his superiors in the CO and keep them informed of all developments in the country, which Sir Percy failed to do. But Sir Percy refused, and there was no way, a successful administrator would go to such length in initiating the removal of a community to a different location without seeking the approval of the CO.

This should have been the case, more especially, in a country where the British government was concerned with the preservation of African land rights. It could be recalled that Winston Churchill had to defend the position of the government, in July 1907, before the Parliament, on the preservation of African land rights and the removal of the Maasai from the Rift Valley to Laikipia.[69] Therefore, any action that would involve the removal of Africans to a different location must be referred to the CO for approval. But Sir Percy refused to seek approval before directing the Maasai to move. As Sir Percy received directives to suspend the move, he complied with the directives, but complained to Hopwood, in a private and confidential letter of 21 April 1910, disguising the fact to Hopwood that the move was in the best interest of the Maasai.[70] But it was clear from the circumstances that culminated in the removal of the Maasai that, as I stated in the preceding paragraphs, the move was not in the best interest of the Maasai, as Sir Percy claimed.

The removal of the Maasai from Laikipia to the ecologically unfriendly extended southern Maasai reserve would not have been otherwise than detrimental to the very best interest of the Maasai. His statement in the letter to Hopwood that he had the Maasai at heart, does not appear to be without doubt as the move was mainly to afford the European farmers access to better farms, while the Maasai would be relocated to an arid area, where shortage of water supply was mentioned as a potential problem that they had to deal with.[71]

But with the intervention of the CO, there seemed to have been a respite for the Maasai, when Crewe, in his confidential dispatch of 22 April 1910, told Sir Percy that the agreement of 1904, signed between the Maasai and the government was "solemn and binding," and implored Sir Percy that in view of the "enduring nature of the 1904 agreement, it could not be revoked without another treaty of equal stature with that of 1904."[72]

Also, Crewe admonished Sir Percy against rumors in London that the Maasai might have been coerced to accept the move, and concluded his dispatch by raising concern that "due to the severe form which the cattle disease had taken, it is probable that the move could not have been undertaken in any case, for fear of infecting the stock on European farms, and in the Loita plains."[73]

Sir Percy complied with Crewe's directives, and also addressed a letter to the farmers waiting for the Maasai move so that they could move into Laikipia, intimating to them that the move was suspended due to cattle disease that Crewe referred to in his dispatch rather than the move was suspended because he did not seek the CO's approval before the commencement of the move. However, Sir Percy defended his action, when he pointed out that the Maasai herds were becoming increasingly large and that the Laikipia reserve was insufficient for their herds to graze.[74] He pointed out that the reserve was extended twice and still, most frequently, the livestock strayed into European farms for more pasture, and the owners of the livestock were in the process "sometimes fined."[75] Also, in his reply to Crewe by a telegram of 6 May 1910, he stated that he had wanted to reunite the Maasai tribes in one area so as to preserve the reserves as well as the authority of the paramount chief Olonana. Sir Percy also added that, "gravest reason for the move was is that paramount chief is losing his power by our having treaty some years ago (which was) absolutely necessary (for) quarantine reasons and owing to impossibility to allow Masai to wander over half a miles through sixty mile of European farms."[76]

The local authorities had earlier assured the Maasai in Laikipia that a cattle route would be beaconed so that they could move their stock without cattle straying into European farms. In addition, the beaconed cattle route would connect the Laikipia Maasai with their kin in the southern reserve. Without the beacon the Maasai could not wander with their cattle nor could they maintain contact with the Maasai in the southern reserve. In view of the significance of the route, the local authorities assured the Maasai that the route would be beaconed. But since early 1910 when the promise to beacon had been made, the local authorities never beaconed the cattle route and intercommunication between the two sections of the Maasai was becoming a distant possibility and that Olonana's power to exercise control over both the Laikipia and the southern reserve was becoming increasingly tenuous. Therefore, the absence of the beacons had made movement of the Laikipia Maasai almost impossible and that was good enough for the Laikipia Maasai to leave Laikipia even if the government had not proposed to remove them.

As to the desirability of procuring an agreement for the Maasai move as recommended by Fiddes, Sir Percy stated that he was already in possession of the agreement, made in presence of witnesses who were the same signatories of the 1904 agreement, and once the agreement was signed, the move might proceed. But Sir Percy told Crewe, in his telegram of 6 May 1910, that he would prefer to place the Maasai in the hands of a board of trustees. The board of trustees, would be composed of the Chief Judge of the High Court, and two Judges, a Bishop, and Secretary of Native Affairs, as members.[77] Sir Percy attempted to deflect blame on his action in the removal of the Maasai, stating different stories that deflected from the main issue. It was not only the question of procuring agreement, but also of the CO consenting to the move. But neither was an agreement procured nor was the CO being informed of the proposed move, which was shrouded in secrecy, and it only came to the knowledge of the CO, when the move collapsed. Sir Percy's action, in this regard caused considerable embarrassment to the CO, and directed their hostility against him, which eventually caused his resignation.[78]

With such subversive administrative action, it would in no way be considered an outstanding performance, and neither would Sir Percy be considered a successful administrator, as the CO should not only to be informed of government activities in the country, but they had to approve of policies that the governor proposed for implementation in the colony. However, Sir Percy was also concerned with his action in the removal of the Maasai, which did not portray him, as an administrator who was following clearly the laid down procedure of administration. He had not been intimating the CO of development in the country, which was an important requirement for effective, efficient and a successful administration.[79] Haunted by his subversive action, Sir Percy also told Hopwood, in a private letter of 21 April 1910, "I would not desire to embarrass government and lam deeply sensible of support accorded but would earnestly point out that if your support is now withdrawn my Government would be completely discredited and, though leaving myself completely in your hands would prefer to be relieved in my government and return presently and explain my reports which I have now almost completed."[80] He suggested further that the present arrangement was that the European farmers would be moving north. With the northern Maasai ready to move south, this must be carried on during May and June, and such arrangement was a reaffirmation of his proposed reserves to be governed by a board of trustees.[81]

In spite of Sir Percy's explanation in self-defense, Crewe refused to budge, when he replied to Sir Percy's telegram of 6 May 1910, and Sir Percy's private letter to Hopwood, of 21 April 1910, in a telegram of 12 May 1910. He stated, "I fear it is not feasible to place the Masai reserve in the hands of trustees for reason which will be explained to you by dispatch."[82] Therefore, Crewe reiterated his commitment to safeguarding African reserves by the British government rather than individuals, when he explained his position to

Sir Percy, in a confidential dispatch of 31 May 1910, that the British government would be the trustee and that the involvement of private persons would be unnecessary complications.[83]

MAASAI TREATY OF 1911

Nevertheless, Sir Percy took the CO instruction seriously and convened a meeting at Ngong and concluded a provisional agreement between the Maasai and the government. The terms of the agreement stated that the tribesmen, being satisfied that it was to their best interest that the Maasai people should inhabit one area, agreed to move from Laikipia to Loita plains.

A conference was convened to sign the agreement between the Maasai leadership and the authorities of the colony. The representatives of the Maasai were Olonana, Ole Masikonde and Ole Gilisho, and Saburi (whose position in the southern reserve was similar to Ole Masikonde in the northern reserve). There were also heads of clans i.e. the principal elders of the northern reserve and the spokesmen of the senior and junior of the coming age group of the warriors. Sir Percy, Hobley, and Lane, provincial commissioners; Combe, the Crown Advocate; Hollis, the Secretary for Native Affairs; and Collyer, District Commissioner of the Northern Reserve, represented the government. Also, in attendance was Reverend Dr. Scott who served as an independent witness. The contents of the agreement were read to the Maasai delegates that the agreement entered into between the government and the Maasai "of their own free will was translated and finally explained to them."[84] Upon listening to the contents of the agreement, Ole Gilisho dissented, and told the conference that the said area was not large enough for their needs. But Sir Percy asked Ole Gilisho and Ole Masikonde to depute representatives to report on the country with Collyer. Sir Percy also promised that if the area was found to be too small, the country across the Amala River would be made over to them.[85]

The two men nominated by Ole Gilisho later reported that the said area was too small for their habitation and that the Sotik would steal their cattle. Also Collyer, who was recommended to Ole Gilisho by Sir Percy as part of the deputation, reported that the "Masai of Laikipia were ready to go if the government ordered them to do so, but that they do not wish to leave Laikipia."[86]

In August 1910, the Maasai convened a meeting with a view to consider the report, and to take a common position. After the meeting, they approached Collyer and told him that they were ready to move out of Laikipia if the government ordered them to do so, "but they did not wish to leave Laikipia."[87] If all these reports were placed before Crewe, he could hardly have been impressed, let alone be convinced sufficiently to approve of the removal of the Maasai to such an ecologically unfriendly southern reserve.[88]

As negotiations were ongoing between Sir Percy and the Maasai, Sir Percy received a strongly worded letter from Leys, dated 25 May 1910. Leys was very critical of Sir Percy over the removal of the Maasai, deploring the nature of land dealing in the protectorate, and how "European influence threatened native lands."[89] Leys told Sir Percy that the Maasai move would confirm the belief that "all specially desirable native reserves would similarly come to be exchanged for more distant, less well watered or less fertile land."[90] Leys was critical of Sir Percy's land dealings which, he pointed out, caused the removal of the Maasai. However, in view of the damaging remark that Leys made against Sir Percy and his administration, he had, upon a second thought, addressed another letter of 27 May 1910 that he wished to withdraw a certain portion of his letter of 25 May 1910; the portion that criticized government for exchanging African lands with far distant and less watered areas.[91] In a reply to Leys, Sir Percy, in a letter of 2 June 1910, assured Leys that he would take the "earliest opportunity afforded by a public occasion to make it unmistakably clear that government policy in resistance of such encroachment was so fixed and strong as to make the hopes of it utterly vain."[92] He assured Leys that as long as he was governor "any proposal from any quarter to move a single native village would have his uncompromising resistance."[93] Sir Percy told Leys that the "breach in those principles shown in his Masai policy was due to circumstances so exceptional."[94]

Sir Percy added that the disunion of the tribe and the circumstances arising out of stock disease meant that he made up his mind that they would have to move whenever he investigated the subject. Sir Percy added that the fulfillment of these assurances would have gone far to neutralize the effect of the move on the minds of the Europeans. Leys' confrontation with Sir Percy was investigated after Sir Percy resigned, in July 1912. The CO received all the details of what transpired between Leys and Sir Percy, when, in September, Harcourt requested the Acting Governor, C. C. Bowring, to submit to him all correspondence between Sir Percy and Leys. Bowring transmitted what transpired between Sir Percy and Leys to the CO. The transcript of discussion between Leys and Sir Percy, exposed altercations over the Maasai move and Sir Percy's defense of his action that clearly was not only a cover up but also a contravention of his proposed policy for the administration of the Africans.

Upon perusal of the correspondences, Read commented, "whether or not Sir Percy gave the assurance in question and whether or not, he made the public statement referred to, "I do not think that Dr. Leys has made his case any better or it affected by the renewed letter of his."[95] Anderson made a pointed accusation that Leys had masterminded the Maasai court case against the government. Anderson became very critical of the Maasai attorney, Alexander

Morrison, whom Anderson described as a "Hungry lawyer."[96] Anderson added that Leys had "placed himself between the lawyer and the delegation and engaged in communication between the two, it will be difficult to agree with Leys."[97] He further added that Leys attitude was reprehensible and that this issue might lead to the end of his service.[98] Anderson concluded, "such a man cannot be retained in the service."[99] Harcourt agreed with Anderson's comments, but not without some reservations; Harcourt's doubt had arisen in connection with the telegram from Sir Percy's successor, Belfield, of 23 May 1912 which threw a "sinister light on Sir Percy Girouard's 'frankness', if not on his motives for action."[100] Harcourt added, "Granting this however, I do not think it affects the disloyal action of Dr. Leys."[101]

Harcourt's statement was without doubt that Sir Percy's motives in this regard must have been informed by certain considerations to remove the Maasai. It could be recalled that Sir Percy, despite his proposed safeguard of African areas, did not live up to his word, when he attempted to compromise African areas. This suggested that he did not have Africans at heart, as he had stated earlier on. His sinister motives of safeguarding African reserves did not go unchallenged, when Leys challenged him and pointed out that there was no sincerity as to African reserves and government would in the long run remove Africans from fertile areas to a less fertile areas to give way for European farms, a policy that Leys considered as a betrayal of the Africans and Sir Percy's cynical motives in defending African rights which he had enunciated in his interim report. Despite the bold step taken by Leys in exposing Sir Percy's unfair deals, the CO failed to support his position simply because the CO was bound to support the governor rather than his subordinate. Precedence showed that listening to subordinates behind the governors could cause resignation, and thus the CO, probably for that reason, refused to support Leys, and the issue was allowed to slide down in an easy way.

However, Sir Percy's attempted Maasai move had to be delayed, as he could not conclude a treaty in 1910. The move was deferred to 1911. But even then, consultations with the Maasai on the proposed move were on going, when, on 7 March 1911, Olonana died. The Blue Book notes that Olonana was suffering from dysentery, though he was getting on well, when he suddenly collapsed.[102] The Blue Book notes, that the Assistant District Commissioner for the southern Maasai reserve, Mr. Crewe-Read, had visited Olonana and discussed various minor questions with him, a few hours before his death.[103] It was reported that Olonana, while in his deathbed, uttered before Crewe-Read, "tell the government to look after my children and to give them the money that I should have earned if I had been alive. Tell my people to obey the government as they have done during my life. Tell the Laikipia Masai to move with their cattle to the Loita plains."[104]

Olonana's 13-year-old son Seggi succeeded his father in a succession selection made in the presence of Provincial Commissioner, C. R. W. Lane. There were also two regents (Nagoya, a cousin of Olonana was selected as regent for the south and Ole Gilisho for the north). This arrangement was necessitated due to the young age of Seggi. The Blue Book reported that during the investiture ceremony, Ole Gilisho stated on behalf of the northern Maasai that he wished to ask that they be permitted to move to the extended southern reserve. Ole Gilisho was said to have stated that the change of opinion was due to the death of Olonana and the dying wish he had left behind. Again, Ole Gilisho stated they also feared of a possible disruption between the two sections of the tribe.[105] Lane, who was present at the meeting, was reported to have told them to consult the government in Nairobi over the issue.[106] As a sequel to their request, Sir Percy convened a meeting of the Maasai representatives in Nairobi on 3 April 1911. The Blue Book notes that Ole Gilisho, speaking on behalf of the Northern Masai, stated that it was their wish to move to the extended southern reserve.[107]

On 4 April 1911, a formal treaty was drafted, and another meeting was convened with the Maasai leadership. The Blue Book notes that members of the executive council and the provincial commissioners were summoned, and, in the presence of all, the Blue Book notes, Sir Percy asked the Maasai leaders "whether or not they wish to move to the extended southern reserve."[108] It further notes that the Maasai were said to have replied that they wanted to move in honor of Olonana's death wish. But a possible water shortage in the southern reserve was raised. The Blue Book account states that Ole Gilisho, acting as spokesperson for the Maasai, stated "if the government would help improve the water supply, they would contribute toward the work by the payment of bullocks."[109] The Blue Book notes that Ole Gilisho requested that all the Europeans living in the area of the southern reserve should be removed, and that the area applied for by Mr. Powy's Cobb, known as "The Promised Land," should be made over to them. The Maasai also asked for protection against possible Sotik raids, and approval for protection was granted. Therefore the Maasai finally asked that they would like to move as soon as possible, and at a time when there was grass along the route to the southern reserve. The Blue Book also states that the Maasai asked that they should be allowed to move slowly, but they were told, "the move was contingent upon the approval of His Majesty, the King. . . ."[110] They were told that if they were permitted to move, they would be allowed to proceed slowly. After all the issues raised had been considered, the treaty was translated and fully explained to them, and the Maasai affixed their marks in the presence of European officials. Thereafter the treaty was sent to Ole Masikonde in Rumuruti and other old men in order to secure his consent and to inform them of the meeting at Ngong.

Thereafter Sir Percy, in a telegram of 5 April 1911, told Harcourt that the Maasai held a meeting in Olonana's old home and have expressed their desire to move to the southern reserve in honor of Olonana's dying wish; that they should move after his death to the southern reserve.[111] Sir Percy also told Harcourt that he had concluded a treaty agreement with the Maasai, on the proposed move, and urged Harcourt to approve the move.[112] Harcourt replied in a telegram of 7 April 1911, and asked Sir Percy to submit full details in a dispatch.[113]

Sir Percy's action caused officials in the CO to tread with circumspection in dealing with any issue he might transmit to them, rather than considering him as a successful and an outstanding administrator. Harcourt demonstrated this when he became suspicious of Sir Percy's correspondence over the case, and because of the deep-seated distrust and hostility the CO officials had against him. Harcourt minuted that Sir Percy might have telepathically inspired Olonana's dying speech and awaited unfolding development.[114] Harcourt's minute raised a very important question on the performance of Sir Percy as an administrator, as there was no way, with such comment from the most senior of Sir Percy's superiors in the CO, that would suggest that Sir Percy was considered not only a successful but also an outstanding administrator.

Another failure of Sir Percy's administration came at a time Harcourt was considering approving the Maasai move, believing that Sir Percy had complied with the CO confidential dispatch of 22 April 1910 which required of him to conclude a treaty between the government and the Maasai. He was also told in the dispatch that the agreement should be in a similar manner to that which Stewart and the Maasai leadership had concluded in 1904.[115] Stewart and the Maasai entered into an enduring treaty agreement that the Maasai would move from the Rift Valley to inhabit Laikipia as long as they existed as an ethnic group. The agreement between Stewart and the Maasai was considered an enduring agreement, and the CO hoped that Sir Percy would enter into a similar agreement, before he could remove the Maasai from Laikipia to the extended southern reserve.

But rumors that Sir Percy promised farms on Laikipia to European farmers before 1911 began to filter to the Commons. A Member of Parliament and leader of the Labor Party, Ramsey MacDonald, addressed a private letter to Harcourt of 18 May 1911 with an enclosure of an anonymous petition addressed to MacDonald.[116] MacDonald told Harcourt that promises of farms in Laikipia had been made to farmers, and challenged Harcourt to inquire from the District Commissioner, Northern Maasai Reserve, Collyer, who was in London on leave.[117] The anonymous petition, allegedly written by Leys, criticized Sir Percy's administration of bowing to settlers. The governor was described as a supporter and advocate of Europeans settlers. Leys wrote, "our governor is not playing fair; his mind and ambition lead him into intrigues and bluffing. It is freely said that he does not mean to listen to the COs admonitions. He thinks himself safe in the favours of wealthy planters and investors."[118]

The disappointment of the CO was clearly demonstrated in a minute by Fiddes, stating, "this, if true, meant that Girouard and his principal officers were in a conspiracy to deceive."[119] The latter minute on Sir Percy did not portray him as an honest administrator, if it proved that MacDonald's allegations were true. But the confirmation of such allegations was just a matter of time, as some of his dealings, shrouded in secrecy, had been exposed to Parliament and the CO.[120]

In spite of the magnitude of the allegations, the CO would most likely be reluctant to investigate Sir Percy on anonymous allegations, and instead, they would rather allow MacDonald to challenge them, by raising the issue on the floor of the Commons. The CO had enough of similar instances in Kenya's past, where subordinate staff reported issues behind the back of the governor, and, upon investigation, it usually provoked anger, unhappy feelings and resignations.[121] The memories of Jackson and Bagge, who informed the Foreign Office of alleged attempts by the protectorate's commissioner, Sir Charles Eliot, to grant land to a syndicate, in the Maasai nominal grazing reserve, were still afresh in their memories. Eliot's travail began, when the Secretary of State for Foreign Affairs, Lord Lansdowne, listened to similar gossips behind Eliot's back, presumably from Jackson and Bagge. The outcome of such gossips over the grants, soured relations between Eliot and Lansdowne, and resulted in the resignation of Eliot, in 1904. These were examples of how listening to gossip from the governor's subordinate staff could lead to unhappy relations between the governor and the CO, which the latter wished to avoid.

There was also the case of Jackson, which the CO could not overlook, when Jackson reported, though to a lesser extent, against Sir Percy's immediate predecessor, Sir James Hayes Sadler. This discredited Sadler and resulted in his transfer to the British colony of the Windward Islands.[122] The CO, however, might also have recalled Sir Percy's Main Report, in which Sir Percy was very critical of nearly all the officials of the protectorate, stating that he would not condone acts of staff reporting to the CO, behind his back.[123] Sir Percy had, without doubt, clearly told the CO that he would not condone staff talking behind his back to his superiors in the CO. Therefore, with previous experience of by passing the governor to listen to the governor's subordinate staff of rumors or anonymous allegations, Harcourt refused to budge on MacDonald's allegations and advise. But at the same time, however, Harcourt did not dismiss MacDonald's allegations outright, as he had heard the same allegations from C. R. W. Lane, whom

Sir Percy had, earlier on, described as liable to utter disloyal statements. Lane had already told Harcourt that Sir Percy promised farms on Laikipia to European farmers.[124]

In view of such allegations, Harcourt delayed approving the move to allow MacDonald to prove his allegations, and stated that if MacDonald could not substantiate his allegations, he would have no alternative course of action open to him, than to approve the move.[125] However, Harcourt stated that the allegations against Sir Percy should be published, and should anyone desire to confront Sir Percy, he would have something to rely upon.[126] He added that to investigate Sir Percy on anonymous charges would provoke him, to tender his resignation.[127] Fiddes agreed, and stated that there was no need to consult Collyer as MacDonald suggested.[128] However, Fiddes suggested further that, even if, the allegations were true, MacDonald might be "pulverized to raise the issue on the floor of the Commons."[129]

Despite the fact that Harcourt was determined to approve the move, however, he did not reject MacDonald's allegations outright. As he was awaiting MacDonald to substantiate his allegations, he enquired from Sir Percy, when he cabled a telegram of 5 October 1911, warning against "the grant of, or promise of, land" and enquiring whether any grants or promises to such land had already been made.[130]

Sir Percy replied to Harcourt, in a telegram of 7 October 1911, that "no such right had been given or promised, but that Europeans who had given up 130,000 acres for the extended southern Masai Reserve had to be accommodated elsewhere."[131] Harcourt knew this statement was false because Lane, Sir Percy's Provincial Commissioner, had already told Harcourt that promises of farms had been made.[132] Harcourt commented on Sir Percy's reply, "we can accept this information for what it is worth, but Lane the District Commr [*sic*] whom I saw the other day thought that farms in the Northern Reserve had been promised."[133]

Despite doubts arising from allegations that Sir Percy promised farmers Laikipia, Harcourt, in his reply to a question from the Commons, on 12 April 1912, stated, "no allocation of land occupied by the northern Masai had yet been made to Europeans."[134] Therefore, the CO shelved the advice of MacDonald, and resigned to their fate, as MacDonald was not forthcoming in substantiating his allegations, On 29 May 1911, Harcourt conveyed his approval to Sir Percy, and the move commenced.[135] The approval of the move reads: "This agreement appears to have fulfilled all the conditions laid down in paragraph 6 of my predecessor's dispatch of 22 April 1910, viz. that the new agreement of 1904, signed by a similar body of chiefs, and similarly attested by the interpreters and leading local officials. I have therefore felt justified in giving my approval to the agreement, and I have informed you accordingly in my telegram of 29th May."[136]

Following the approval of the move, a tour of the southern Maasai Reserve was made, and a final decision was also made to remove the Laikipia Maasai. But the report on the area was not encouraging, and noted, in addition to previous doubts about the reserve, that the area was too small. An additional area across the Amala River was made over to the Maasai so that they could be fully accommodated. With approval granted, and the move was resumed. Soon after it commenced it collapsed in June and was suspended. Sir Percy reported, in a telegram of 10 August 1910, that the move had been suspended due to cold and rains on the Mau plateau.[137]

Additional information was received in a dispatch with a report from the Director of Agriculture of the protectorate, MacDonald, stating that all the Maasai livestock had been sent back to Laikipia. But he denied that there were livestock losses and suffering, and regretted that the move failed.[138] But in reporting the collapse of the move, Sir Percy disguised the true position as to why the move was suspended, when he told Harcourt that the move was suspended to allow the Maasai cattle to graze before it could be resume. He added that the move had been hurried up.[139] In the CO, Harcourt disagreed with Sir Percy upon reading his reason for the suspension of the move. Harcourt stated, "this was a piece of monstrous impertinence" coming from Sir Percy.[140]

The proposed Maasai move from Laikipia to the southern reserve had been widely known in the protectorate, and at the commencement of the move, the mission had been accomplished, with opening up of a fine grazing land for European farmers. It was widely presumed that the Maasai were removed from Laikipia to the extended southern Maasai Reserve to give way to the European farmers, but the circumstances in which, the move was conceived in secrecy, and attempted execution of the move failed, and the disguising of information on the move to the CO, was later disclosed to the shock and consternation of Harcourt and officials in the CO. These dealings disclosed vague correspondences on important issues, which Sir Percy wrought in telegrams; providing little information, and, in some instances, he had to be told to write in a dispatch. If the latter were the problems, still Sir Percy could be considered a successful administrator. But in a situation where nearly all his dealings on this issue were disguised, it disclosed not only the dishonesty of the administration, but also the sinister motives relating to the purpose and intent of the removal of the Maasai.

All these dealings were not disclosed to the CO, that had the power and authority to decide on these matters, as Sir Percy refrained from transmitting information and seeking approval on the proposed Maasai move and the promise of farms. With these actions, Sir Percy not only failed to prove the presumed notion of him being an outstanding and a successful administrator, but he demonstrated that he was an administrator whose superiors in the CO would not repose their confidence in him. Instead of his performance earning him respect and good working relations with the CO, qualities that were indispensable for a successful administrator, his action earned him the hostility of his superiors.[141]

Sir Percy's failure in this aspect of his administration caused considerable disappointments and embarrassments to the CO, and it was the chief cause for his resignation. Sir Percy was forced to resign not because he was a successful administrator, but because he failed to administer in a manner consistent with the expectations of the CO, which was vested with powers and authority to decide policies for His Majesty's dominions.[142] Irked by his performance, Harcourt nursed considerable reservations against him, and had been waiting for an opportunity to ventilate his grievances against Sir Percy's promise of farms to farmers and the handling of the Maasai move without his consent.[143]

Thereafter, the opportunity came in the aftermath of the failed Maasai move, which disclosed to Harcourt, in the ensuing correspondence between Sir Percy and the CO, how Sir Percy concealed information on the proposed removal of the Maasai from Harcourt.[144] An angered Harcourt was aware that Sir Percy made the promise, as Lane had already told him the same.[145] Harcourt also learned that MacDonald's allegation was the truth, but as the fact had been disguised from him, he acted based on false information, as he had no option other than to believe Sir Percy.[146]

Harcourt found himself in a very difficult situation over the affairs of the protectorate; he was pained that Sir Percy misled him, in the administration of the affairs of the country.[147] But he had no option other than to live with it, and to wait for an opportune time to confront Sir Percy.[148] The most important thing was that he had a hint that his governor was disguising the facts of the matter from him, which forced him to deal with whatever Sir Percy might report to him, with great circumspection.[149]

In spite of the fact that his mishandling of the Maasai had been disclosed, Sir Percy sought to cover up, when he told Harcourt, in November 1911, that, in the past, there had been no well-defined policy over the Maasai, and that had been responsible for the delay in the Maasai move. He therefore told Harcourt of the need to come up with a well-defined policy on the Maasai. Unbeknown to Sir Percy, Harcourt had already been angered over his deceitful correspondence over the Maasai move. Harcourt was dissatisfied with the whole arrangement and had been waiting for an opportunity to ventilate his grievance, and his disappointments to Sir Percy, and this might had been part of the opportunity occasioned to Harcourt to address Sir Percy, on the question of the Maasai move. Harcourt told Sir Percy, the extent of his disappointment, when he stated: "It is clear that on the most favourable construction the whole arrangements for moving the tribe have been grossly mismanaged. There had been no adequate preparation before the move any proper supervision to control it during its progress you will understand that my confidence in the future handling of the matter has been greatly shaken."[150]

Harcourt's statement suggested that he had lost confidence in Sir Percy's handling of the Maasai move. However, as Sir Percy had directed that the Maasai should return to Laikipia following the failed move, Sir Percy reported to Harcourt that, the Maasai had been told to return to Laikipia, and they had returned since August. Sir Percy also reported in November that the Maasai were sent back to Laikipia, but some of them, were left on European farms.[151] Such conflicting reports raised doubts in the CO; Fiddes doubted if the information they had been getting from Sir Percy was the truth.[152] Fiddes also asked of the whereabouts of the Maasai? He added, "this most interesting part of the story wd. be the part that we are not allowed to know."[153] Frustrated, Harcourt stated, "this is always so with Sir Percy Girouard.... I give it up; I can't waste the remnants on my brain on his riddles."[154] Harcourt's anger could be seen not only from his comments but also from his writing. He used, "on my brain," rather than "of my brain."[155]

In May 1912, when Sir Percy was home on leave, Harcourt seized the opportunity and confronted him, over the issue. In the ensuing discussion between Sir Percy and Harcourt, in Harcourt's office at the CO, Sir Percy admitted that promises had been made to the European farmers who gave up their farms for the Maasai move.[156] Harcourt was astonished hearing Sir Percy admitting that promises had been made to the farmers. Still, Harcourt asked him, if he could comment on his telegram of 7 October 1911, in which Sir Percy told Harcourt that no promises had been made to the farmers, which was a reply to Harcourt's telegram of 5 October 1911, in which, Harcourt warned against the grant of or promise of, land, asked if promises of farms had been made to the farmers.[157]

But Sir Percy couldn't comment; he became speechless at last. He said nothing other than he saw no inconsistency in what he said in the telegram of 7 October 1911, and his admission of the promise in Harcourt's office. Harcourt was stunned and embarrassed that Sir Percy had intentionally misled him. In fact, the interview between Harcourt and Sir Percy was, in the main, the last altercation that ended Sir Percy's Kenya governorship, in an uncelebrated and most disappointing performance, on the Maasai question.[158]

It was reported that, at that very moment Sir Percy tendered his resignation to Harcourt, which he accepted, some sources hinted that Harcourt forced him to resign.[159] Harcourt clearly lost confidence in Sir Percy. Harcourt's frustrations over the move stemmed from how secretly Sir Percy arranged the removal of the Maasai without informing the CO, which caused Harcourt to demand a resignation from Sir Percy.[160] Harcourt, dissatisfied with his performance, was no longer willing to continue with him, as he could not vouch of his confidence. The following was the draft of the discussion that ensued between Harcourt and Sir Percy:

> Mr. Harcourt's discussion with Sir Percy today brought to light a curious misunderstanding. He said in reply to a question that the (South African) farmers who gave up their land in the south in order to make room for the Masai were promised that if the Laikipia lands were thrown open they wd. be considered (apparently they have been hanging about, on other peoples farms, ever since, waiting the fulfillment of this promise.) He was reminded of the telegraphic enquiry made by the Secretary of State on this point and of his reply, and said that he had stated nothing inconsistent with the above. It is difficult to reconcile this with our telegram of 5/10/11(31623) and his reply 32728(cf. the Secretary of State minute on the later).[161]

A copy was telegraphed to Bowring together with copies of the former two to refresh his memory.[162] Therefore, Fiddes drafted another letter addressed to Bowring, Officer Administering the Government, reiterating the warning given to Sir Percy that no dealing must be undertaken or promises made, concerning the Laikipia lands until they had been submitted to Harcourt and approved by him.[163] For the benefit of the doubts, the CO enclosed Harcourt's telegram of 5 October 1911 warning against promises of land and enquiring whether promise had been made, and Sir Percy's reply, in a telegram, dated 7 October 1911 that no promise of land had been made.[164] His resignation was a further confirmation that his performance had not been successful, it was a failed administration and neither could he consider an outstanding administrator as claimed by Kirk-Greene.[165]

The fact that Maasai were forcibly removed out of Laikipia was confirmed in the Maasai case against the government. In a sworn affidavit of Stephano Ole Hongop before a High Court of Justice sitting in Mombasa, in 1912, Hongop told the High Court that the Maasai were being forced to move out of Laikipia by the government.[166] Stephano told the Court that the Maasai agreed to move out of Laikipia, not because they wanted to move, but they had to move because of fear of government.[167] Huxley in *Whiteman's Country* pointed out that Sir Percy was not dismissed but resigned to take a better offer in an ammunition factory.[168] But Huxley's position was indefensible from archival manuscripts that detailed correspondence between Sir Percy and Harcourt on the Maasai question to the last, when he encountered Harcourt in the CO. The correspondence between Sir Percy and Harcourt and Sir Percy's interview with Harcourt, showed that Sir Percy lied, and he had lost the support and confidence of Harcourt and officials in the CO.

It was out of these circumstances that Harcourt viewed that Sir Percy could not be retained. Therefore, he asked him to resign.[169] With this failing in his administration and in dealings with his superiors in London, his performance was unsatisfactory. In dealing with the CO, Sir Percy was expected to keep it informed of his activities in the colony and to seek approvals through dispatches of actions he might execute in the colony. He should ensure that he complied with the directives of the CO as instructed in their approvals as well as other directives to carry through certain tasks in the colony. This failing in the Maasai case was not the only case where his performance was criticized. There was also the case of a European farmer, Galbraith Cole, whom the CO directed Sir Percy to deport, having shot and killed a suspect, and admitted, before a jury, of doing so to kill. The CO feared his presence could pose a threat to peace and order and directed for his deportation but Sir Percy created administrative and legal difficulties to block the deportation.

In the second Maasai move, despite their friendly relations with the local authorities, the Maasai resisted their removal from Laikipia to the southern reserve. The Maasai complained that the proposed second move for the extended southern reserve was not in their own best interest. They pointed out that in the southern reserve, there was no adequate water for their cattle and that Sotik would steal their cattle. But Sir Percy did not present the concern of the Maasai to the CO, when he intimated to Harcourt that they agreed to move. Even then, the CO told Sir Percy that the Maasai would have to agree to move and that he should enter into a treaty with them, similar to the treaty Stewart entered with the Maasai in 1904. But that never happened, as in the first failed Maasai move, he did not enter into agreement. It was following the failed first move that the CO told him that he must enter into agreement. Sir Percy initiated agreement with the Maasai but before he could conclude it, he was transferred out. It was his successor, Sir Conway Henry Belfield who concluded the agreement with the Maasai, and directed their removal to the southern reserve. The Maasai leaders tried to reverse their removal to the southern reserve, by resorting to a court proceeding to block their removal from Laikipia. Their application failed and they had to stay the southern reserve.

CONCLUSION

The removal of a portion of the Maasai from the Rift Valley to Laikipia in 1904 was successful and it was done in agreement with the Maasai leadership. Stewart's agreement with the Maasai brought the Maasai groups to inhabit Laikipia as long as they existed. But the agreement could not be sustained as the local authorities in concert with influential settlers were working to reclaim Laikipia by removing the Maasai to the extended southern Maasai reserve. Upon Sir Percy's assumption of the government of the protectorate, he should have stopped the proposed move, as it conflicted with his proposed safeguard of African reserves, but he failed to do so. Instead,

Sir Percy acquiesced in the proposed removal of the Maasai, coming under pressure of the settlers who wanted fertile Laikipia land for their farming. Sir Percy failed to make agreement with the Maasai as Stewart did, and failed to seek the CO's approval, and directed the Laikipia Maasai should move to the extended southern Maasai reserve in 1910. On the commencement of the move it collapsed, and the CO intervened to suspend the move and asked Sir Percy to make agreement with the Maasai before he could remove them.

He could not make agreement with the Maasai within a short period of time, when he happened to be in the CO, in early 1912, when Harcourt asked him of the removal of the Maasai without the approval of the CO. Harcourt's interview with Sir Percy on the removal of the Maasai, in the CO, resulted in the resignation of Sir Percy. Harcourt believed that Sir Percy was not forthcoming in his discharge of duty, especially the circumstance that surrounded the Maasai move had cause him to place Sir Percy in a very unenviable position. The CO believed that Sir Percy was not forthcoming in telling the truth surrounding the secret proposed removal of the Maasai from Laikipia.

Therefore Maasai were not comfortable with the removal, but they were compelled to move. This caused Maasai to seek redress in a court of law against the government eviction without their consent. Their application failed, and they were compelled to move to the southern reserve. Sir Percy's action in thc removal of the Maasai caused the government court action, disappointed the CO, and embarrassed himself before his superiors. He left the service of the EAP as a failed administrator, who worked out his own way in dealing with the Maasai against the CO's expectation.

NOTES

1. B. A. Ogot, "Kenya Under the British, 1895 to 1963," *Zamani: A Survey of East African History*, ed, B. A. O. got (Nairobi: East African Publishing House Ltd., 1974), 258.
2. Williams, *Running the Show: Governors of the British Empire* 1857–1912 (London: VIKING an imprint of Penguin Books, 2011), 360.
3. Ibid.
4. Ibid. Sir Charles Eliot was the son of a Wiltshire clergyman, a brilliant scholar, linguist and diplomat, who had served in Russia, Tangier, Constantinople and Washington.
5. Hughes, *Moving the Maasai,* 63.
6. Ibid.
7. Sir Percy to Crewe, Interim Report, confidential, 13 November 1909, CO 533/63.
8. Wright to European Farmers, private, 3 June 1909, CO 533/62.
9. Ibid.
10. Ibid.

11. Ibid.

12. Sorrenson, *Origins of European Settlement in Kenya*, 126.

13. Wright to Montgomery, 7 July 1910, enclosure in Montgomery to Sir Percy, memorandum, 7 June 1910, CO 533/108; Sorrenson, *Origins of European Settlement*, 126–27.

14. Ibid.

15. Ibid.

16. Ibid.

17. Wright to Montgomery, 15 April 1910, CO 533/73.

18. Montgomery to Sir Percy, 24 April 1910, CO 533/73.

19. Montgomery to Sir Percy, private, 7 April 1910, CO 533/73; Sorrenson, *Origins of European Settlement in Kenya*, 127.

20. Minute by Wright to Montgomery, 15 April 1910 CO 533/73; Sorrenson, *Origins of European Settlement in Kenya*, 127.

21. L. M. Dundas to Wright, 27 April 1910, CO 533/73.

22. Ibid.

23. Ibid.

24. Ibid.

25. Sir Percy to Crewe, telegram, 30 April 1910, CO 533/73.

26. Wright to Farmers, private, 18 April 1910, CO 533/73.

27. Sir Percy to Crewe, Interim Report, confidential, 13 November 1909, enclosure in Sir Percy to Crewe, confidential, 13 November 1909, CO 533/63.

28. Wright to Farmers, private, 3 June 1909, CO 533/62; G. R. Sandford, *An Administrative and Political History of the Masai Reserve* (London: Waterlow & Sons, 1919), 26. The Blue Book is a government official account of the administration of the Maasai.

29. Sandford, *An Administrative and Political History of the Masai Reserve* 26.

30. Ibid.

31. Ibid.

32. Ibid; Leys, *Kenya,* 104.

33. Sandford, *An Administrative and Political History of the Masai Reserve*, 26–27.

34. Ibid.

35. Ibid.

36. Ibid.; Hughes, *Moving the Maasai*, 35.

37. Hughes, *Moving the Maasai*, 35.

38. Leys, *Kenya*, 104.

39. Ibid.

40. Ibid.

41. Ibid.; Mungeam, *British Rule in Kenya,* 220.

42. Sir Percy to Crewe, Secret, 6 May 1910, CO 533/73; Leys, *Kenya,* 106; Hughes, *Moving the Maasai,* 35–6.

43. Sir Percy to Hopwood, confidential, 21 April 1910, CO 533/73.

44. Ibid.

45. Sir Percy to Hopwood, private, to Sir Percy, confidential, April 1910, CO 533/73.

46. Norman Leys to Professor Gilbert Murray, private, 3 February 1910, CO 533/72.

47. Mungeam, *British Rule in Kenya,* 261.

48. Ibid.

49. Ibid.

50. Ibid.

51. Ibid.

52. Mungeam, *British Rule in Kenya* 260; Sorrenson, *Origins of European Settlement in Kenya*, 127; Hughes, *Moving the Maasai*, 44; Bennett, *Kenya*, 31.

53. Minute by Fiddes, 14 April 1910, on Sir Percy to Crewe, confidential, 10 March 1910, CO 533/72.

54. Ibid.

55. Ibid.

56. Ibid.

57. Ibid.

58. Ibid.

59. Mungeam, *British Rule in Kenya,* 261.

60. Ibid.

61. Ibid., 262.

62. Ibid.

63. Ibid.

64. Ibid.

65. Crewe to Sir Percy, telegram, 21 April 1910, CO 533/73; Sorrenson, *Origins of European Settlement in Kenya,* 174.

66. Sir Percy to Crewe, telegram, 22 April 1910, CO 533/73; Sorrenson, *Origins of European Settlement in Kenya,* 174.

67. Maxon, "Judgment on a Colonial Governor," 90–93.

68. Sorrenson, *Origins of European Settlement in Kenya*, 206; Mungeam, *British Rule in Kenya,* 201; Hughes, *Moving the Maasai,* 37.

69. Great Britain, *Parliamentary Debates* (Commons), Fourth series, Vol. 7 (11–24 July 1907); 683–4.

70. Sir Percy to Hopwood, private, 21 April 1910, CO 533/73.

71. Ibid.

72. Crewe to Sir Percy, confidential, 22 April 1910, CO 533/73.

73. Ibid.

74. Hughes, *Moving the Maasai,* 34–5.

75. Ibid.

76. Sir Percy to Crewe, telegram, 6 May 1910, CO 533/73.

77. Ibid.

78. Mungeam, *British Rule in Kenya*, 268.

79. Ibid.

80. Sir Percy to Hopwood, private, 21 April 1910, C O 533/73.

81. Sir Percy to Crewe, telegram, 6 May 1910, CO 533/73.

82. Crewe to Sir Percy, telegram, 12 May 1910, CO 533/73.

83. Crewe to Sir Percy, confidential, 31 May 1910, CO 533/7; Mungeam, *British Rule in Kenya,* 223.

84. Sandford, *An Administrative and Political History of the Masai Reserve,* 30.
85. Ibid.; Leys, *Kenya*, 108.
86. Sandford, *An Administrative and Political History of the Masai Reserve,* 31; Leys, *Kenya,* 108.
87. Sandford, *An Administrative and Political History of the Masai Reserve,* 31.
88. Leys, *Kenya,* 108.
89. Leys to Sir Percy, private, 25 May 1910, CO 533/74.
90. Ibid.
91. Leys to Sir Percy, private, 27 May 1910, CO 533/74.
92. Sir Percy to Norman Leys, 2 June 1910, transcript of a conversation, enclosure, in Bowring to Harcourt, confidential, 20 October 1912, enclosure of transcript of conversation between Sir Percy and Leys, private, 2 June 1910, CO 533/108.
93. Ibid.
94. Ibid.
95. Minute by Read to Fiddes, 22 October1912, on Ibid.
96. Minute by Anderson to Harcourt, 23 October 1912, on Ibid.
97. Ibid.
98. Ibid.
99. Ibid.
100. Minute by Harcourt to Fiddes, 25 October 1912, on Leys to Bowring, private, 25 May 1912, 20 September 1912, enclosures in Bowring to Harcourt, confidential, 26 September 1910; CO 533/108.
101. Ibid.
102. Sandford, *An Administrative and Political History of the Masai Reserve,* 31.
103. Ibid.
104. Ibid., 32.
105. Ibid.
106. Sorrenson, *Origins of European Settlement in Kenya,* 202–204.
107. Sandford, *An Administrative and Political History of the Masai Reserve,* 31.
108. Ibid.
109. Ibid.
110. Sandford, *An Administrative and Political History of the Maasai Reserve,* 31–32.
111. Sir Percy to Harcourt, telegram, 5 April 1911, CO 533/86.
112. Ibid.
113. Harcourt to Sir Percy, telegram, 7 April 1911, CO 533/86.
114. Minute by Harcourt, 16 March 1911, on Sir Percy to Harcourt, telegram, 15 March 1911, CO 533/85.
115. Crewe to Sir Percy, private, 22 April 1910, CO 533/ 73.
116. Sorrenson, *Origins of European Settlement in Kenya,* 129.
117. Ramsay MacDonald to Harcourt, private, 18 May 1911, CO 533/86.
118. Ibid.
119. Minute by Fiddes to Harcourt, 11 June 1911, on MacDonald to Harcourt, private, 18 May 1911, CO 533/86.
120. Sorrenson, *Origins of European Settlement in Kenya,* 129.
121. Mungeam, *British Rule in Kenya,* 211.

122. Sir Percy to Crewe, telegram, 16 October 1909, CO 533/62; Mungeam, *British Rule in Kenya,* 211.

123. Sir Percy to Crewe, Main Report, confidential, 26 May 1910, CO 533/74.

124. Sorrenson, *Origins of European Settlement in Kenya,* 129.

125. Harcourt minute, 23 May 1911, on MacDonald to Harcourt, private, 18 May 1911, CO 533/86.

126. Harcourt to MacDonald, private, 24 May 1911, CO 533/86.

127. Ibid.

128. Minute by Fiddes to Harcourt, 22 May 1911, on MacDonald to Harcourt, private, 18 May 1911, all in CO 533/86.

129. Minute by Fiddes, 22 May 1911, on Ibid; Sorrenson, *Origins of European Settlers in Kenya*, 129.

130. Harcourt to Sir Percy, telegram, 5 October 1911, CO 533/90; Maxon, *Struggle for Kenya*, 41.

131. Sir Percy to Harcourt, telegram, 7 October 1911, CO 533/90.

132. Sorrenson, *Origins of European Settlement in Kenya,* 129.

133. Minute by Harcourt, 10 October 1910, on Sir Percy to Harcourt, telegram, 7 October 1910, CO 533/90.

134. Sorrenson, *Origins of European Settlement in Kenya,* 129.

135. Ibid.

136. Ibid.

137. Ibid; Mungeam, *British Rule in Kenya,* 265.

138. Mungeam, *British Rule in Kenya,* 265.

139. Sorrenson, *Origins of European Settlement in Kenya*, 206.

140. Ibid.

141. Maxon, "Judgment on a Colonial Governor," 90–91.

142. Ibid.

143. Sorrenson, *Origins of European Settlement in Kenya*, 129; Mungeam, *British Rule in Kenya,* 268.

144. Ibid.

145. Ibid.

146. Ibid.

147. Mungeam, *British Rule in Kenya,* 268.

148. Ibid.

149. Ibid.

150. Harcourt to Sir Percy, telegram, 3 November 1911, CO 533/90.

151. Sorrenson, *Origins of European Settlement in Kenya*, 206.

152. Mungeam, *British Rule in Kenya,* 267.

153. Ibid.

154. Minutes by Fiddes to Harcourt, 27 November 1911 and Harcourt to Fiddes, 28 November 1911, on Sir Percy to Harcourt, telegram, 25 November 1911, CO 533/91; Mungeam, *British Rule in Kenya,* 267.

155. Ibid.

156. Mungeam, *British Rule in Kenya,* 267.

157. Maxon, *Struggle for Kenya*, 41.

158. Mungeam, *British Rule in Kenya,* 267; Sorrenson, *Origins of European Settlement in Kenya*, 174.

159. Maxon, *Struggle for Kenya,* 41.

160. Sorrenson, *Origins of European Settlement in Kenya*, 174.

161. Mungeam, *British Rule in Kenya,* 267.

162. Harcourt to Bowring, telegram, 11 May 1912, CO 533/103; Mungeam, *British Rule in Kenya,* 267.

163. Ibid.

164. Harcourt to Bowring, telegram, 11 May 1912, CO 533/103; Harcourt to Sir Percy, telegram, 5 October 1911, CO 533/90; Sir Percy to Harcourt, telegram, 7 October 1911, CO 533/91; Mungeam, *British Rule in Kenya,* 267.

165. Kirk-Greene, "Canada in Africa, 211–13; Maxon, "Judgment on a Colonial Governor, 90–1; Maxon, *Struggle for Kenya,* 36.

166. Stephano Ole Hongop to W. S. Wright, affidavit, 25 June 1912, CO 533/108; Leys, *Kenya*, 119. Hangop is one of the principal witnesses in the Maasai case against the local authorities.

167. Ibid.

168. Huxley, *White Mam's Country,* 269–70.

169. Maxon, *Struggle for Kenya,* 41; Sorrenson, *Origins of European Settlement in Kenya*, 129; Mungeam, *British Rule in Kenya,* 268.

Chapter 9

The Galbraith Cole Case

The Cole case was a test on Sir Percy's sense of justice and fairness, but at the same time, it showed how his support of settlers had an impact on his sense of justice in the discharge of his official functions. When Cole was docked before the jury for shooting to kill a suspected thief who stole a sheep from his farm, he admitted of shooting to kill. Despite his testimony, which was viewed a threat to peace and good governance; the jury acquitted him against the advice of justice Hamilton to return a guilty verdict against Cole.

The CO, concerned about a reprisal from the Africans in view of his testimony, directed Sir Percy to deport Cole. Sir Percy refused to adhere to Harcourt's deportation order and sought to block the order by creating administrative and judicial difficulties. Earlier on, he refused to appeal against the verdict of the jury, causing anger in the CO. Thereafter, the CO directed deportation. Even then, Sir Percy continued to cause difficulties to block deportation.

It caused anger in the CO before Sir Percy could issue deportation against Cole, and even then, he issued the deportation order in the name of Harcourt, which suggested that, it was Harcourt who directed the deportation not him. Sir Percy wanted to shield Cole of deportation, knowing fully that Cole was an influential person in London, a relative of the Earl of Enniskilin. Sir Percy's failure to issue the order caused embarrassments to the CO, and further placed Sir Percy in a very unenviable position with the CO.

The Cole case was a contributing factor in Sir Percy's resignation. Sir Percy's action in this case suggested that he was not willing to obey the instruction of his superiors in London, and such an act of insubordination would not be condoned as the CO expected its governor to comply with the directives emanating from the CO, and also to inform the CO of any development in the protectorate. In this case, Sir Percy failed to do so, and it became a factor that contributed in the CO's view about him.

THE INCIDENCE AND THE CASE

The history of Cole and the government was mainly on a case of an African suspected to have stolen a sheep from Cole's farm. Cole, a prominent settler in Kenya, shot a suspected African he alleged to have stolen a sheep from his farm, abandoned the dead body, and never reported the case to the police. The nearby Africans who witnessed the shooting reported the case to the government after 12 days. On receipt of the report, a physician, Dr. Boedeker, performed an autopsy which confirmed that the deceased died as a result of his bullet wound.[1]

In a five minutes trial, the jury acquitted Cole of a murder charge, despite his admission of shooting to kill. The jury returned a not guilty verdict on the case, despite objection from Justice Hamilton.[2] Alarmed by the degree of miscarriage of justice, and the fact Cole's testimony established that he could be a threat to peace and order, the CO directed Sir Percy to take all the necessary steps to deport Cole back to England.[3]

But the deportation took a dramatic turn, when Sir Percy refused to comply with the deportation directives, and raised administrative and judicial difficulties to block the deportation of Cole. Sir Percy's action provoked indignation in the CO, for his refusal to comply with the deportation directives. It caused frustration of Harcourt and all the senior officials of the CO, before Sir Percy could issue the deportation warrant. On issuing the warrant, Sir Percy was greeted with protest against the deportation order, especially from Cole's counsel, and Lord Delamere, as well as in London. The protest was the cause of prolonged altercations between Sir Percy and the CO, which provoked anger, disappointment, and placed Sir Percy in a very unenviable position.

Cole's action in 1911 followed from an attempt to trace the whereabouts of some Africans he believed to have stolen a sheep from his farm. When he came across a number of Africans skinning a sheep not far away from his house, Cole assumed that it was his stolen sheep, which was being skinned, and he opened fire on them, as they ran away.

The bullet hit the back of one of the suspects and penetrated through his stomach, pulling out his intestine, which lay waste on the ground.[4] The other two suspected thieves ran for their lives and escaped unhurt.[5] Thereafter, neither Cole nor the escaped Africans reported the incident, until 12 days later, when some Africans reported the incident to the local authorities.[6] Cole was arrested following discovery of the body and police investigations showed that the man had died from Cole's actions. Following a preliminary inquiry, Cole was committed to the high court at Nakuru, in the heart of the white highlands, to stand trial for murder. The trial began on 31 May 1911 as the protectorate presented testimony from both European and African witnesses that clearly pointed to Cole as having caused the death of another human being. It was left to a jury of nine European men to decide the guilt of the defendant. As noted earlier, the all white jury quickly acquitted Cole.

Therefore, Sir Percy reported to Harcourt, in a telegram of 7 June 1911, the verdict of the jury, and stated that he had contemplated appealing against the verdict but his attorney advised him that appeal was not possible in a case where the defendant was acquitted of the charges against him.[7] Sir Percy also told Harcourt that the case was "due to the prevalence of stock theft."[8]

The CO had actually learnt of the case in a press report of 26 April 1911, and officials were alarmed with the degree at which the jury miscarried justice.[9] Read had already read the press report and upon perusal of Sir Percy's report, disagreed with Sir Percy's argument that appeal cannot be made in a case where a defendant was acquitted.[10] Read stated, "In spite of Sir P. Girouard's apologetics, it seems to me murder is murder and that it is out of the question to allow the matter to slide in the easy manner he appears to contemplate."[11] Fiddes and Harcourt agreed, and a telegram of 12 June 1911, was addressed to Sir Percy, directing him to appeal against the verdict. In the telegram, Harcourt stated, "a callous and unjustifiable murder had been committed and that there had been a gross miscarriage of justice."[12]

Therefore the CO disagreed with the jury and the advice of Sir Percy that appeal was not possible in a case where the defendant was acquitted. Harcourt directed Sir Percy to appeal against the acquittal verdict, if he was advised that was possible, but Sir Percy had earlier on, told Harcourt that he was advised that appeal was not possible, in an acquittal case, decided by a jury.[13] Sir Percy replied to Harcourt's telegram, in a confidential dispatch of 24 June 1911, with an enclosure of a copy of the court's proceedings, and a private letter, addressed to Harcourt.[14] In the dispatch, Sir Percy refused to comply with Harcourt's instructions, when he reiterated that the "crime was due to prevalence of unchecked stock thefts."[15] However, Sir Percy disguised the true position of the Naivasha district, when he told Harcourt that the crime was due to the prevalence of stock theft. In fact, there was no prevalence of stock theft in the Naivasha district. Therefore, his allegations of stock theft was a cover up against Cole's acquittal verdict, as he was determined to shield Cole from further litigation or any attempt at deportation. Sir Percy also stated that it was undesirable to appeal, but he preferred, however, to consider any proposal which might be submitted to him.[16]

However, Sir Percy's allegations could not be taken seriously, as available statistics of stock theft in Naivasha, showed it was comparatively insignificant. In fact, from the available statistics of stock theft, which Bowring transmitted to Harcourt, in a confidential dispatch of 25 May 1912, with an enclosure of a Returns of Stock Thefts Reported to the Police, Naivasha, for Fifteen Months Ended 31 March 1912, indicated that, for a 15-month stock theft, ending on 31 March 1912, comparatively insignificant number of cases of stock theft in the Naivasha district, which could not be described as prevalent.[17] In fact, the total numbers of cattle stolen during the 15-month period were only six cases. Out of the latter, one was recovered, one person was convicted, one person was arrested, one case had been established, and only a few cattle stolen.[18]

As for sheep and goats, there were 30 cases, out of which 25 convictions had been obtained, 67 persons had been arrested, 44 persons had been convicted, 82 head of sheep and goats were stolen, and 42 head of sheep and goats recovered.[19] Bowring pointed out that stock theft appeared to have been over blown by the white farmers to block Cole's proposed deportation.[20] Bowring also told Harcourt that as for agitation against the stock thefts, "It has become increasingly evident during the last few month that this matter is by no means of such importance as was contended in certain quarters in 1911. In fact, there is reason to believe that the public agitations engineered in the interest of the accused in the Cole case."[21] In the CO, Fiddes was disappointed with the figures relative to Sir Percy's references of prevalence of stock theft during Cole's case. Fiddes stated that despite all the talk about stock theft during Cole's case, the number presented in Bowring's dispatch was insignificant to warrant references being made to stock theft.[22]

As to Sir Percy's private letter addressed to Harcourt in 1911, he proposed two options which, if adopted, could ease the strain caused over the verdict. The first option was the suspension of trial by jury and the second, was the deportation of Cole.[23] Sir Percy's recommendations were informed by the court proceedings, in which he noted that the defense attorney had not done his job of defending his client.[24]

Shocked by the action of the defense attorney, and the miscarriage of justice, Batterbee was stunned to learn that the defense counsel refused to defend his client.[25] Batterbee stated that the defense counsel made no attempt to "set up any defense and evidently relied upon the Jury to acquit simply because he was a white man."[26] Out of the two possible options Sir Percy proposed to Harcourt, Anderson, in his minute, recommended the second option; deportation of Cole.[27] Anderson believed that section 25.1 of the 1902, East Africa order-in-council applied to Cole. The court proceedings, and particularly the action of the defense attorney in not even bothering to put up a defense for his client, shocked many in the CO. The outcome of the case outraged civil servants in the colony and such outrage was not inconsequential in the way the CO decided to deal with the case. The outrage over the verdict certainly impacted the way in which the CO decided to deal with the Cole case. Anderson took the lead in suggesting the CO response after they had seen the transcript of the trial. Of the two possible options Sir Percy proposed to Harcourt, Anderson, in his minute, recommended the second, the deportation of Cole.[28]

DEPORTATION

Therefore, Anderson stated that the protectorate could order deportation, once a sworn affidavit attesting to Cole's testimony had been made.[29] Again, Anderson's choice of a deportation option on Cole's case was informed by his concern that the court proceedings of the case was public knowledge, and Harcourt might be asked in the parliament as to why Cole had not been deported, a question to which, according to Anderson, "it would be difficult to frame a satisfactory reply."[30] Harcourt agreed, and stated, "it was a very horrible case.... Cole must be deported."[31]

Thereafter, Harcourt, in a telegram of 28 July 1911, told Sir Percy, "I have come to the conclusion that he must be deported under section 25.1 of the order-in-council. If you have any observation to make telegraph them at once as I wish to direct deportation immediately."[32] The Parliamentary Undersecretary of State for the Colonies, Lord Lucas, expressed his satisfaction with Harcourt's decision to deport Cole. Lucas minuted, "I am glad you decided for Cole's deportation."[33] Lucas added, "this will show the settlers that we mean business...."[34] The wisdom behind the CO decision to deport Cole lay in the protectorate's racial formations. A protectorate where black and white live in separate settlements, and the Cole case being a case between the white farmer and a black African suspect killed, it was feared that Cole's presence in the colony might ignite racial tension and provoke reprisals from the Africans.

To avoid the latter course of action, Harcourt's telegram of 28 July was categorical, and an expression of urgency to effect deportation was also very clear. But since the said telegram had been sent to Sir Percy, nothing was forthcoming from him. The long lull caused Harcourt to dispatch two telegrams of 3 and 7 August 1911, reminding Sir Percy to respond to his telegram of 28 July 1911.[35] However, silence greeted such telegrams, as there were no replies received in the CO. Harcourt and the CO's officials were not only embarrassed, but they were disappointed with Sir Percy's disregard to such telegrams. In fact, Harcourt was outraged, and at once, directed that a telegram must be dispatched to Sir Percy to respond at once. A strongly worded telegram of 9 August 1911 was dispatched to Sir Percy, demanding of him to respond to Harcourt's telegram of 28 July 1911 at once on receipt of this telegram, and provide an explanation as to why he omitted to do so, earlier on.[36]

On the receipt of the said telegram, Sir Percy reluctantly replied to Harcourt, in a telegram of 10 August 1911, objecting to Harcourt's deportation directives and raising possible difficulties to be encountered, if a deportation order was to be executed. Sir Percy stated that, upon consultations with the High Court Judges and his Executive Council, he came to the conclusion that a person acquitted in a criminal case could not be deported.[37] Sir Percy observed that, if Cole applied for a writ of habeas corpus, and it was granted, no deportation could ensue.[38] The CO were astonished that Sir Percy went out of his way to consult judges on a matter that might go before them, in due course.[39] Harcourt strongly disagreed with his arguments, and in a telegram of 10 August 1911 told Sir Percy that the Order-in-Council empowered the governor to order a deportation of any individual "conducting himself so as to be dangerous to the peace and good order in East Africa. . . ."[40]

Believing that Sir Percy did not understand his argument, Harcourt explained the relevant section of the case as contained in the 1902 Ordinance.[41] Harcourt also told Sir Percy, in the telegram, that he seemed to have entirely misapprehended as to why Cole must be deported. Harcourt stated that the need to deport Cole stemmed from the fact that the testimony he made in court established that he was "conducting himself so as to be dangerous to peace and good order whose continued presence in the protectorate may provide reprisal by natives," and not because his court case had any connection with the deportation.[42]

Harcourt also dismissed Sir Percy's argument when he told him that, the CO legal adviser held that no appeal could be made against a deportation order under section 25.1 of the 1902 Order-in-Council.[43] Therefore, Harcourt instructed Sir Percy to affect all the necessary process to institute the deportation of Cole.[44] Harcourt's explanations notwithstanding, Sir Percy refused to budge. He told Harcourt, in a telegram of 22 August 1911, that he doubted that section 25 and 26 of the Order applied in the Cole case.[45] However, to prove his objection and also to exonerate himself of blame Sir Percy enclosed a sworn affidavit by an Acting Crown Advocate, and stated that, if the lawyers in the CO considered the evidence in the affidavit adequate, he would issue the deportation order.[46] But the CO refused to refer the case to their legal adviser, and instead, told Sir Percy, in a telegram of 29 August 1911, to affect the deportation order. With the latter, the Colonial Office believed that Sir Percy would affect the deportation order as he had promised to do so, in his telegram of 22 August 1911.[47] The telegram instructed Sir Percy to comply with the instruction of the deportation order Harcourt transmitted to him, in the previous telegram.[48]

Sir Percy replied to Harcourt, in a telegram of 5 September 1911, that after consultations with his Executive Council, he is issuing the deportation order under protest, and only on orders from London.[49] Sir Percy added that as "the order-in-council of October 1906 directs me to carry out your instructions, I am issuing a deportation warrant ordered in your telegram of July 28."[50] In the CO, Read stated that Sir Percy was trying to divest himself of any responsibility in connection with this matter.[51] The CO officials were stunned by Sir Percy's reply, and Harcourt consulted with the CO legal adviser before instructing for a strongly worded telegraphic reply of 9 September 1911, asking Sir Percy to comply with the section 25.1 of the order-in-council. In the telegram, Harcourt also asked Sir Percy if he had complied or ordered the deportation in his [Harcourt] name, as he had stated, in his telegraphic reply of 5 September 1911.[52]

In a sequel to Harcourt's telegram of 9 September 1911, Sir Percy reported, in a telegram of 15 September 1911, that Cole had been served with the deportation order.[53] But the CO was not impressed since before Sir Percy could reply to Harcourt, already the CO learnt from the *Times* of 9 September 1911 that Sir Percy publicly suggested that Harcourt issued the deportation order.[54] In a minute by Read, he stated, "this is not very convincing."[55] Thereafter, Lord Lucas, said "Sir Percy's dispatch furnished no justification or explanation."[56] Harcourt replied to Sir Percy, with a telegram that was critical of his conduct in the Cole case. Harcourt reflected Read's minute and accused Sir Percy of refusing to cooperate, and attempting to divest himself of the responsibility in the deportation of Cole.[57] Harcourt concluded his telegram by reflecting on the difficulties occasioned to him by Sir Percy's refusal to cooperate in effecting the deportation order. He told Sir Percy, in a private letter, "I regret that throughout this case I have failed to receive from you the co-operation to which I consider myself entitled."[58] Harcourt added, in a private letter of 24 October 1911, "So far from lending me ready assistance, you continued to raise difficulties which appeared to me to be adequately covered by the instructions and opinions already sent to you."[59]

Thereafter, there were objections to the deportation by the settlers in the protectorate. Cole's British counsel, Sir Edward Carson, advised him to disregard the deportation warrant and to continue with his life in Kenya.[60] Also, Lord Delamere cabled the *Daily Mirror* to protest the deportation.[61]

The case earned wide publicity, and opposition against the local authorities mounted both in the protectorate and in London. In the protectorate, there was opposition against the local authorities on how they handled the case. The latter came from Dr. Norman Leys, who might have got insight into the case through Dr. Boedeker, a friend and a co-worker, who performed an autopsy on the deceased's body.[62] Leys, known for his controversy in the Maasai move, communicated the information to a friend, Harvey, and asked him if they are getting the official report published.[63] Leys was more hopeful of the usefulness of the Cole case against the local authorities than the hopeless case of the Maasai.[64] It was believed that Harvey told Ramsey

MacDonald, leader of the Labor Party, and Member of the Commons, who raised the issue with the CO, and subsequently, on the floor of the Commons, and embarrassed the CO.[65]

The Cole case was also of interest to the Pastoralists Association, EAP, who petitioned Harcourt for the rescission of the deportation warrant. But the petition raised other concerns than addressing the problem, which it was intended to address. The petition was defective, as the CO expected every person mentioned in the petition to append his signature against his name, and the absence of such, raised doubts on the originality of the petition.[66] In the said petition, there were some names of the petitioners whose signatures were not appended against their names.

On receipt of the petition, Sir Percy did not initiate to address the petitioners on the circumstances surrounding the deportation of Cole, other than acknowledgement of receipt of the petition, stating that he would forward their petition to Harcourt. Thereafter, he transmitted the petition to Harcourt to address the problem, a problem, which he should have addressed. His action was to demonstrate to Harcourt the consequence of the deportation that he was not willing to attend to, and instead, Harcourt should attend to it, as he has ordered for the deportation. Therefore, Sir Percy, in a confidential dispatch of 15 September 1911, told Harcourt, he was forwarding a petition from the Pastoralists Association as an enclosure to his dispatch.[67]

In the CO, Butler minuted that Sir Percy was forwarding the petition to Harcourt to decide over a case that should have been disposed of by Sir Percy. Sir Percy must have been trying to divest himself of responsibility in the deportation of such an influential settler, as he felt more safe and comfortable in the midst of planters than in executing his job accordingly. Read stated that Sir Percy, instead of responding to a petition, decided to send it to Harcourt to respond on the petition.[68] Also, enclosed in Sir Percy's dispatch, was a copy of an acknowledged receipt of the petition, addressed to the petitioners that the petition will be forwarded to the Secretary of State[69] In reacting to Sir Percy's action, Butler, in his minute, suggested as a response; "Harcourt sees no reason in modifying the action which has been taken in the case of Cole."[70] Butler also doubted any need to reply to the petitioners, and pointed out that "the petitioners would have long ceased to expect any reply."[71] However, Butler suggested a less obvious reason to reply; that all those whose names were appended to it did not sign the petition. Butler also doubted what Sir Percy's private secretary had described as petition, which according to Butler, a petition; "I understand will be signed by all members of the Pastoralists Association."[72] Anderson was sarcastic when he stated, "he can tell the petitioners that their petition has been sent to the Secretary of State."[73] Fiddes stated, that the petition should be sent back for petitioners to append their signatures. Fiddes added that in the future, Sir Percy should be told to wait, until all petitioners appended their signatures against their names before dealing with a similar petition.[74] In a minute by Harcourt, he expressed his concurrence with Butler, and stated, "Sir Percy should be told to wait until petitions are signed before dealing with or making promises about them."[75] However, Harcourt added that "such a communication as that of Sir Percy might be used to induce signatures to the petitioners."[76] Harcourt observed that, the "whole thing is dead now, the row has been less, and the effect better, than some of us dared to hope."[77]

Therefore, in a reply to Sir Percy's dispatch, a confidential dispatch of 4 December 1912 was addressed to Sir Percy, stating the need to append all signatures to a petition before he could forward it to the CO.[78] Harcourt informed Sir Percy to communicate to the members of the Pastoralists Association that "I have received their petition dated 1 October 1911, but that I see no reason for modifying the action which has been taken in the case of Cole."[79] Harcourt added when he referred to a letter from Sir Percy's secretary, and stated that, it appears from W. J. E. Lawson – Walton's letter of the 12 October 1911, when the petition was submitted to you, "it had not actually been signed by all those whose names were appended to it."[80] Harcourt commented further, when he stated that, "I consider it desirable to wait until all the signatures to a petition have been actually appended to, before dealing with it, or undertaking to forward it for consideration."[81] Harcourt implored Sir Percy to adhere to the latter, when he stated that, "I have to request that this practice may be followed in the future."[82]

CONCLUSION

In the Cole case, the CO finally compelled Sir Percy to budge to their terms. His action in the Cole case was a good example of insubordination to his superior officers in the CO. It also suggested unwillingness or reluctance in the execution of appropriate action as ordained in the relevant ordinance to deport Cole. His action of engaging in subversive correspondence over the deportation of Cole was a clear testimony to his partiality toward the settler community, which caused exasperation in the CO. The end of Cole's case disappointed the CO. With this performance, it would be nearly impossible to commend Sir Percy, as he has engaged in subversive action to frustrate the CO, in their attempted efforts to deport Cole. His action soured relations between him and the CO, which had already lost confidence in him, believing that he had failed them, and there would be no better description of Sir Percy as far as Cole case was concerned other than, he failed to carry out the duty assigned to him, which discredited him, before the CO.

The compensation issue, the Maasai move and Galbraith Cole's case tested Sir Percy's sense of fairness in the administration of the colony. Sir Percy's administration of the colony was judged to be a successful administration, especially by Kirk-Greene, suggesting that Sir Percy administration brought order and economic prosperity in the colony. Mungeam's *British Rule in Kenya* considered that Sir Percy brought order in the chaotic administration of the colony, and considered Sir Percy as a successful administrator. However, Sir Percy's administration could not be in any way be considered an outstanding performance in view of the way he handled the compensation question, the Maasai move and the Galbraith Cole case.

NOTES

1. Hughes, *Moving the Maasai,* 67–68
2. Maxon, *Struggle for Kenya,* 38.
3. Hughes, *Moving the Maasai,* 67.
4. Ibid.
5. Ibid.
6. Maxon, *Struggle for Kenya*, 38.
7. Sir Percy to Harcourt, telegram, 7 June 1911, CO 533/88.
8. Ibid.
9. Maxon, *Struggle for Kenya*, 38.
10. Minute by Read to Fiddes, 9 June 1911, on Sir Percy to Harcourt, telegram, 7 June 1911, CO 533/88.
11. Ibid.
12. Harcourt to Sir Percy, telegram, 12 June 1911, CO 533/88.
13. Sir Percy to Harcourt, 7 June 1911, CO 533/102.
14. Sir Percy to Harcourt, confidential, 24 June 1911, CO 533/88.
15. Ibid.
16. Ibid.
17. Bowring to Harcourt, confidential, 25 May 1912, CO 533/104.
18. Ibid.
19. Ibid.
20. Ibid.
21. Ibid.
22. Ibid.; Minute by Fiddes to Harcourt, 14 June 1912, on Bowring to Harcourt, confidential, 25 May 1912, CO 533/104.
23. Sir Percy to Harcourt, private, 24 June 1911, enclosure in Sir Percy to Harcourt, confidential, 24 June 1911, CO 533/88.
24. Court proceedings; Crown vs Galbraith Lowey Egerton Cole, criminal case, 94 of 1911, enclosure in Sir Percy to Harcourt, confidential, 24 June 1911, CO 533/88; Maxon, *Struggle for Kenya*, 38.
25. Minute by Batterbee to Read, 27 July 1911, on Ibid.

26. Ibid.
27. Minute by Anderson to Harcourt, 27 July 1911, on Ibid.
28. Ibid.
29. Ibid.
30. Ibid.
31. Minute by Harcourt to Read, 28 July 1911, on Ibid.
32. Harcourt to Sir Percy, confidential, 28 July 1911, CO 533/88.
33. Minute by Lord Lucas to Harcourt, 4 August 1911, on Sir Percy to Harcourt, confidential, 24 June 1911, CO 533/88.
34. Ibid.
35. Harcourt to Sir Percy, telegrams, 3, and 7 August 1911, CO 533/88.
36. Harcourt to Sir Percy, telegram, 9 August 1911, CO 533/88; Maxon, *Struggle for Kenya*, 39.
37. Sir Percy to Harcourt, telegram, 10 August 1911, CO 533/89.
38. Ibid.
39. Maxon, *Struggle for Kenya*, 39.
40. Harcourt to Sir Percy, telegram, 10 August 1911, CO 533/89.
41. Ibid.
42. Ibid.
43. Ibid.; Maxon, *Struggle for Kenya*, 40.
44. Ibid.
45. Sir Percy to Harcourt, telegram, 22 August 1911, CO 533/89; Maxon, *Struggle for Kenya*, 40.
46. Ibid.
47. Harcourt to Sir Percy, telegram, 29 August 1911, CO 533/89.
48. Ibid.
49. Sir Percy to Harcourt, telegram, 5 September 1911, CO 533/90.
50. Ibid.
51. Minute by Read to Fiddes, 8 September 1911, on Sir Percy to Harcourt, telegram, 5 September 1911, CO 533/90.
52. Harcourt to Sir Percy, telegram, 9 September 1911, CO 533/90.
53. Sir Percy to Harcourt, confidential, 15 September 1911, CO 533/90.
54. *Times*, 9 September 1911.
55. Minute by Read to Fiddes, 11 October 1911, on Sir Percy to Harcourt, confidential, 15 September 1911, CO533/90.
56. Minute by Lucas to Harcourt, 10 October 1911, on Sir Percy to Harcourt, confidential, 15 September 1911, CO 533/90.
57. Harcourt to Sir Percy, telegram, 9 September 1911, CO 533/90.
58. Ibid.
59. Harcourt to Sir Percy, private, 24 October 1911, CO 533/90.
60. Hughes, *Moving the Maasai*, 68.
61. Ibid.
62. Ibid.
63. Ibid.
64. Ibid.

65. Ibid.

66. Sir Percy to Harcourt, confidential, 15 September 1911, CO 533/90.

67. Ibid.

68. Minute by Butler to Fiddes, 2 February 1912, on Sir Percy to Harcourt, confidential, 5 January 1912; J. E. Lawson-Walton to the Secretary of the Pastoralists Association, 12 October 1911, all in CO 533/101.

69. J. E. Lawson-Walton to the Secretary of the Pastoralists Association, 12 October 1911, enclosure in Sir Percy to Harcourt, confidential, 5 January 1912, CO 533/101.

70. Minute by Butler to Fiddes, 2 February 1912, on Sir Percy to Harcourt, confidential, 5 January 1911, CO 533/101.

71. Ibid.

72. Ibid.

73. Minute by Anderson to Harcourt, 5 February 1912, on Sir Percy to Harcourt, confidential, 5 January 1911, CO 533/101.

74. Minutes by Fiddes to Harcourt, 2 February 1912, Harcourt to Fiddes, 6 February 1912, Sir Percy to Harcourt, confidential, 5 January 1911, all in CO 533/101.

75. Minute by Harcourt to Read, 6 February 1912, on Ibid.

76. Ibid.

77. Ibid.

78. Harcourt to Sir Percy, confidential, 9 February 1912, CO 533/101.

79. Ibid.

80. Ibid.

81. Ibid.

82. Ibid.

Chapter 10

Conclusion

In the end, Sir Percy's action or failure to follow the dictates of the CO did not save Galbraith Cole as he was deported from the EAP in September 1911. Partly as a result of London's loss of confidence in Sir Percy occasioned by the Maasai move and the Cole affair, he followed suit the following year. Sir Percy held office as governor less than three years that were critical in Kenya's history. No doubt Sir Percy had performed considerably well prior to his Kenya service in the Sudan, Egypt, Transvaal and Northern Nigeria and with relative success. But in Kenya, it was an entirely different story. There, his performance was not only embarrassing to the CO but it was also disappointing. In view of the latter, he failed to deliver successfully as claimed in many of the sources mentioned in this work. The criteria I have used in assessing his performance and determining his success or failure are generally the yardstick that the CO wanted officials in the British colonies to adhere to, for the success in the administration of those colonies.

In reflecting on the CO's expectations for Sir Percy's performance and on the assessment of his policy of government administration in the protectorate, it becomes, clear that he failed to deliver as the CO proposed and as expected of him. Sir Percy proposed to institute government standing orders, restructure government administration and departments, improve and strengthen the machinery of government and amalgamate Uganda to the EAP. Not much was achieved in the latter aspect; he improved the condition of administration by providing government circulars and schedule of duty of administrative staff. But the success was below his proposed recommendations for improvement of the condition of the administration.

As to the strengthening of the machinery of government, Sir Percy had not been able to trim the size of staff members of the protectorate. In the latter case, the CO refused to give way, stating that the staff past service during the pioneer years of the protectorate had to be recognized. They should not be cut adrift, therefore, with the exception of the retirement of heads of public works, agriculture and the conservator, the CO refused to pension off or superannuate some of the staff Sir Percy recommended to be relieved from the service of the protectorate.

Sir Percy also proposed the merger of the coast provinces of Seyyedie, Jubaland and Tanaland into one provincial administration. It did not only fail to resonate with the CO, but was refused approval as the separate existence of the provinces outweighed their amalgamation for economic consideration and strengthening of the machinery of government of the provincial administration. The existence of the coast provinces was considered as administration expediency. The merger of the provinces could have been detrimental to the very best interest of the minority ethnic groups and could have led to nationalist feelings. Therefore, the CO forbade Sir Percy's proposed merger for economy and strengthening in the interest of enduring in the political and administrative expedience for safety and acquiescence in the political atmosphere to prevail.

This was one of the failings in his policy reviews that suggested that Sir Percy failed to appraise the position of the coast provinces and the rationale for their separate existence. If he had done so, he would not have recommended for their merger.

The institution of official government circulars to govern the conduct of day-to-day government action in the administration of the colony was also proposed for reform. Sir Percy sought to provide order and direction for political officers in carrying out government functions, including the administration of taxation which, other than in the Nyanza Province, he considered chaotic throughout the colony and recommended for its reform.

Sir Percy succeeded considerably in affecting certain administrative reforms, especially in official government circulars, giving order, direction and similarity of action in carrying out government functions and he improved the method of tax collection in the coastal provinces, especially among the Mijikenda. The relative successes, however, were much less insignificant in proportion to his proposed administrative reform, and they were limited to the coast. For a colony with a swath of land stretching from the southern tip of the head waters of the white Nile to over 1,000 miles to its southern extremity bordering the shores of the Indian Ocean, with a population of over two million subjects of the crown in 1909.

In reviewing the condition of the machinery of government, Sir Percy proposed to pension off or superannuate some of the senior, as well as junior, officials of the colony and to merge or scrap some of the departments he considered redundant, incompetent, lazy and supine or duplicating functions of other departments of government administration. The latter reforms,

Sir Percy told Crewe, would strengthen the machinery of government administration and the economy of the colony. The CO requested details of how Sir Percy intended to effect the latter, taking into consideration adjustment of officials to occupy offices of the retired officials, adjustment of claims and pension benefits in a time when the annual budget of the colony had not made provision for these retirements and when the British Treasury did not provide any assistance to a retiring colonial official in the colony.

For Sir Percy to effectively address the latter question was an uphill climb and after a prolonged hesitation, he asked the CO for the proposed reform to be approved. But the CO told him that it would not act on pieces of information in a telegram. The officials reiterated their earlier position that they needed more details on how the retirees could be paid and vacancies and claims of adjustment settled. There was a deadlock and Sir Percy, instead, chose to press for the transfer of Jackson to Uganda and the appointment of Bowring to the newly created post of a colonial secretary. The CO agreed and promoted Jackson to the post of governor of the Uganda Protectorate. The CO also considered his proposed reform on the executive, legislative and the judiciary powers of the protectorate. His recommendations were not approved. However, the CO approved the appointment of six unofficial members on the Legislative Council.

Other than the latter, the CO refused to give way for staff and administrative reforms. The status quo was maintained, as the CO believed that the existing staffs were appropriate for the colony at the time and nothing was discussed further. In addition to the latter, the CO was skeptical to implement the recommendation, believing that Sir Percy had not mastered the political, administrative and racial landscape of the colony to warrant his hefty recommendation, so they treaded cautiously on these reforms. Sir Percy's failing to secure the approval of his policy reforms were not only a measure of the doubts expressed by the CO, but his recommendations were not in tandem with the required policy of His Majesty's government in the administration of the Crown's dominions.

His Majesty's government expected policy such as this to provide a good working relationship with the CO, and the executive, legislature and the judiciary branches so as to achieve the full results desired by the CO and the subjects in the colony. But the CO viewed that Sir Percy's uncomplimentary comments on nearly all the officials of the colony and his proposed restructuring would not only fail to provide the desired results of a quiescent, effective and efficient administration, but it could lead to complications between him and the staff members of the colony and derail the administrative drive for better service to the colony. At the time the CO refused his proposed reforms, the officials in the CO admonished Sir Percy to be patient and accommodate all the staff members of the colony as the CO could not weed them out without benefits and considering that these staff had served the colony meritoriously in its pioneer years.

The weeding of some staff members of the protectorate and the strengthening of the machinery of government, as well as the extension of the restructuring government departments became his proposed restructuring of staff of the protectorate. In the restructuring of government departments and their functions, Sir Percy considered amalgamating Uganda Protectorate to the EAP when he was asked by the CO to report on its administration. Sir Percy considered the amalgamation of the EAP and the Uganda Protectorate for the development of the region's economy and the strengthening of the machinery of government of British possessions in East Africa. He held that the amalgamation of the two protectorates under the administration of the EAP would strengthen the machinery of government, provide economy in expenditure, and facilitate the development of the Uganda. But the CO upon perusal of his reports on the EAP and Uganda came to a clear opinion that amalgamation would not be in the best interest of Uganda Protectorate, and the CO opined that Sir Percy must have been under misapprehension to suggest that EAP was more developed and could assist in the development of Uganda. The CO also concluded that Uganda was more prosperous and should be left alone to develop independent of the EAP. Sir Percy's recommendation for the amalgamation was not informed by knowledge of the two colonies but by his desire for relevance and for having a large expanse of land under his command.

The failure to provide genuine assessment that could be used to improve the condition of the colony was no less a short coming in an administration that was seeking a way for effective administration for the conduct of its multiracial society, especially the European settlers and the Indians residents. In considering the application of government policy on the inhabitants of the country, Sir Percy observed that the European settlers were confronted with the problem of access to land. He considered that the existing legislation did not afford the settlers opportunity of easy access to land. To this, he proposed to relieve the situation by coming up with a land policy that could afford them access to land for agricultural cultivation. In addition to access to land, they should be included in other government bodies as advisory persons, especially in the government agricultural department so that their advice should be part of the government policy as the decision of the executive could not necessarily reflect the views and wishes of the settlers as to their agricultural pursuit. Sir Percy also considered that the Europeans, who intended to make the colony home, should be allowed to participate in the government of the country especially at country and local government level.

The highlands settlement should be exclusive to them and be carved out as an independent settlement exclusive to other races with its own administration. He advocated the increased participation of the settlers on the legislative council. The settlers also had the leverage to put forward certain demands especially when they formed a political association, under which they sought to have elective representation. But the government was able to keep a tight control over their activities with a view to curtail their excessive political demand. Despite the favorable disposition and proposed policy toward the Europeans settlers, the condition of the settlers was not better off than it had been. This was because some of his proposed policies were not approved, and in some instances, Sir Percy never followed up with the Colonial Office, on his requests.

As to the Indians, the administration had not adopted a favorable disposition toward their demands, and policy by which they could be governed was proposed. Therefore, the government, instead of mitigating the difficult position of the Indians, chose to accentuate their difficulty by recommending the suspension and later on, removal of the representative on the Legislative Council. The Indians demands for immigration of more Indians into the colony, seeking equality of rights and treatment as British subjects, ending racial discrimination in land distribution, and judicial procedures. These demands were refused by the colony and the Indians continued to suffer such disabilities, which provoked an interview by Jeevanjee in London on the Indian condition, causing the intervention of the Secretary of State for India and the All-Muslim League on behalf of the Indians. Despite the interventions, nothing changed for the better and their struggle continued.

The effective administration of these races required a policy to guide officials in the administration of not only the Indian subjects of the crown but also of the European settlers. In this Sir Percy noted, there was no defined policy of administration of the settlers, and he desired to create a policy to govern the conduct of the settlers. He therefore, proposed for their greater involvement in the legislative council, county and local government administration, and establishment of a separate area for their settlement, distinct from other races.

He recommended for their participation in the government agricultural department and in other analogous bodies to better their cause, especially for those who wished to make the colony their home. He recommended that the settlers should be taken into confidence and should be afforded all rights and privileges that the government could afford.

The CO approved these recommendations when it reappointed Lord Delamere as settler representative on the Legislative Council. The CO also increased the unofficial representation on the Legislative Council to six. The CO also accepted that the settlers should be held in confidence and should be allowed participation in counties and local governments as well as in other government bodies, such as the agriculture department. The question of the participation of settlers in the government of the colony, especially county and local government was not achieved by the administration despite the CO's approval. Sir Percy, transmitting details of the process and pressing on the CO to act on the proposal, caused the latter policy to fail. By the time he left the colony, the question of settlers involvement in the administration for their own affairs had not been achieved.

As to the Indian policy of administration, Sir Percy inherited a large body of Indians in the colony without a defined policy on their status and rights within the administration. The Indians had been living with disabilities since the entry of the white settlers into the protectorate, as successive local authorities adopted a different approach to the welfare and prospects between the settlers and the Indians, favoring the settlers and accentuating the difficult position of the Indians in the colony. This had been in existence prior to Sir Percy's arrival into the colony, and he had not devised any means to alleviate their suffering. Instead, he accentuated their difficult position.

Sir Percy had not proposed any measure to alleviate the difficult position of the Indians despite their numerous disabilities, and instead recommended for the dropping of their representative on the Legislative Council. He also opposed Indian access to land in the highlands, refused to reconsider the question of Indian immigration into the colony and towed the line of his predecessor when he refused to accept Indian demands for equal government opportunities with settlers and for fair treatment through trial by jury as applied to the settlers, attending the same markets, owning land in strategic market areas, and using the same streamers with the settlers on the Uganda Railways.

Sir Percy as with his predecessors, refused to give way to any of the Indian demands. The favoritism he had shown to the settlers and his anti-Indian position accentuated the racial divide and created a structure similar to that of the apartheid South Africa to bear on the colony. The latter development had in no way created peace, harmony and acquiescence, and had, instead, led to the feeling of racial animosity and the rise of nationalism on the part of the Indians to reassert their rights in a colony they claimed that without them it would not had been the way it was. They also claimed that because of the numerical and cultural influence they had established that the colony should be amalgamated to the Indian viceroy. The question of race and administration was an important policy question in the colony as there were Africans, in addition to the settlers and the Indians.

As to the Africans, Sir Percy considered the introduction of a separate policy of administration, in which African chiefs and elders government their people to be supervised by European officials. This was similar to a system of administration Lord Lugard introduced in Northern Nigeria Protectorate where African chiefs were allowed to decide on their own affairs but subject to moderation by British colonial officials in the persons of residents and district officers. Sir Percy's proposed policy was accepted by the Colonial Office with a request to furnish further details as to the process of the policy. In detailing the process, Sir Percy introduced a different element from his earlier proposal when he stated that he would place the Africans under a board of trustees. But the Colonial Office viewed that the involvement of private persons in the administration of the subjects of the Crown would be unnecessary complication, and therefore, refused to approve the policy. Thereafter, Sir Percy revised his proposal, which conferred administrative responsibilities on African chiefs and elders to govern the people with supervision by European officials.

The administrative reform provided official circulars to provincial and district commissioners on the conduct in the discharge of their functions with a view to achieving similarity in the discharge of government function as opposed to individual idiosyncrasy that characterized the administration. This administrative reform was achieved by Sir Percy, but it had not gone far to alleviate the disabilities which Sir Percy had proposed to alleviate, especially as to safeguards of African land against interest and business groups. In spite of the fact that it was an administrative measure which had not gone far and was faced with a challenge of the High Court involvement in the administration of African areas, African youth were not favorably disposed to his African policy administration as they preferred the European model of administration they considered better than their own traditional method of administration.

Therefore, Sir Percy's African policy of administration, despite the CO's acceptance of the policy, failed to provide acceptable process of the policy to the CO, causing the rejection of the proposed policy outright. Not much had been achieved and the proposed safeguards and efficient African policy became a distant possibility. The inhabitants of the colony, Sir Percy viewed, were not better off, and proposed to introduce an economic policy to alleviate the condition so that the colony could obtain sufficient receipts to balance its budgets, and the settlers should have economic prosperity by means of developing agricultural production for exports. The remaining races of the protectorate were left to their own devices, as government had no economic development policy for their prosperity.

The Africans also lacked a policy of administration and Sir Percy sought to put one in place. His African policy recommendation of the safeguarding of African land and the introduction of an indirect rule system was accepted in the first instance. The CO agreed upon the question of African land safeguards, but subsequent developments originating from the settler quest for more fertile land compelled Sir Percy to compromise his policy when he offered to remove the Maasai from Laikipia, in violation of an enduring agreement between the Maasai and the government, and to grant the same land to European farmers.

As to the introduction of indirect rule, the CO subsequently rejected it as Sir Percy sought to involve private persons in the administration of crown subjects of the empire. The CO objected to the recommendation as it would have amounted to His Majesty' government abandoning responsibility to a private board of trustees which would have been an embarrassment to the imperial government. Sir Percy failed to provide the desired safeguards on land out of pressure from the European settlers, who demanded more land for cultivation, and thereby compelled him to break his promise of safeguarding African land within their own reserves. His Majesty's government desired effective administration for subjects of the empire, especially maintenance of law and order, so that the economy of the colony could prosper for the betterment of the colony and its inhabitants.

The economic policy, which Sir Percy also believed would provide prosperity of the colony, was to induce famers to produce for export so that revenue receipts from the export of the colony could ease the colony's dependence on an annual grant-in-aid from the British Treasury. The detail of the process involved was that the Treasury would lower rates on the Uganda Railway for export goods. The Treasury agreed and lowered the rates, but by the end of Sir Percy's administration of the colony, his policy failed to provide the economic solvency he proposed it would afford the protectorate. Certainly it was during Sir Percy's tenure that the colony attained economic solvency, but it was not his policy that produced the economic prosperity that the colony witnessed from 1913 onward.

The economic success of the colony lay in African peasant farmers from the Nyanza basin who had produced more for consumption and exported the surplus. This earned the government part of the revenue receipts. In addition to the latter, receipts on goods from other colonies exported through the EAP's port of Mombasa and shipped on the Uganda Railway, and receipts from poll and hut taxes being paid by African peasants also contributed to the salvation of the EAP economy. The latter receipts were instrumental in the colony's attainment of economic independence. Sir Percy's policy failed to provide the desired relief, as the settlers were not numerically strong enough to produce sufficient exports that could earn the desired revenue to support its administration.

This failing is viewed as a shortsighted proposed economic policy, limiting production for export to a few individuals that could not provide the relief sought. Had Sir Percy assessed the economic position of the colony more fully, he would have broadened his policy to include other races of the colony for more production and more revenue. But the limitation he placed on his policy was the main factor that caused the policy to fail. Therefore, the administration of economic policy, as in other aspects of his administration noted in the preceding paragraphs, suggests that Sir Percy lacked knowledge of the economic potential of the colony for more production so as to afford relief for an administration that needed more receipts to cater for the development of a poor colony, such as the EAP.

In addition, Sir Percy must had been under racial influence of affording his kith and kin the most favored treatment in economic development which placed him under a misapprehension, that the same policy would also afford relief to the colony, irrespective of the inclusion of other races of the colony. In addition, Sir Percy viewed that the economic development of the colony would be a success story, if railway development could be undertaken with a view to ease the difficulty in the shipment of export products. The construction of Nairobi-Thika railway was reconsidered and the Magadi railway was welcomed.

The Nairobi-Thika railway became an important line in the shipment of products for export, even though the initial purpose for the line was to provide relief to the area in the emergency period when the area had no means of communication to other parts of the colony. The Magadi railway was initiated by a soda company for the shipment of their products, but as a colony seeking investment from private enterprise for the development of the colony, the government paid the cost of the construction of the railway.

Both the Nairobi-Thika and the Magadi railway were brought under the administration of the Uganda Railway and were used by peasants to ship their products to the port for exports. The provision of adjunct railways had eased the movement of goods to the port for export and had afforded the government receipts that went a long way in alleviating its difficult financial position. In addition to these receipts, there were receipts from the land grants, especially in the form of land tax, which also formed part of the colony's receipts. Though it did not form a significant share of the receipts, but the land question in general formed an important aspect of the administration, as it was in land administration that Sir Percy's inefficiency in policy administration became clearly visible.

The administration of land policy was held off as there was no adequate land ordinance to guide the conduct of land dealings, but there were land regulations that governed the conduct of land grants and administration in the form of the Elgin regulations, which had to be included in any amendment of the land ordinance. In the process of the inclusion, Sir Percy refused to support these regulations that had formed the working regulations in dispensing crown land in the colony since 1907. Doing this was interpreted as shielding the settlers from legislation that would require them to pay taxes on land they held as Sir Percy had asked that the land tax should be dropped.

The land tax, revision of rents after 33 years on a 99-year lease and transfer of land after development conditions, as enunciated by Elgin, were the working regulations on land administration in the colony. Sir Percy refused to apply these regulations in his administration of land and refused their inclusion in the revision of the land ordinance to the consternation of the CO. This condition accentuated land speculation and dummying, producing difficulty in accessing land to prospective immigrants who had to resort to buying exorbitantly from speculators, thereby undermining the prospects of government receipts from the increased land value of the colony. Prospective immigrants suffered as land became accessible only a few influential farmers.

These influential farmers became a problem in the administration of lands in the protectorate. They sought large acres of fertile land to develop estates, and in doing so, they revisited the question of Laikipia land, which they were being compensated for, and reclaimed the land. The local authorities approved the Laikipia land for them without the knowledge of the CO and when Sir Percy sought to remove the Maasai so that these farmers could take over, the Maasai move failed. This disclosed the secrecy and sinister motive behind his action. The move displaced the Maasai and the farmers who had left Guaso Nyiro, presumably to occupy Laikipia, failed to secure Laikipia as the Maasai had to return to Laikipia following their failed move.

This brought in the question of land compensation for the two; Maasai and the farmers. The Maasai were never offered any compensation, but the farmers were offered compensation for relinquishing their Guaso Nyiro farms to take up farms in Laikipia. The manner of the administration of compensation to the settlers by Sir Percy's government left some of the farmers, who felt they were not fairly compensated, with no option other than to go back to South Africa. These actions also discouraged some prospective immigrants to the colony.

While the question of the Maasai move was unfolding, the case of Cole came forth. Cole shot a suspected thief and killed him and refused to report it to the authorities. Cole was tried and even though he was exonerated by a jury, testimony suggested the he was a threat to peace and security. The CO directed Sir Percy to deport him. Sir Percy refused and continued to create administrative and judicial difficulties to block his deportation to the dismay of the CO officials. The question of compensation, the Maasai move and the deportation of Cole portrayed Sir Percy's administration in a bad light and were the main factors that led to his dismissal from his enviable post of governor.

By the time Sir Percy left the colony most of the policies he had enunciated had not been implemented, even if they were approved by the CO. Sir Percy's Kenya tour of duty could best be remembered by a legacy of unfulfilled promises. He failed to resolve the knotty land question, accentuated the racial divide between the settlers and the Indians, and he interfered with the African reserves. This was caused by his favoritism for the settlers and his dislike for the Indians. He afforded the settlers all opportunities in government and businesses but denied the Indians, following a similar policy of his predecessor on the Indians of the protectorate. The Indians never had what they wished, especially allowing further immigration of Indians into the protectorate, trial by jury, land in the highlands, equal opportunities in the government with the European settlers and grants of land in a suitable business district in Nairobi, among other things.

Despite Sir Percy's successful tour of duty in the Sudan, Transvaal and Northern Nigeria, his failings in the administration of the EAP were clearly visible in affecting policy of government administration, dealing with the races of the protectorate, economic development and, the worst of all, in his performance in dispensing crown lands. These failings occasioned to Sir Percy because of the historical antecedent of the protectorate. The EAP had had a succession of ineffective governors and staff members further compounded by the entry of European settlers, some of them very influential in London, casting their eyes on every fertile land for agricultural cultivation, making a fair and equitable dispensing of crown land a difficult matter not only for Sir Percy but also for his predecessors. Personal interest of those settlers was an important factor in accentuating the difficulty in the administration of the protectorate and causing governors to leave behind complicated administration and in some case, governors had resigned, especially Sir Percy, having resigned over the Maasai land dealings. In view of the difficult circumstance of the protectorate, Sir Percy had by the time he was forced to resign, not done much to impress the CO and instead the CO was disappointed. The CO could not hide their disappointment and frustration with Sir Percy. A senior official in the CO, W. C. Bottomley, summarized Sir Percy's tour of duty in the protectorate, when he stated, "the mark he left on the protectorate at the end of his administration in 1912 was rather one of promise than of performance. His promises in fact were the chief difficulty in the way of his successor and Sir Henry Belfield was continually in a position of having to refuse to recognize alleged promises made to settlers by Sir Percy Girouard.... There is nothing in his [Girouard's] record in East Africa to shew [*sic*] his efforts would be directed to the permanent welfare of the country rather than to the expediency of the moment and his own popularity."[1] This was a befitting assessment of Sir Percy's rush to failure; having failed to deliver his proposed reform and left behind promises rather than performance.

Sir Percy's rush to failure was not only a personal disaster, but by devoting his energies to the expediency of the moment he made critical and long lasting impacts on Kenya. As this book has demonstrated, Kenya was at crossroads during his administration. The decision he made and refused to make, such as supporting African peasant production and pursuing discriminatory policies towards the colony's African and Indian residents, had long term and negative effects.

The result of these actions and non-actions worked themselves out in Kenyan history over subsequent years with many unhappy consequences. Kenya was at a crossroads in 1909–12, but Sir Percy took many wrong turns.

NOTE

1. Maxon, *Struggle for Kenya,* 41.

Bibliography

PRIMARY SOURCES

Great Britain, The National Archives, Colonial Office Records,
CO 533/29, 44, 56, 62, 63, 64, 65, 66, 67, 68, 69, 70, 71, 73, 74, 75, 76, 77, 78, 79, 82, 85, 86, 87, 88, 90, 91, 94, 101, 102, 103, 104, 108. These documents were consulted at the Bird Library, Syracuse University, New York and Wise Library, West Virginia University, Morgantown, West Virginia.

GOVERNMENT PUBLICATIONS

East Africa Protectorate. Department of Agriculture British East Africa Annual Report 1911–1912. Nairobi: Government Printer, 1913.

BOOKS

Eliot, Sir Charles. *The East Africa Protectorate*. London: Fisher T Unwin, 1905. East Africa and Uganda/Great Britain Foreign Office: Correspondence relating to the resignation of Sir Charles Eliot.

Girouard, P. C. Cranwill. *History of the Railways During the War in South Africa, 1899–1903*, London: HMSO, 1903.

Hardinge, A. H. *The Diplomatist in the East*. London: Jonathan Cape Limited, 1928.

Hindlip, Lord. *East Africa Protectorate: Past, Present and Future*. London: Fisher T Unwin, 1905.

Mungeam, G. H. *Kenya, Select Historical Documents, 1884–1923*. Nairobi; Kenya: East Africa Publishing House, 1978.

SECONDARY SOURCES

Unpublished Papers

Dissertations and Theses

Cashmore, T. H. R. "Studies in District Administration in the East Africa Protectorate, 1895–1918." Ph. D., Dissertation, Jesus College, Cambridge University, 1965.

Kohlman, Carl L. "A History of German Colonization of East Africa, 1871–1914, With Emphasis on Germany's Change in Native Policy." M. A. Thesis, Duquesne University, Pittsburgh, 1969.

Mwaruvie, John Mwaniki. "Political Economy of Railway Extensions in Kenya: the case of the Uasin Gishu railway, 1901–1910," Ph.D., Dissertation, West Virginia University, Morgantown, 2005.

Naseem, Abdul Waheed. "Indian Enterprise along the East African Coast and Subsequent Role in the Development of Kenya, 1840–1905." St. Johns University, New York, Ph. D., 1975.

Simpson, George L. Jr. "On the Frontiers of Empire: British Administration in Kenya's Northern Frontier District, 1905–1935." Ph. D., Dissertation, West Virginia University, Morgantown, 1994.

Smith, Cynthia B. "*Giriama Rising* 1914: Focus for Political Development in the Kenya Hinterland, 1850–1963." University of California, Los Angeles, Ph. D., 1973.

Spear, Thomas Turner. "The Kaya Complex: A History of the Mijikenda Peoples of the Kenya Coast to 1900." Ph. D., Dissertation, University of Wisconsin, Madison, 1974.

Books

Abour, C. J. Owando. *White Highlands No More: A Modern Political History of Kenya Vol. 1.* Nairobi: Pan African Researchers, 1970.

Amutabi, Maurice Nyamanga, Ed. *Studies in the Economic History of Kenya: Land Water, Railways, Education, and Entrepreneurship.* Lewiston: The Edwin Mellen Press, 2009.

Bennett, George. *Kenya, A Political History: The Colonial Period.* London: Oxford University Press, 1963.

Berman, B. J. *Control and Crisis in Colonial Kenya.* Athens, Ohio University Press, 1999.

Berman, B., & Lonsdale, J. *Unhappy Valley: Conflict in Kenya and Africa: Book One: State and Class.* Athens, Ohio University Press, 1992.

Bodelson, C. A. *Studies in Mid Victorian Imperialism.* New York: Alfred A. Knopf, 1924.

Brantley, Cynthia. *The Giriama and Colonial Resistance in Kenya, 1800–1920.* Berkeley: University of California Press, 1981.

Brown, M. Judith & Louis Wm. Roger. Ed. *Oxford History of the British Empire: Volume IV: The Nineteenth Century.* London: Oxford University Press, 2001.

Burwash, Nathanael. *Lord Elgin: The Makers of Canada Egerton Ryerson, 1837–1902*. Toronto: Morgan & Co, Ltd., 1912.

Clayton, Anthony & Savage Donald. *Government and Labour in Kenya, 1895–1963*. London: Frank Cass, 1974.

Cransworth, Lord. *Kenya Chronicles*, London: Macmillan & Co., Ltd., 1939.

Collins, Robert O. *Document from the African Past*. Princeton: Markus Wiener Publishers, 2001.

———. *Eastern African History in Document*, Vol. 2. New York: M. Wiener Pub, 1990.

Cox, Richard. *Kenyatta's Country*. London: Hutchinson of London, 1965.

Croft, Henry Page. *Path of Empire, 1881–1947*, Vol. 5. 1988.

Church, Major Archibald. *East Africa: A New Dominion, A Crucial Experiment in Tropical Development and Its Significance to the British Empire*. West Port, Connecticut: Negro University Press, 1970.

Dracopoli, Ignatius, Nicholas. *Through Jubaland to the Lorian Swamp; An Adventurous Journey of Exploration & Sport in the Unknown African Forests & Deserts of Jubaland to the Unexplored Lorian Swamp, 1887–*. Philadelphia: J. B. Lippincott Company, 1928.

Dundas, Sir Charles. *African Crossroads, 1884–1956*. London: Macmillan, 1955.

Fieldhouse, D. K. *Economics and Empire, 1830–1914*. Ithaca, New York: Cornell University Press, 1973.

Flint, John E. & Williams Glyndwr. *Perspectives of Empire: Essay Presented to Gerald S. Graham*. New York: Barnes & Noble Books, 1973.

Galbraith, John S. *Mackinnon and East Africa, 1878–1895: A Study of New Imperialism*. London: Cambridge University Press, 1972.

Gregory, Robert G. *Quest for Equality: Asian Politics in East Africa, 1900–1967*. New Delhi: Orient Longman, 1993.

———. *India and East Africa: A History of Race Relations within the British Empire*, 1890–1939. Oxford: Clarendon Oxford, 1971.

Harcourt, Lewis. *Lou Lou: Selected Extracts From the Journals of Lewis Harcourt (1880–1895)*. Cranbury, New Jersey: Associated University Presses, 2010.

Harlow, Vincent et al. *History of East Africa*. 2. Oxford: Clarendon Press, 1965.

Himbara, David. *Kenyan Capitalists, the State and Development*. London: Boulder & Rienner, 1994.

Hughes, Lotte. *Moving the Maasai: A Colonial Misadventure*. New York: Palgrave Macmillan, 2006.

Huxley, Elspeth. *Whiteman's Country: Lord Delamere and the Making of Kenya*. London: Macmillan and Co., Ltd., 1968.

Hyam, Ronald. *Elgin and Churchill At the Colonial Office*. New York: St. Martin's Press, 1968.

Inglehart, Ronald. *Modernization and Post Modernization: Cultural, Economic, and Political Change in 43 Societies*. Princeton: Princeton University Press, 1997.

King, A. & Zwanenberg, R. M. A. Van. *An Economic History of Kenya and Uganda, 1800–1970*. Atlantic Highland, NJ: Palgrave Macmillan, 1975.

Kipkorir, B. E. ed., *Biographical Essays on Imperialism and Collaboration in Colonial Kenya*. Nairobi: Kenya Literature Bureau, 1980.

Kirk-Greene, A. H. M. *On Crown Service: A History of HM Colonial and Overseas Civil Services, 1837–1997*. London: I B Tauris Publishers, 1999.

Le May, G. H. L. *British Supremacy in South Africa, 1899–1907*. Oxford: Clarendon Press, 1965.

Leakey, L. S. B. *Kenya Contrasts and Problems*. London: Methuem & Co., 1936.

Leys, Norman M. *A Last Chance in Kenya*. London: The Hogarth Press, 1931.

———. *Kenya* London: The Hogarth Press, 1931.

Lloyd, T. O. *The British Empire 1558–1995 (Short History of the World of the Modern World)*. 2nd Ed. New York: Oxford University Press, 1997.

Low, D. A. *Mind of Buganda: Documents of the Modern History of an African Kingdom*. Berkeley: University of California Press, 1971.

Lugard, Lord F. *Dual Mandate in British Tropical Africa*. London: Archon Books, 1965.

Magnus, Philip. *Kitchener. Portrait of an Imperialist*. New York: E. P. Dutton & Company, Inc., 1959.

Mangat, J. S. *A History of the Asians in East Africa, c. 1886 to 1945*. Oxford: Clarendon Press, 1969.

Marlow, John. *Cromer in Egypt*. New York: Praeger Publishers, 1970.

Maxon, M. Robert. *Struggle for Kenya: Loss and Reassertion of Imperial Initiative, 1912–1923*. Cranbury: Associated University Press, 1993.

———. *John Ainsworth and the Making of Kenya*. Washington: University Press of America, 1980.

McDermott P. L. *British East Africa or IBEA: History of Formation or Works of the Imperial British East Africa Company*. London: Chapman & Hall LD, 1893.

Morton, Fred. *Children of Ham* Freed Slaves and Fugitive Slaves on the Kenya Coast, 1873 to 1907. Boulder: West View Press, 1990.

Mungeam, G. H. *British Rule in Kenya, 1895–1912: The Establishment of Administration in the East Africa Protectorate*. Oxford: Clarendon Press, 1966.

Mwakikagile, Godfrey. *Kenya: Identity of a Nation*. Pretoria, South Africa: New Africa Press, 1997.

Mwaruvie, J. M., *Ewart Scott Grogan and Politics of Railway Development in Kenya: The Case of Uasin Gishu Railway: 1901–1930*. Saarbrucken: GVDM Verlag, 2010.

Nicholls, C. S. *Red Strangers: The White tribe of Kenya*. London: Time Well Press, 2005.

———. *The Swahili Coast: Politics, Trade on the East African Littoral, 1798–1856*. New York: Africana Publishing Corporation, 1971.

Ogot, B. A. ed. *Kenya in the 19th Century*. Nairobi: Bookwise Ltd., and Ayange Press Ltd., 1985.

———. "Kenya Under the British, 1895 to 1963," in *Zamani: A Survey of East African History*, ed. B. A. Ogot. Nairobi: East African Publishing House, 1974: 249–94.

Parkinson, Cosmo. *The Colonial Office from Within*. London: Faber & Faber, 1947. Parsons, Neil. King Khama, *Emperor Joe and the Great white Queen: Victorian Britain through African Eyes*. Chicago: University of Chicago Press, 1998.

Pope-Hennessy, James. *Lord Crewe the Likeness of a Liberal, 1858–1945*. London: Constable, 1955.

Porter, Andrew. *Oxford History of the British Empire: Volume 111: The Nineteenth Century*. London: Oxford University Press, 2001.

Prakash, Jain C. *Racial Discrimination Against Overseas Indians: A Class Analysis*. New Delhi: Concept Publication Company, 1990.

Robinson, R. Gallagher, J. *Africa and the Victorians: The Climax of Imperialism in the Dark Continent*. New York: St. Martin's Press, 1961.

———. *Africa and the Victorians: The Official Mind of Imperialism*. Los Angeles: Macmillan, 1961.

Ross, W. McGregor. *Kenya From Within: A Short Political History*. London: Cass, 1968.

Salim, I. A. *Swahili Speaking People of Kenya's Coast, 1895–1965*. Nairobi: East African Publishing House, 1973.

Sandford, G. F. *An Administrative and Political History of the Masai*. London: Waterlow & Sons Ltd, 1919.

Stichter, Sharon. *Migrant Laborers*. London: Cambridge University Press, 1985.

Sorrenson, M. P. K. *Land Reform in the Kikuyu Country: A Study in Government Policy*. London: Oxford University Press, 1967.

———. *Origins of European Settlement in Kenya*. London: Oxford University Press, 1968.

Spear, Thomas T. *Kaya Complex: A History of the Mijikenda Peoples of the Kenya Coast to 1900*. Nairobi: Kenya Literature Bureau, 1978.

———. *Kenya's Past: An Introduction to Historical Method in Africa*. London: Longman Group Ltd., 1981.

Walker, Eric A. *The British Empire: Its Structure and Spirit*. London: Oxford University Press, 1947.

Wrench, Evelyn Hohn. *Alfred Lord Milner: Man of No Illusions, 1854–1925*. News Brunswick, NJ: Eyre & Spottiswoode, 1958.

Articles and Chapters in Books

Ake, Claude. "Modernization and political instability: Theoretical Exploration," *World Politics* 26, 4 (July, 1974).

———. "Notes on the Political Economy of Africa," *Journal of Modern African Studies* 14, 1 (Mar., 1976).

Bennett, George. "Settler and Politics in Kenya," *History of East Africa*. 2, ed. V. Harlow & E. M. Chilver. Oxford: Clarendon Press, 1965.

Kirk-Greene, A. H. M. "Canada in Africa: Sir Percy Girouard, Neglected Colonial Governor," *African Affairs*, Vol. 83, No. 331 (April. 1984).

Lonsdale, John & Berman, Bruce. "Coping with the Contradictions: The Development of the Colonial State in Kenya, 1895–1914," *Journal of African History* 20 (1979): 491.

Maxon, M. Robert. "Judgment on a Colonial Governor: Sir Percy Girouard in Kenya," *Transafrican Journal of History*, 18 (1989).

Mwaruvie John M. "Kenya's Forgotten Engineer and Colonial Proconsul: Sir Percy Girouard Departmental Railway Construction in Africa, 1896–1912 (Biography)," *Canadian Journal of History* (March 22, 2006).

Ogot, Bethwell A. "Kenya Under the British, 1895 to 1963," *Zamani: A survey of East African History*. New ed., Kenya: East African Publishing House Ltd., 1974.

Royal African Society, "Dinner of the society" *Journal of the Royal African Society* 7, 28 (July 1908).

Index

About the Author

Abdullahi Sara is Adjunct Instructor of History at West Virginia University.

Lightning Source UK Ltd.
Milton Keynes UK
UKOW03n1253060117
291521UK00007B/274/P

9 781498 510653